AF477677

Changing Directions
of the
British Welfare State

Changing Directions of the British Welfare State

Edited by

Gideon Calder, Jeremy Gass
and Kirsten Merrill-Glover

UNIVERSITY OF WALES PRESS
CARDIFF
2012

www.uwp.co.uk

British Library Cataloguing-in-Publication Data
A catalogue record for this book is available from the British Library.

ISBN 978–0–7083–2546–9
e-ISBN 978–0–7083–2547–6

Typeset by Marie Doherty
Printed in the UK by MPG Books Group Ltd

FOREWORD

Huw Edwards

I was delighted when approached by the University of Wales, Newport to write a foreword to this publication. The welfare state is something that the British public has always been proud of and, indeed, it has been the envy of other countries throughout the world.

In 1942, William Beveridge (1879–1963) published his report on the way forward for Britain after the Second World War. Beveridge's report identified five 'giant evils' that were prevalent at that time – Want, Disease, Ignorance, Squalor and Idleness. These are addressed in the first part of the book. The year 1945 brought about a tremendous change in government policy when Winston Churchill's Conservative Party was defeated by a Labour Party headed by Clement Attlee. In 1948, Beveridge's 'welfare state' was established with the key elements of social security; health; housing; education and social services (welfare and children). What a tremendous legacy for both Beveridge and Attlee, and, of course, Aneurin Bevan (minister of health at that time) who was tasked with the operational details.

For more than sixty years you and I have benefited from living in a welfare state. In that period of time other challenges have evolved in areas such as gender, ethnicity, disability, devolution and the start and end of life. These are debated in the second part of this publication.

Alongside this publication, the university organised a series of public lectures and debates, various film projects, and at the heart of the project was a website providing a forum for the sharing of views, perceptions and for critical debate.

I am sure that this publication will provide an excellent reference on a wide-ranging and accessible set of reflections on the past, present and future of welfare provision in Britain.

ACKNOWLEDGEMENTS

The editors would like to thank the contributors to this book for their commitment to it amid the usual array of hurdles and distractions – and some tricky personal challenges. We would also like to thank our colleagues on the Welfare State 2008 project, and all of those who contributed to its vibrancy in one way or another, via submissions to the website, contributions to events or encouraging it along in other ways. We owe particular gratitude to Matthew Evans for the energy he invested in the project during his time at the Community University of the Valleys (East), and to Scott Hazell for his invaluable work on the IT side.

Gideon Calder dedicates his share of the book to the memory of his father Angus, who was born in the year of the Beveridge Report, died a month before the sixtieth anniversary of the National Health Service, and whose writings, in different ways and registers, echo many of this book's concerns.

Jeremy Gass dedicates his share of the book to Katrina, who was born in the year of the National Health Act, and their daughter Beth, one of 'Thatcher's children', both of whom work in different ways for social justice and women's rights.

Kirsten Merrill-Glover dedicates her share of the book to the memory of her brother Karl, a proponent and defender of welfare service provision, and to her sons Nye and Billy whose generation holds the future of the British welfare state.

CONTENTS

Foreword   v
Huw Edwards

Acknowledgements   vii

List of figures and tables   xi

Notes on contributors   xiii

Introduction   1
Gideon Calder, Jeremy Gass and Kirsten Merrill-Glover

Timeline   15

Part 1: The 'five giants'   **17**

1. WANT: 'What the British people desire': the rise and fall
of insurance-based social security   19
Peter Kenway

2. DISEASE: Social democracy, health inequalities and
the welfare state   44
Michael Sullivan

3. IGNORANCE: Combating ignorance: education, social
opportunity and citizenship in Wales   65
Gareth Rees

4. SQUALOR: Shifting boundaries: people, homes and the state
since 1945   84
John Puzey

5. IDLENESS: 'No longer a problem of industry'? Principles,
practice and policy in the early twenty-first century   98
David Byrne

Part 2: Five challenges   **123**

6. Gender: Continuity and change: gender and welfare   125
Sandra Shaw

7. Race: A very 'British' welfare state? 'Race' and racism   141
Charlotte Williams

8. Disability: What rights for disabled people in a welfare state? Need-fulfilment versus identity-assertion and the 'problem of dependency'   160
Steven R. Smith

9. Devolution: Devolution and the welfare state: the case of Wales   177
Mark Drakeford

10. The start and end of life

Part 1: The welfare of children since 1948   195
Ian Butler

Part 2: The welfare of older people since 1948   203
Liz Lloyd

Conclusions: Taking Stock   213
Victoria Winckler

References   221
Index   247

LIST OF FIGURES AND TABLES

Figures

1.1 Real value of selected National Insurance benefits and
family allowance, 1948 to 2010   31

1.2 Real value of selected national assistance benefits and
the state retirement pension, 1948 to 2010   33

1.3 The proportions of children, pensioners and other adults
in poverty since 1961   37

Tables

1.1 Requirements for adults of working age, and retired
persons (at 1938 prices) (Beveridge, 1942: paras 222
and 225, tables IX and X)   25

1.2 Rates of benefit per week in the 1942 report and the
1946 Act (Beveridge, 1942: para. 401; Owen, 1948:
para. 11, p. 10)   29

1.3 People in households below low-income thresholds,
1961 to 1963   36

NOTES ON CONTRIBUTORS

Ian Butler is a qualified social worker. Formerly Professor of Social Work at Keele University and Visiting Professor in the Department of Child Health at the University of Wales College of Medicine, he is Professor of Social Work at Bath University. In 2005, he was seconded to the Welsh Assembly Government where he was a special advisor to the first minister until 2012. He is an Honorary Member of the Council of the NSPCC and was elected to the Academy of Social Sciences in 2004. In 2009, he was appointed to the Board of Cafcass (England). He has published widely on social work policy and practice with children and families.

David Byrne is Professor of Sociology and Social Policy at Durham University. His main interests include methods for understanding complex systems, and the nature of post-industrial societies. Among his publications are *Social Exclusion* (2nd edn, Open University Press, 2005), and, edited with Charles Ragin, *The Sage Handbook of Case Based Methods* (Sage, 2009).

Gideon Calder is Reader in Ethics and Social Philosophy at University of Wales, Newport and Director of the Newport Social Ethics Research Group. He has a special interest in the application of social, ethical and political theory to issues of pressing contemporary social concern – and recent published work has addressed a range of such contexts, including environmental politics, citizenship, the normative justification of European Union institutions and the ethics of sporting boycotts. He is currently president of the UK Association for Legal and Social Philosophy.

Mark Drakeford is Assembly Member for Cardiff West. Previously he was Professor of Social Policy and Applied Social Sciences at Cardiff University. Between 2000 and 2009 he was the Cabinet's special adviser on health and social policy at the Welsh government.

Jeremy Gass is a visiting lecturer at the University of Wales, Newport, where he was formerly Head of Community Learning. Previously, he was a social worker and welfare rights worker before becoming a tutor/organiser with the Workers Educational Association in south Wales. He has recently completed doctoral research in adult education and active citizenship.

Peter Kenway is Director and co-founder of the New Policy Institute (NPI), an independent think tank focusing on evidence-based analysis of social justice issues. Formerly an economist at the University of Reading, he has also worked as a manager, consultant and planner in public transport. Recent work by the NPI has included a 2011 report produced with the Bevan Foundation and the Equalities and Human Rights Commission, bringing together data on inequalities between different groups, and how these inequalities differ between England and Wales.

Liz Lloyd is Senior Lecturer in Social Gerontology at the School for Policy Studies, University of Bristol. She is an experienced higher education teacher and researcher in gerontology and social care policies and practices. Her research and publications reflect her particular interest in the end of life in old age and the role of care. Prior to taking up academic work, Liz was a community worker and maintains an active interest in voluntary sector management.

Kirsten Merrill-Glover is Head of Community Learning within the University of Wales, Newport's Centre for Community and Lifelong Learning, having previously worked as a community-based senior lecturer in psychology and a curriculum development officer. Prior to joining the university she taught both sociology and psychology in further education and for the Workers Educational Association. She is currently undertaking a professional doctorate in education within Cardiff University's School of Social Sciences.

John Puzey has been Director of Shelter Cymru since 1990. He was a member of the Welsh Assembly Homelessness Commission that drew up the first Homelessness Plan for Wales and a founder member of Rough Sleepers Cymru and Housing Forum Cymru. He is currently a member of the Welsh Assembly Government Supporting People and Homelessness Strategy working group, he also represents housing interests on the Welsh Assembly Government Third Sector Partnership Council. In 2012, John was appointed to two Welsh Government ministerial advisory groups, on tackling poverty and ageing. John has written or contributed to a wide range of reports and publications concerning housing and homelessness and is a frequent public speaker and broadcaster on housing and related matters. He is chair of the Pontardawe Film Society and skipper of the Shelter Cymru Sharks Cricket team.

Gareth Rees is Director of the Wales Institute of Social and Economic Research, Data and Methods (WISERD) and Professor at the Cardiff School of Social Sciences, Cardiff University. He has held visiting appointments at the University of British Columbia and the University of New South Wales. He has researched and written extensively on participation in lifelong learning, the relationships between education and training and regional economic development, and the governance of education policy. He has also been a consultant to a wide variety of organisations, including the OECD, the European Commission, the Welsh Assembly Government and Education and Learning Wales (ELWa).

Sandra Shaw is Senior Lecturer in Social Policy at the University of Salford. She has been teaching and researching in the area of social policy for over twenty years, since completing a Ph.D. on lone parents at the University of Sheffield. Her research interests include families, children and young people; gender and welfare and comparative and global social policy. Recent publications include *Parents, Children, Young People and the State* (Open University Press, 2010). She is joint editor of a new introductory Social Policy textbook due for publication in 2013.

Steven R. Smith is Professor of Political Philosophy and Social Policy at the University of Wales, Newport, and a founding member of the Newport Social Ethics Research Group (SERG). His main research interests are contemporary political philosophy, egalitarian theory, policy and practice, the philosophy of disability, recognition and identity politics, and the philosophy of the welfare state. As well as two books, he has published widely on these themes in journals and edited collections. His most recent book is *Equality and Diversity* (Policy Press, 2011); he is currently working on well-being.

Michael Sullivan is Professor of Policy Analysis at Swansea University and a specialist policy adviser to the Welsh Government. He has researched and written, over the last twenty-five years, on the relationship between social democracy and modern social policy, on the Labour Party and social reform, on the politics of the welfare state and on the politics and social policy implications of devolution.

Charlotte Williams OBE is Professor in the School of Global Studies, Social Sciences and Planning at RMIT University, Melbourne. A qualified social worker, she taught previously at the universities of Bangor and Keele. She has written and researched extensively on equalities issues in Wales and her publications include *A Tolerant Nation? Exploring Ethnic Diversity in Wales* (University of Wales Press, 2003) and *Social Policy for Social Welfare Practice in a Devolved Wales* (Venture Press, 2011). Professor Williams is author of the memoir *Sugar and Slate* (Planet, 2002), which won Welsh Book of the Year in 2003. In 2007 she was awarded the OBE for services to equal opportunities and ethnic minorities in Wales.

Victoria Winckler is Director of the Bevan Foundation, a think tank, founded in 2001, with a focus on social justice in Wales. She joined the foundation in 2002 from the Welsh Local Government Association where she was Head of economic and environmental affairs. She has worked for many years in research and policy, including at Mid Glamorgan County Council and at the Social Research Unit at Cardiff University.

INTRODUCTION

*Gideon Calder, Jeremy Gass
and Kirsten Merrill-Glover*

The British welfare state has never been a simple 'given' – a static thing, with fixed purposes, agreed-upon parameters, a single guiding strategy or ideological guarantees. Rather it has been a shifting project, in all such respects. It remains so. As we pass the seventieth birthday of the Beveridge Report, fast-moving, controversial reforms of, for example, health, welfare benefits and legal aid are under consideration. On the one hand, throughout these shifts, the idea that the state should set minimum standards of welfare – in health, housing, education and primarily income – has persisted. Yet on the other hand, what those standards should *be*, what kinds of agency should rightly pursue them and how they might best be realised, have been matters of ongoing contestation. We write, in late 2011, amid a series of skirmishes around each of these issues as the Westminster Conservative/Liberal Democrat coalition government enacts a programme of radical neoliberal reforms. The Health and Social Care Bill 2011 is widely perceived – by concerned Liberal Democrats such as Baroness Shirley Williams (Helm, 2011) as much as by critics from other parties, and by doctors and nurses themselves – as an attempt gradually to privatise the National Health Service and to undermine the commitment to deliver a comprehensive public health service, free at the point of need. Meanwhile similar concerns apply in other spheres of welfare provision. The Welfare Reform Bill, equally contentious in its reception by campaigning groups, social policy analysts and indeed the House of Lords, will, by the time this book appears, have become an Act of Parliament. For its critics, it will have the effect of dismantling key aspects of the welfare safety net.

So, while the structure and nature of welfare provision has always been up for debate, at the present conjuncture the very *idea* of a welfare state is, in new and important ways, under scrutiny. This is an especially fitting, vital time at which to consider how the 'story so far' of the British welfare state relates to its future prospects. That story might be traced to various possible starting points. Some of these – and some of the most significant – lie in Wales.

'A burning luminous mark'

'It was no abstract question for us,' writes Aneurin Bevan near the beginning of *In Place of Fear*: 'The circumstances of our lives made it a burning luminous mark of interrogation' (Bevan, 1952: 1). The 'it' he refers to is power – and, specifically, where it lies. The 'us' is the miners of the south Wales coalfield, in the years following the First World War. Whatever illumination on questions of power might emerge from debates among political theorists, their urgency for Bevan lay precisely in their proximity to people's lives, and the struggles in which they were enmeshed. Society viewed from that angle was, as Bevan puts it, 'an arena of conflicting social forces' (ibid.: 2). Part of the job of what has come to be called the 'welfare state' was, if not to resolve those conflicts, to minimise their harmful impact on the least powerful. This book sets out, from various angles, to explore the extent to which that mission has been successful – and also the ways in which the nature of the mission itself has changed since the inception of the British welfare state.

A key moment in that inception is 5 July 1948, when the National Health Service – in so many ways a product of Bevan's own labours – formally came into being. This book was conceived on its sixtieth anniversary, as part of a public project – Welfare State 2008 – inaugurated in Bevan's home town of Tredegar and comes to fruition seventy years after the publication of the Beveridge Report in 1942. The surrounding landscape has changed since the 1940s, of course, in ways mapped and explored in several of the chapters in this book. The miners now are very few. The health service is in very different shape, as are the benefits system, education and other aspects of state service provision established by the post-war Labour administration. Struggles have switched their focal points and scope since then. Conflicts have in some ways shifted. Social movements have diversified. Migration has made British civil society a far more multicultural place to be. Globalisation has changed the kinds of things states can do. Domestic set-ups have adapted and become more fluid. Work – how it is done and the stability of labour markets – is in many ways markedly different. The lexicon of social welfare and the terms of theoretical debates have, in crucial ways, moved on. For many commentators (see e.g. Pierson and Castles, 2006; Cooper, 2008; Rustin, 2008; Fraser, 2009; Devine et al., 2009; Castles et al., 2010) the 'modernisation' of welfare which began in the era of the Thatcher governments has amounted to a fundamental break with the 'post-war settlement' and an unravelling of the 'British model' of the welfare state.

For others, we need a new settlement not because the goals of the welfare state are somehow obsolete, but because they can no longer be achieved along the lines envisaged by Bevan or Beveridge – climate change, for example, is hitting the poorest and least powerful in new and grave ways (see Coote 2009; Coote and Franklin, 2009). Again, the landscape has changed in substantive ways, and to overlook these changes is to risk misconfiguring the nature both of problems and of their possible resolution. Even so, our recognition of such shifts, as well as the forms they have taken, is, in large part, down to the momentous impacts on that landscape of the welfare state itself. It is among the most important additions to the social, political and economic times through which, in Britain, we have recently been living – perhaps the most, however taken for granted its achievements might have come to be. The purpose of the book is to capture – and critically explore – the nature of that importance, those impacts and those achievements.

Of course, any such assessment will be coloured by its own historical context. As already noted, we write as the Conservative/Liberal Democrat coalition has embarked on a massive programme of public sector cuts in the wake of the banking crisis and the subsequent recession, and is part-way through a sweeping reorganisation of the welfare state, including the National Health Service. These measures are presented as a response to Britain's budget deficit. Yet, they represent, at the same time, the latest embodiment of New Right hostility to the model of post-war welfare provision – and of that critique which, as Claus Offe has put it, sees the welfare state as the illness of which it pretends to be the cure. Established welfare provision is caught in a squeeze between economic imperatives and ideological antagonism. Yet, we find at the same time a flourishing of fresh perspectives on social welfare: a wave of in-depth explorations of inequality, and of the social forces which engender it. Richard Wilkinson and Kate Pickett's best-selling study *The Spirit Level: Why Equality is Better for Everyone* (2009) – with its systematic analysis of how all aspects of social life, from health to crime to literacy, are conditioned by how equal a society is in terms of the gap between rich and poor – has found a ready audience among academics and policymakers, but also well beyond the sphere of those whose job it is to discuss such things. In January 2010 a major government-commissioned report (Hills et al., 2010) found that the divide between rich and poor (exacerbated by gender, location, ethnicity and other differentiating factors) was wider than forty years previously, and often 'colossal'. A month later, a government-commissioned review of health inequalities led by the president of the British Medical Association, Sir Michael Marmot, issued a groundbreaking report – *Fair Society, Healthy Lives*. It revealed a clear, often drastic 'social gradient in health' (9), so that the lower a person's social position, the poorer his or her health is likely to be. It concluded that these inequalities result from social inequalities – and that as such, they are avoidable. Shortly after that, Daniel Dorling's *Injustice: Why Social Inequality Persists* (2010) offered a forceful argument that the ongoing maldistribution of resources is now best explained by the undue influence of five key, unacknowledged, contestable tenets: that elitism is efficient, exclusion is necessary, prejudice is natural, greed is good and despair is inevitable. For Dorling, each presumption has emerged and worked its dominance despite the endurance of the welfare state, its shifts and evolutions, and its achievements.

Yet, as already noted, the 'welfare state' is not a given, either as ideal or as policy. Notions of 'social welfare' – what it is, and what enables or thwarts it – are themselves, of course, contested. And even were that not so, questions about the means by which the state might best support welfare, or promote it – what a welfare state should look like and what exactly it should do – would remain very much open.

And so it has been, since 1948. In place of consensus about the nature and scope of the welfare state or its desirability, we find debate, shifts of orthodoxy and – as we enter the second decade of the twenty-first century – complex fissures in what once seemed rather more predictable terms of the ideological debate. This is the case across Europe, where as Peter Taylor-Gooby makes the point, factors such as 'globalization, technological unemployment, fewer children and more older people, new patterns of migration, shifts in political ideology' have all challenged the original terms on which welfare states were set in place (Taylor-Gooby, 2001: ix).

In light of all this, marking sixty years of the British version might seem a slippery, risky kind of project. If we cannot agree about what the 'welfare state' is – and if the figure regarded as its chief architect, William Beveridge, came himself to 'loathe' the term (Kynaston, 2007: 26) – then the subject at stake might seem rather compromised. Even to use the phrase is, as Nicholas Timmins observes, 'to set artificial frames'. Timmins goes further: 'as an entity [the welfare state] does not exist – it is a collection of services and policies and ideas whose boundaries expand and contract over time' (Timmins, 1995: 7). Yet, these shifts and complexities are of course what make the tackling of this subject so vital. For in those services, policies and ideas – in debates about what a welfare state might, or might not, achieve, and its place in accounts of social justice – 'the circumstances of our lives' are, of course, at stake. 'Welfare' is difficult to define, and find consensus about, because it is so crucial a notion. The widespread coverage, throughout 2008, of the sixtieth anniversary of Britain's welfare state was itself a testament to the unfinished, difficult and urgent nature of all of these issues and debates. The questions remain luminous, in the lives of Bevan's everyday people as much as in the field of academic debate.

Aims and outline of chapters

This book has three main aims. One is historical: to consider the record of the British welfare state since the late 1940s – with an emphasis, in some chapters, on the Welsh context. A second is critical: to evaluate the aims, principles and ambitions of the welfare state as conceived by government, social commentators and other agencies. And a third aim is to consider the priorities of welfare provision as we face the future. We have opted to tackle these aims by taking ten different themes, and separating them out in the chapters which follow. Through them, the contributors explore (in different ways) the extent to which the achievements of the welfare state have matched its aims, whether those aims themselves have been adequately conceived, and which issues, in each area, are currently most urgent.

Part 1 addresses the 'five giants' identified by Beveridge as the prime threats to British society, and thus the core priorities for responsible government:

> It [social security] is one part only of an attack upon five giant evils: upon the physical Want . . ., upon Disease, which often causes that want and brings many other troubles in its train, upon Ignorance, which no democracy can afford among its citizens, upon Squalor, . . . and upon the Idleness which destroys wealth and corrupts men. (Beveridge, 1942: 170)

The welfare state was founded amid an overriding concern with class inequality as a barrier in fields such as education and health (Briggs, 1961). If its aim was the elimination of those barriers, the results, as the different chapters show, are mixed. The gap between rich and poor has risen; the notion that one's social circumstances might be rendered irrelevant to one's standard of health remains an aspiration, rather than an outcome of the work the welfare state has done. But at the same time, other challenges and priorities, marginal at best for Beveridge and Bevan, have emerged as crucial to the working out of the promotion of equality. Part 2 considers five prominent themes in more recent political discourse, the tackling of which require, for many, important departures from the Beveridge agenda. Here we confront questions of values and policy posed by diversity, by identity, by devolution and aspects of our social relations – such as gender, age and disability – which seem not to be simply addressable through discussion of the distribution of economic resources. To what extent can the welfare state, in its customary forms, address the issues which confront current and future generations of British society? Again, many of our chapters here use Wales as a chief reference point. But these issues and challenges, while felt in particular ways in the current Welsh context, have a clear resonance across the British welfare state.

In chapter 1, Peter Kenway tackles what seems unavoidably the first, key question: how far has the British welfare state achieved its original aims with respect to the abolition of 'want'? The answers which emerge are significantly ambiguous. Kenway outlines Beveridge's own agenda for eradicating want: the Plan for Social Security. He analyses its architecture, and the assumptions on which it was based. The chapter then explores the various means by which the plan itself was put into practice by the Labour governments of 1945–51, and its history through subsequent changes of political direction, and wider circumstances. He tracks rises and falls in benefits, and also shifts in orthodoxy between three periods: 1948–73, 1973–90 and then from 1990 to the present. In tracking these changes Kenway identifies a sea-change in the final period, as means-testing supplants dwindling universal provision. So, to what extent has 'want' been abolished? Answering this question is complicated by absences in terms of both information and an agreed yardstick by which to judge it. Figures suggest that fresh anti-poverty strategies are vitally urgent. We are some distance away now from the terms of Beveridge's original agenda. The targets of the 1997–2010 Labour government in reducing child poverty, for example, were not met. Kenway concludes that while a 'return to Beveridge' is not an option, there are advantages, despite subsequent orthodoxy, in many of Beveridge's key assumptions – especially when it comes to addressing the needs of 'part-working' families and those affected by unemployment.

Michael Sullivan, in chapter 2, addresses health – or rather the designated 'giant', Disease, to which the establishment of the National Health Service was the eventual response. The purpose of the NHS was 'to vanquish disease and ill health irrespective of the social standing of the patient', but simultaneously and just as importantly, to ensure equal access to the healthcare provided. Stances on how best to achieve the latter have changed across the decades since 1948 – and are surveyed throughout the chapter. We move from the broad post-war political consensus on government's responsibilities to ensure a regime of entitlements to welfare, through various debates about how the NHS might best evolve, to the explicit departure from that consensus position, with the Conservative governments of the 1980s and 1990s – and New Labour's rhetoric around individual responsibility for healthcare outcomes. What is striking, as Sullivan notes, is that the provision of health services 'free at the point of use' has not succeeded in resolving health inequalities. 'The health of the "rich"', as he puts it, 'has improved at a much faster rate than the health of the "poor"'. Thus the effects of disease do not do their work 'irrespective of the social standing of the patient'. How to address this? As Sullivan concludes, the impetus of New Labour policy has been in the direction not of government solutions to structural inequalities, but of targeted strategies for 'individually focused behaviour change'. This shift places much of Beveridge's analyses, aims and recommendations at a clear distance from current political orthodoxy – both under New Labour and under the Conservative/ Liberal Democrat coalition since May 2010.

'Ignorance' – which, for Beveridge (1944: 7), 'no democracy can afford among its citizens' – is the focus of chapter 3. Gareth Rees charts the relationship between education and the welfare state with a particular focus on Wales. Identifying the significance and endurance of key decisions made during the post-war period, he highlights the different ways in which successive governments have maintained a commitment to provide access to education. Consequences of these different versions of that commitment are discussed, along with examples of structural, social and geographical inequalities that have prevailed and still remain. Also explored is the extent to which educational policy and practice is driven by an economic imperative and the pitfalls inherent in doing so. Rees discusses how historical legacies in Wales contributed to a pledge to provide the widest possible access to education and argues that this can still be evidenced today in the policies agreed by the National Assembly for Wales. The chapter succinctly encapsulates the complexity of the debates facing policy makers. Questioning the efficacy of placing too much emphasis on employing education as a tool for achieving social justice, the chapter then goes on to caution against the commodification of education and concludes by advocating a reaffirmation of Beveridge's ideals.

Noting the 'rather ambiguous relationship' between housing as a public service and the welfare state, in chapter 4 John Puzey traces the changing fortunes of social housing from the post-war period up until the contemporary recession in the context of the ideological shifts of the last sixty years which have seen it become a largely residual function. The chapter begins with the view that the post-war Labour government recognised the key role that decent housing could play in achieving other social policy goals in relation to health and education as well as contributing to economic prosperity and tackling fundamental inequalities. Whilst Labour aspired to council housing becoming the tenure for all, the Conservatives envisaged it being restricted to the working class and primarily serving the needs of the poor. Highlighting the role of the market throughout the period, Puzey suggests that, since a third of homes were owned at the end of the war, Labour's aspirations were unlikely to materialise. Puzey reviews both the ideological differences between the main political parties and their apparent similarities. Ironically, it was in 1953 and 1954 under a Conservative government that the greatest number of council houses were built. Subsequent dismantling of council housing through the right to buy and the lack of investment initiated by the Thatcher government was not reversed by New Labour. The chapter also considers the differentiated approaches of the devolved administrations before suggesting that there may be a new role for social housing in the light of a Keynesian approach to the current recession.

David Byrne, in chapter 5, reflects on Beveridge's solution to the 'evil' of idleness: full employment. In doing so, he charts the impact and scale of social and associated policy changes since the 1940s and their impact on consensual understandings of dependency. Noting that, for Beveridge, the value of both employment and the ability to support a partner and child were self-evident, Byrne evidences how many individuals and families are trapped in working poverty as a result of low wages and benefit eligibility rulings. Identifying the UK as a post-industrial society where service and financial industries have advanced – at least up until the recent crisis – as employment in man-ufacturing has receded, he goes on to consider the regional impacts of these shifts in employment and how formerly industrial urban and coalfield localities have suffered worst within regions. Indeed, at the time of writing Blaenau Gwent, a former industrial heartland in south-east Wales, has been identified in a report published by the social research charity the Joseph Rowntree Foundation as having the largest numbers of those claiming job-seeker's allowance in the UK. Byrne explores who 'the idle' might now be, in a contemporary environment of vastly reduced job security and tenure, and considers the dramatic increase in families headed by a single parent. Thus the chapter both articulates and challenges the assumptions and guiding principles of policy makers in Beveridge's wake.

As Sandra Shaw states in her introduction, each area of the welfare state might be assessed in relation to gender – on a scale, of course, beyond the scope of a single chapter. Even so she pinpoints a range of key issues that have characterised the welfare state since its inception and continue to be of contemporary concern. Not least of these is women's poverty. Beveridge's design for the welfare state was predicated on a particular set of prevailing values and assumptions about the nuclear family comprising a male breadwinner, who was also the head of the household, and his wife whose role was to care for the home and his needs and rear children. This is the starting point for chapter 6, in which Shaw explores how this concept of an ideal family unit and the sexual division of labour has underpinned the welfare state. The chapter starts with a feminist analysis of the welfare state, citing examples of how the welfare benefits system has 'taken for granted' women's caring work. However, Shaw also alludes to the ambiguity of women's relationships with the welfare state when she suggests that the possibility of claiming benefits and result-ant dependence on the state may be preferable to relying on a man for a stable income, as well as highlighting the extent to which the welfare state is dependent upon women's paid labour. The relation-ship between gender and citizenship is also considered, particularly in relation to the contemporary emphasis on the notion of citizen-ship as economic activity, as manifested – for example – through the centrality of paid work and increased conditionality in New Labour's welfare reform.

In chapter 7, on 'race', Charlotte Williams concludes that 'there is no one welfare state but more accurately states of welfare in newly evolving societies'. The central tenet of the chapter explores how laudable and radical post-war ambitions to implement universalist state welfare provision failed to develop a coherent strategy for multicultural welfare. Drawing on a breadth of research and experience of ethnic minorities, Williams brings to the fore the injustice that in addition to the exploitation of cheap labour from Commonwealth countries, which was relied on in the establishment of the NHS apparatus, the British care industry would be unsustainable without migrant labour. This is coupled with a body of long-standing evidence of discrimination, racism and a neglect of rights in welfare provision. Crucially, Williams notes how race remains a major determinant of life chances and how policy guided by whimsical ideology and populist fears about immigration (often created and exacerbated by the media) have served to characterise political discourse on 'race' and welfare. Acknowledging the steps taken by New Labour to strengthen equalities frameworks, Williams argues that the authoritarian assimilation processes implicit in citizenship tests and ceremonies, while representing a shift from ethnic differences to shared values, remain problematic. She argues that devolution – for example, via the notion of 'progressive universalism' adopted in Wales – has the potential to more appropriately meet the needs of a diverse population. However, scepticism remains, as experience teaches us that organisations are slow to change – and without adequate financial support for third sector initiatives as well as public services, inequalities are likely to prevail.

Chapter 8 addresses disability – and, specifically, debates and ambiguities surrounding ideology and policy with regard to 'welfare rights' for disabled people, since the inception of the British welfare state. On one familiar view, as Steven R. Smith suggests, the state's responsibility is to meet the needs, and address the vulnerabilities, of disabled people. On another, it is to empower them to live independent lives. These two views reflect two doctrines of 'disability rights': prioritising, respectively, entitlements to 'needs-fulfilment' and to 'independent living'. These two doctrines in turn link up with different understandings of disability itself. On the one hand, disability can be viewed medically, as an unfortunate, perhaps tragic deficiency inherent in the individual, and causing them to live in a state of dependency on others. In contrast to this, proponents of a social model of disability locate the condition not in individual impairments but in social environments – so that what makes a particular medical condition a disability is not the impairment itself, but perceptions, barriers, exclusions and other aspects of social life engendered by ignorant or condescending assumptions about the lives of people with impairments. Smith finds both understandings reflected in disability policy and politics. He suggests that each, by itself, is partial and inadequate – and that an alternative, reciprocal understanding of rights is both more theoretically coherent and more productive as a model for social welfare.

Mark Drakeford begins chapter 9 with a review of the history of the Labour Party in Wales, on the grounds that the welfare state and devolution in Wales are inextricably linked with it. This involves consideration of both the formative ideas of the welfare state and the devolution debate from Attlee to Blair. He identifies four core elements of the 'Beveridge-derived' welfare state as a context for an assessment of the policy preferences of the first three Welsh assembly governments. Acknowledging the extent to which he draws on his experiences as an adviser to successive assembly cabinets, which makes this an 'explicitly insider view of policy making' rather than an academically objective account, he claims to avoid a directly party political partisanship. Asserting that Wales, amongst the nations of the United Kingdom, has a unique left-of-centre political tradition, he acknowledges that, whilst Labour has had 'the most practical influence over the policy developments', the underlying 'ideological impulses' would be shared amongst a wider range of assembly parties.

Chapter 10 – addressing the welfare of children and older people since 1948 – has two parts, written respectively by Ian Butler and Liz Lloyd. Each begins with an outline of the positive outcomes of the welfare state for the age group in question, especially in relation to health and, in the case of older people, life expectancy. Yet, whilst infectious diseases no longer present the threat that they used to, either for young or older people, new health issues such as obesity amongst children and dementia have emerged to pose their own challenges. Despite overall improvements in reducing premature deaths, class inequalities remain and Lloyd questions the capacity of welfare services to combat these. Increased life expectancy, combined with a fall in the birth rate, have resulted in the population aged under sixteen to fall below that of pension age in 2008 for the first time. This altered age structure has led to concerns over the affordability of welfare and the perception of older people as a burden on the rest of society. Similarly, negative perceptions apply to young people who, Butler argues, are 'systematically represented as dangerous, difficult, unbiddable or worse'. Both authors highlight parallel concerns about their respective age groups in terms of citizenship, in that children and young people are 'politically neutered' without a voice in the way the welfare state is designed or operated, and that services for older people do not always promote their independence and dignity. However, Butler highlights policy divergence in Wales, including the appointment of the UK's first Children's Commissioner, a move now mirrored with the creation of a Commissioner for Older People.

Victoria Winckler closes the book by reflecting back on key themes in the foregoing chapters, and highlighting present challenges.

Marking the welfare state

Many chapters in this book make mention of a special connection between Welsh political traditions and the welfare state. While this is easy to romanticise, there is clear substance in it. The project from which the original idea for this book emerged – Welfare State 2008 – was an initiative conceived at the Community University of the Valleys East, in Tredegar, part of the Centre for Community and Lifelong Learning at University of Wales, Newport. The aim was to combine academic analysis of the legacies and significances of the British welfare state at its sixtieth anniversary – a critical celebration of its achievements – with public engagement with those same themes. Initiatives included public lectures in Risca and Newport, a film competition, vox pop interviews on the streets of Tredegar exploring people's perspectives on the value of the NHS – and on the largest scale, a website (*http://welfarestate2008.newport.ac.uk/*) including a huge array of contributions, from all kinds of angles, reflecting on the issues raised. Those issues are many, various and, of course, complex. Contributions came from professors of international renown, but just as often from those with no previous experience of making interventions of this kind. The work of the project became inspiring to those involved, and was, we hope, exemplary of the kinds of barrier-removal that the original welfare state was itself designed to achieve. We hope as well that it offered, in its own way, a contemporary echo of the 'interrogation' of power which Bevan, in the passage quoted above, had in mind. The legacies of Beveridge and Bevan – always contested and critiqued, often by the sympathetic as much as by ideological opponents – are now, through Westminster policy and orthodoxy, under direct and pressing threat. It is the view of the editors and of other contributors to this book that in times like these, the work of interrogation is as much a priority as ever.

TIMELINE

1942	Beveridge Report: *Social Insurance and Allied Services*
1945	Family Allowances Act
1946	National Insurance Act National Insurance (Industrial Injuries) Act National Health Service Act New Towns Act
1948	National Assistance Act Children Act 5 July: establishment of integrated welfare state
1951	Macmillan's 'Housing Crusade'
1959	National Insurance Act (introduces earnings-related pensions) Mental Health Act
1963	Children and Young Persons Act
1965	Circular 10/65 on comprehensive education Founding of Child Poverty Action Group Founding of Disabled Income Group
1970	School leaving age raised to sixteen Chronically Sick and Disabled Persons Act
1972	Housing Finance Act
1973	Employment Training Act
1974	Circular 4/74: compulsory comprehensive education
1975	Employment Protection Act (introduces maternity benefit) Child Benefit Act Social Security Act Introduction of State Earnings-Related Pension Scheme (SERPS)
1976	Education Act (ends direct grant schools)
1979	Education Act (cuts in school meals and transport)

1980   Social Security Acts (reform of supplementary benefit;
        freezing of child benefit)
        Education Act (scraps Circular 4/74; introduces Assisted
        Places Scheme)

1983   Mental Health Act (revises social workers' role and
        responsibilities)

1986   Social Security Act (introduces income support, family credit)

1988   Education Act (introduces 'opt out' and national curriculum)

1989   Children Act

1990   NHS and Community Care Act (introduces 'internal market')

1992   Education Act

1994   Commission for Social Justice

1995   Disability Discrimination Act

1996   Nursery Education and Grant Maintained Act (introduces
        vouchers for nursery education)

1998   Government of Wales Act; Scotland Act (devolves powers to
        Cardiff and Edinburgh)
        Human Rights Act
        National Minimum Wage Act

1999   Disability Rights Commission Act

2006   Equality Act (establishes Equality and Human Rights
        Commission)

2012   Health and Social Care Act

2012   Welfare Reform Act

2012   Social Services (Wales) Bill

PART I

THE 'FIVE GIANTS'

I

WANT

'What the British people desire': the rise and fall of insurance-based social security

Peter Kenway

Introduction: want and the welfare state

To ask, after the passing of its sixtieth anniversary, how far the British welfare state has achieved its original aims with respect to the abolition of 'want' was to ask a question with acute contemporary relevance. For at the start of 1999, a still new Labour prime minister declared the goal of eliminating child poverty within a generation. The fact that Labour's principal tool for doing this was the welfare state means that, looking back after the 2010 general election, we are in a position to offer a post-mortem on this new attempt to reach the old goal.

This new adaptation of the play whose original script was written by Beveridge and his co-founders is both a homage to them and a challenge. It is a homage because the modern attempt to end child poverty shares the founders' view not only that want exists and that its existence is intolerable, but also that alongside employment, a state-directed system of income transfers is the key to solving the problem. And it is a challenge not only because the fact that the adaptation is necessary at all is a sign that the old attempt had failed, but also because the rewriting itself suggests serious defects. What makes a contemporary assessment of the 60-year-old scheme of topical rather than just historical interest is that the challenge works both ways. For while the heavily revised nature of the modern attempt to end want may represent a reproach to the original, so does a coherent, vigorous original represent a standard against which the modern attempt can be measured.

This chapter is divided into three sections. The first examines the plan for ending want as set out in the 1942 Beveridge Report (Beveridge, 1942). As well as showing what was meant by 'want', it explains the main features of the scheme of social insurance by which want was supposed to be abolished. It also tries to offer some insight into the feel of the report and the context in which it appeared. The second section examines how the plan was put into effect through Acts of Parliament introduced early in the life of the post-war government. Subsequent developments over the life of the welfare state are then presented using a three-period framework, corresponding to a quarter century when the 'Beveridge consensus' held followed by two periods of equal length, the first of which saw the breakdown of the old consensus and the second the emergence of a new consensus. Drawing on this material, the third section offers conclusions to a number of key questions about the success of the welfare state, both in its original and its new forms, in abolishing want.

The Beveridge Report
Social insurance and allied services

Formally speaking, the Beveridge Report contained the findings of the Inter-departmental Committee on Social Insurance and Allied Services. Appointed in 1941, the committee was asked 'to undertake, with special reference to the inter-relation of the schemes, a survey of the existing schemes of social insurance and allied services, including workmen's compensation, and to make recommendations' (Beveridge, 1942: para. 1). If these terms of reference appear mundane or prosaic, the fact that the report stood in the name of Sir William alone shows that this was far from so:

> All the members of the Committee other than the Chairman are civil servants. Many of the matters dealt with in the Report raise questions of policy, on which it would be inappropriate for any civil servant to express an opinion except on behalf of the Minister to whom he is responsible; some of these matters are so important as to call for decision by the Government as a whole. (Ibid.: para. 4)

Yet, the fact that something so portentous as a scheme to abolish want is born within a report on insurance reform is problematic. For example, the report is certainly aimed at the abolition of want, which is defined, measured and explained. But why want should be defined as it was or why its abolition should be a proper object for public policy is barely discussed.

The report also devotes little attention to the issue of why the method chosen for achieving this end should be a scheme of social insurance rather than something else. With hindsight, this looks like a serious weakness in view of the subsequent decline in political support for the insurance principle in favour of the alternative of means-tested assistance (to use the 1940s terminology). Yet, in a report whose very subject is the reform of insurance, such an evaluation is obviously very difficult. The report deals briskly with differences of opinion. Where such differences are reported, they are done so briefly and even-handedly, but when this happens, the report moves swiftly to accept some and reject others.

Two reasons may lie behind this brisk style. The first is that the report is really a detailed plan of action for a unified system of national insurance to replace the numerous voluntary and state schemes that had grown up piecemeal, chiefly since the 1890s (although also going as far back to the Elizabethan Poor Laws). As a result, most of the material deals with practical matters. In particular, about one-third of the main report is devoted to explaining the principal changes needed to create the unified system. A further third is devoted to the plan for social security, including the implications for the social security budget. By contrast, more reflective discussions on the level of benefits and the thorny problem of rent occupy less than a tenth of the report.

The other reason for the report's brisk style is more speculative, namely, that Beveridge clearly saw this as a momentous opportunity, a time ripe for change and decisive action. At such times, the debates about 'problems' and 'difficulties' that preoccupy policy makers, academics and interest groups in normal times have to end: action demands that decisions and choices be made. Beveridge clearly saw this as a revolutionary moment:

The first principle is that any proposals for the future, while they should use to the full the experience gathered in the past, should not be restricted by consideration of sectional interests established in the obtaining of that experience. Now, when the war is abolishing landmarks of every kind, is the opportunity for using experience in a clear field. A revolutionary moment in the world's history is a time for revolutions, not for patching. (Beveridge, 1942: para. 7)

Want and its causes

'Want' in the Beveridge Report is defined, precisely, as lacking the means of healthy subsistence (1942: para. 11). When the report comes later to estimate the minimum income that would be necessary to avoid want, it is made clear what the means of healthy subsistence consist of, namely food, clothing, fuel, light, household sundries and rent. A certain leeway for 'inefficiency of spending' was included (ibid.: para. 217). In taking this approach, Beveridge was drawing on a long tradition of social research which had sought to establish the extent of want in Britain via surveys of living conditions. From several studies conducted before the war in different British cities, Beveridge drew a key conclusion about the cause of want:

Of all the want shown by the surveys, from three-quarters to five-sixths, according to the precise standard chosen for want, was due to interruption or loss of earning power. Practically the whole of the remaining one quarter to one sixth was due to failure to relate income during earning to the size of the family. (Ibid.: para. 11)

This finding – that want is due either to loss of earnings or to large family size – has direct practical implications. First, a household where nobody is earning must be provided with an income sufficient to provide at least a subsistence standard of living. Secondly, families need to be provided with additional money to cover the cost of bringing up children. The 'abolition of want', Beveridge concluded, 'requires a double re-distribution of income, through social insurance and by family needs' (ibid.).

The Plan for Social Security

The Plan for Social Security that Beveridge set out for abolishing want was based on a number of principles. These included a flat rate of benefit, set at a level to meet subsistence principles; a flat rate of contribution, and comprehensiveness, which means that everyone is to be covered by the plan. Comprehensiveness, though, did not mean uniformity; rather, the population was divided into six classes with different benefits and contributions (in some cases none) applying to each. These six classes were employees, employers and the self-employed; housewives; others of working age not gainfully employed; below working age, and retired above working age. With the exception of the benefits for class V, that is children, whose needs (except those of the first child) were to be met by children's allowances paid for directly by the Exchequer (Treasury), all other benefits were to be provided by a scheme of social insurance, funded by individual, employer and government contributions. The largest range of benefits (and the highest rates of contribution) applied to class I (employees) who were entitled to benefit for unemployment and disability, pension on retirement, medical treatment and funeral expenses. Class II (the self-employed) were entitled to all but the first of these. Class IV (other non-working adults) were entitled to all but the first two. Class III (married women) were entitled to maternity grant, provision for widowhood and separation and retirement pensions on the basis of their husbands' contributions. Class VI were entitled to retirement pensions.

One striking feature of this system of classification and its attendant benefits is the differential treatment of men and women, and in particular of married women. While it is beyond the scope of this chapter to examine the reactions to the Beveridge Report, it is of note that this particular aspect of the plan was subject to criticism at the time. One particularly interesting version of this criticism was that the plan's great innovation, of requiring every male citizen and every unmarried female citizen to contribute to a national insurance fund, was less radical – and complete – than it could and should have been precisely because this requirement was not extended to over 9 million married women, who were therefore shut out, or exempted from direct participation in the scheme. The error – an error that lies in the moral rather than the economic sphere – lies in denying to the married woman, rich or poor, housewife or paid worker, an independent personal status. From this error springs a crop of injustices, complications and difficulties, personal, marital and administrative, involving in the long run men both married and unmarried, and the married as well as the unmarried woman (Abbot and Bompas, 1943).

Insurance not means-testing
While Beveridge acknowledged that the complete abolition of want would also require national assistance and voluntary insurance, albeit as 'subsidiary methods', the centrepiece of his plans was a scheme of insurance built around a Social Insurance Fund. This decision, to base the plan on insurance rather than assistance (to use the 1940s terminology), is of profound importance. There are two key differences between insurance and assistance. The first is that, with insurance, benefits are paid as of right, that right having been earned by virtue of having contributed to the Social Insurance Fund. By contrast, with assistance, benefits are paid only if the recipient's income (and usually the income of their household as a whole) is sufficiently low, something that is determined as a result of a means test. The second key difference is that with insurance there is a fund. By contrast, means-tested benefits are paid for directly out of general government revenues.

While our modern system of social security is still a mixture of insurance and means-testing, it is one in which means-testing is very much to the fore. Given that, it is worth dwelling on the principal reason why Beveridge opted for social insurance as opposed to national assistance as the vehicle for delivering freedom from want. This was, he said, because 'benefit in return for contributions, rather than free allowances from the State, is what the people of Britain desire'. He went on:

This desire is shown both by the established popularity of compulsory insurance, and by the phenomenal growth of voluntary insurance against sickness, against death and for endowment, and most recently for hospital treatment. It is shown in another way by the strength of popular objection to any kind of means test. This objection springs not so much from a desire to get everything for nothing, as from resentment at provision which appears to penalise what people have come to regard as the duty and pleasure of thrift, of putting pennies away for a rainy day. Management of one's income is an essential element of a citizen's freedom. Payment of a substantial part of the cost of benefit irrespective of the means of the contributor is the firm basis of a claim to benefit irrespective of means. (Beveridge, 1942: para. 21)

If there is one paragraph in the Beveridge Report against which the modern system of social security in this country might be judged, this paragraph would be it.

Minimum incomes to avoid want

As a plan of action, the Beveridge Report had to come up with precise figures for the amount of money that is actually needed to provide subsistence and so avoid want. To illustrate what was involved, table 1.1 presents estimates for adults of working age and also, for comparison, retired couples. These figures are shown at 1938 prices. The categories of spending are those previously defined as constituting subsistence, along with an allowance ('margin') for what Beveridge calls inefficiency in spending.

TABLE 1.1: Requirements for adults of working age, and retired persons (at 1938 prices) (Beveridge, 1942: paras 222 and 225, tables IX and X)

	Food	Clothing	Fuel, light and sundries	Margin	Rent	Total
Working-age man	7s. 0d	1s. 6d	2s. 6d	1s. 6d	6s. 6d	19s. 0d
Working-age woman	6s. 0d	1s. 6d	2s. 6d	1s. 6d	6s. 6d	18s. 0d
Working-age man and wife	13s. 0d	3s. 0d	4s. 0d	2s. 0d	10s. 0d	32s. 0d
Retired man and wife	11s. 6d	2s. 8d	5s. 0d	2s. 0d	8s. 6d	29s. 8d

Three points of detail are of note here. First, comparison of the rows for a single man and a single woman shows a slightly higher total for men, reflecting the view that a man needs more food than a woman. Secondly, comparison of the two rows for a man and wife shows a higher total for the working-age couple, reflecting their greater need for food and clothing, only partly offset by the retired couple's greater need for fuel.

Despite these differences, Beveridge concludes that simplicity as well as the 'strong public opinion in favour of securing for the aged something more than bare subsistence' dictate that there should actually be no differentiation in benefits either between men and women or between working age and retired persons (Beveridge, 1942: 251). At 1942 prices, the resulting minimum incomes were estimated at 40s. a week for a couple and 24s. a week for a single adult. Thirdly, the use of a single figure for rent for each given family type – in effect, across the whole country – is a major problem. All prices vary somewhat across the country but whereas food, clothing, fuel and light were found by Beveridge to vary by about 5 per cent either side of the average, rent ranged from 30 per cent below average in Scotland to 50 per cent above average in London. Rents in agricultural areas were also much lower than rents in industrial areas.

The report debated whether the benefit should be allowed to vary according to the actual rent paid. In contrast to its normally decisive tone, the decision to reject that idea was described as provisional, and left open for the possibility of review at a later date by a successor committee. The trouble with this is that it undermines a key requirement of the scheme, namely that an insurance benefit should provide the means for healthy subsistence. Given the size and the variation in rent across the country, a uniform benefit would mean that a couple in some parts of the country would be 8s. a week, or 25 per cent, better off than the same couple in London.

Children's allowances

Beveridge also estimated the amount of money required to provide healthy subsistence for a child. After allowing for the provision made indirectly through school meals and free school milk, the report suggested an average figure of 8s. a week per child. One important point about the proposal for children's allowances was that such a sum was not to be paid in respect of every child. The argument advanced for this was that the allowances were there to help parents but not to relieve them of all financial responsibility for their children. One way of putting this into effect would have been to have set the allowance at a lower level than the amount required for subsistence. Another was to set the allowance at the required amount but pay it only for some but not all children. On the grounds that 'very few men's wages are insufficient to cover at least two adults and one child' (Beveridge, 1942: para. 417), Beveridge opted for setting the allowance at the subsistence level, but to be paid for the second and subsequent children only. If neither parent was working, however, the allowance would be paid to the first child as well.

The maintenance of employment

Beveridge was explicit that a scheme of social insurance could only eliminate want as part of a comprehensive policy for social progress. Both child allowances and a comprehensive health and rehabilitation service were parts of that comprehensive policy. So too was the assumption that employment would be maintained. This phrase – 'the maintenance of employment' – is best understood in terms of what it rules out and what it does not. It does not, for example, rule out what could be called short-term unemployment, arising (say) from seasonal fluctuations or from the closure of individual firms, or the decline of particular industries. What it does rule out is 'mass unemployment and . . . unemployment prolonged year after year for the same individual' (Beveridge, 1942: para. 441).

Beveridge set down several reasons why this was so important. One was that mass unemployment might make the cost of the whole plan insupportable. Another was that the only satisfactory test of unemployment was the offer of another job, something that with mass unemployment is not a general remedy. A third was the demoralising, and indeed debilitating, effect of any but the shortest spells of unemployment. The most important, however, was that on its own, income security, which was all that social insurance could deliver, was not enough for human happiness. Instead, social insurance 'should be accompanied by an announced determination to use the powers of the state to whatever extent may prove necessary to ensure for all, not indeed absolute continuity of work, but a reasonable chance of productive employment' (Beveridge, 1942: para. 440).

This last point is of paramount importance. The idea that social insurance only ends want conditional on there being a sufficiently high level of employment is one that could just as well have been espoused in 1922 or 1932 as in 1942. But the idea that the state actually has it within its power to ensure that this condition is fulfilled – that is, to maintain employment at the required level – is an expression of the Keynesian doctrine which only came into being with the publication of Keynes's 'General theory of employment, interest and money' in 1936. In believing that what he proposed was practicable, Beveridge therefore depended upon Keynes.

Implementation: sixty years of the welfare state
The 1946 National Insurance Act

The Beveridge Report was put into effect by the 1946 National Insurance Act. The fact that such an important piece of legislation could be enacted so quickly after the end of the war is itself a legacy of the report, which had argued that planning for peace should take place in war. Had this not happened, such a rapid move to legislate would not have been possible. But how faithfully did the 1946 Act follow the report? In particular, did the Act set the benefits at levels that were consistent with what Beveridge calculated as representing subsistence?

Table 1.2 shows weekly rates of benefit both as set out in the report and as eventually introduced in the Act. The first two cases are the benefits, for unemployment, disability or training, for a single working-age man or woman, followed by the same benefits for a working-age man and wife. The third case is the state retirement pension for a couple.

In all three cases, the rates introduced by the 1946 Act were two shillings a week higher than the figures shown in the 1942 report (respectively 9 per cent, 5 per cent and 5 per cent). The table also

Table 1.2: Rates of benefit per week in the 1942 report and the 1946 Act (Beveridge, 1942: para. 401; Owen, 1948: para. 11, p. 10)

	1942 report	1946 Act
Single man or woman aged 21 and upwards	24s. 0d	26s. 0d
Man and not gainfully occupied wife (joint benefit)	40s. 0d	42s. 0d
Man and not gainfully occupied wife (joint pension)	40s. 0d	42s. 0d

shows that the Act adhered to two key principles of the report, namely that single men and women should receive the same benefit and that retired people should receive the same benefit as those of working age. The Act also followed the report in the rates of contribution that it set, although it is of note that the amount by which contribution rates are higher in the Act than the report (for example, by 12 per cent for men and by 10 per cent for women for class I) is slightly more than the amount by which benefits are higher (Beveridge, 1942: para. 443; Owen, 1948, para. 6, p. 8). It is, presumably, a desire to take account of price inflation that accounts for the Act's higher levels of benefit and contribution. Modern data shows that consumer prices rose by about 3 per cent a year in each of the last three years of the war.[1] On that basis, the 1946 figures should have been around 10 per cent higher than the 1942 ones. Although the actual rise in benefits, at least for couples, was rather less than this, the shortfall is only about 5 per cent, or a shilling a week, hardly a significant departure from the standard that Beveridge set.

Importantly, however, the Act did not come into force until 1948 and in the two intervening years price inflation accelerated, from the 3 per cent per year in the last of the war years to 7 per cent. As a result, by the time the Act came into force in July 1948, prices were roughly 25 per cent higher than in 1942. That means that, after allowing for inflation, benefit rates for single adults were about 15 per cent below the level of the report while those for couples were around 20 per cent below.

The 1945 Family Allowances Act
Legislation to introduce family allowances, which had been championed by the campaigning reformer Eleanor Rathbone, was brought in

by the post-war government in 1945. Despite the difference in name, Beveridge's children's allowances and Rathbone's family allowances were actually very similar. In particular, family allowances were to be paid only for the second and subsequent children of families whenever a parent was earning. To complete this part of the Beveridge plan, the 1946 National Insurance Act included a payment to be made for the first child to families when earnings were interrupted.

But were family allowances high enough? Beveridge had recommended an average of 8s. per week in 1942 prices. With 25 per cent inflation between 1942 and 1948, the required figure by the latter year would have been 10s. Yet, the value of the allowance for the first child of a family without earnings was set in the National Insurance Act at just 7s. 6d, effectively 25 per cent below the Beveridge level. Furthermore, the Family Allowances Act set the family allowance for second and subsequent children at just 5s., a level at which it remained throughout the rest of the 1940s. On that basis, by the time the welfare state came into being in 1948, children's allowances for families with earnings fell short of Beveridge's estimate of subsistence by 50 per cent.

The Beveridge consensus: 1948 to 1973

Figure 1.1 is the first of two pictures that summarise how Beveridge's plan for abolishing want has fared over the sixty years since its implementation. Two types of quantity are shown on the graph. The first is the value of selected National Insurance benefits as well as the value of the family allowance, adjusted for inflation and turned into an index that is set equal to 1.0 in 1948. All three series exhibit a saw-tooth pattern, reflecting a continuous erosion of the real value of the benefit by inflation, interspersed with upward spikes corresponding to the periodic uprating of benefits. The other quantity shown on the graph is an index of real (that is, inflation adjusted) consumption per head of UK population, in effect, a proxy for the average standard of living.

The big patterns of interest correspond to three distinct periods: the first twenty-five years to 1973; then two equal length periods of seventeen years, from 1973 to 1990, and 1990 to the present.

Figure 1.1: Real value of selected National Insurance benefits and family allowance, 1948 to 2010[2]

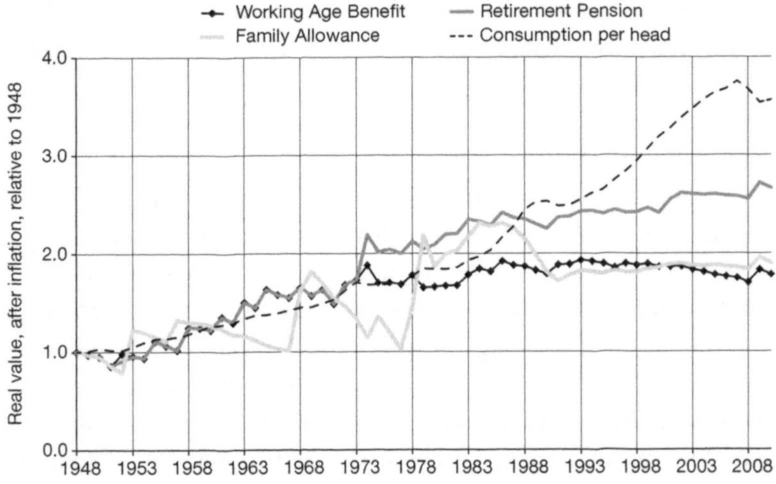

Looking at the twenty-five years between 1948 and 1973, three main things stand out. First, apart from one tiny glitch in the early 1950s, the indices for the two National Insurance benefits, for working age and retired, move in step with one another (to such an extent that the two lines are as one). This shows clear adherence to the Beveridge principle that the two should be equal despite the fact that subsistence for retired people was calculated as being slightly below that for those of working age. Secondly, from the mid-1950s onwards, the value of these benefits was increased not just to keep up with inflation (a horizontal line) but also with increases in the average standard of living. Close inspection of the graph for the 1950s and 1960s suggests a quite marked divergence from this standard over short runs of years, to which a detailed history of the politics of those times would probably assign importance. Here, though, the key point is that by 1973, and after allowing for inflation, National Insurance benefits were worth 70 per cent more than they had been in 1948, exactly in line with the growth in the average standard of living. Thirdly, and by contrast, the value of family allowances does not show any sustained increase over the twenty-five years. Indeed, by 1967, its value after inflation was no higher at all than it had been in 1948. The same low point was reached again a decade later in 1977. This failure to achieve any sustained uprating for family allowances beyond that necessary to keep up with inflation is especially striking given the very low level (compared with what Beveridge thought necessary) at which they were introduced.

Breakdown: 1974 to 1990

The consensus that prevailed since 1948 began to break apart, piece by piece, in 1974. The changes that caused that break-up, though, were by no means all attacks upon, or retreats from, that consensus: on the contrary, some were clearly advances. The first principle to go was the idea that working-age and retirement benefits should be of the same value. What broke this principle, in 1974, was a much larger increase in the state retirement pension than in the working-age benefit. The gap that opened up between the two benefits, of some 15 per cent, was never to close again. Secondly, the idea that benefits should rise in line with the average standard of living also came to be abandoned. This idea was never explicitly part of Beveridge, but it had clearly become custom and practice in the quarter century up to 1973. Yet, between 1974 and 1990, during which the average standard of living rose by just under 50 per cent, the real value of the retirement pension rose by less than 10 per cent, while working-age benefit did not rise at all. Thirdly, after a continued further decline to 1977, family allowances and their replacement, child benefit, doubled in value between 1977 and 1979. After some further rises up to 1984, its value after inflation fell back to a level about 70 per cent above what they had been in 1948. Although that was a marked improved on the pre-1973 period, this was still below the level that Beveridge had thought necessary in 1942.[3]

The modern consensus: 1991 and beyond

In contrast to the hiatus of the years from 1974, the period after 1990 is a very clear and simple one, namely, that the basic rule is that insurance benefits for working-age and retired people, and universal benefits for children, rise only in line with prices. So, over the period from 1990 to 2006, while the average standard of living rose by more than 40 per cent after inflation, the state retirement pension rose by just 15 per cent while working-age benefits and child benefit did not rise at all.[4]

It is important to note that in itself, this indexing of benefits to prices rather than earnings or living standards, while a break with the pre-1973 consensus, is not of itself a break with Beveridge. This is because the question of how the minimum income standards should be uprated over a long period of time was not addressed in the 1942 report.

But, in one respect, the post 1990 consensus has broken with Beveridge in a fundamental way by shifting the system in favour of means-tested, rather than insurance-based benefits. Figure 1.2 presents the evidence for this as far as working-age and pensioner means-tested benefits are concerned, labelled here using the 1940s terminology of national assistance.

In 1948, when the Beveridge scheme came into effect, national assistance provided 40s. a week for a couple and 24s. a week for a single adult, exactly 2s. a week less in each case than the comparable insurance benefits (table 1.2). In general, such a differential between the two types of benefit prevailed all the way through to 1973. After

Figure i.2: Real value of selected national assistance benefits and the state retirement pension, 1948 to 2010[5]

that, however, the picture changes. For working-age people, just as increases in the insurance benefit quickly shifted to follow prices rather than earnings or average living standards (figure 1.1), so too did increases in the corresponding means-tested benefit (figure 1.2). The degree of similarity between the values of the insurance and means-tested benefits is such that if they were shown on the same graph, their paths would be almost indistinguishable.

For a while after 1973, the means-tested pension benefit continued to follow closely the insurance equivalent. But from about 1990, this ceased to be so. Instead of rising much more slowly than average living standards (as did the state retirement pension), the means-tested benefit for pensioners started to rise more or less in line with that average. As a result, by 2007, the means-tested 'pension credit' (for a single person) was worth around 30 per cent more than the insurance-based equivalent.

Were it possible to reduce the effects of the various different schemes of means-tested, in-work support for children to a simple line, this would also show a strong bias in favour of the means-tested tax credits over the universal family allowance/child benefit. The fact that the first of these schemes (family income supplement) began in 1971 is evidence that at least one crack in the Beveridge system was opening up even before the twenty-five-year consensus had quite ended. To give an idea of the scale of the bias, in 2007, the value of the means-tested child tax credit was almost exactly twice the value of the universal child benefit.

Summary judgement and modern lessons
Did the welfare state succeed in abolishing want?
It may seem that a scheme aimed at abolishing want should simply be judged on whether want was indeed abolished following its introduction. But in the case of the welfare state and Beveridge's plan that idea does not really work.

For a start, suitable data to help answer the question are sparse. Seebohm Rowntree's third study of poverty in York (Rowntree and Lavers, 1951) is one of the few sources of information that is potentially comparable to the studies undertaken before the Second

World War upon which Beveridge drew for insight and inspiration. Although later analysis of the same data cast some doubt on the conclusion, Rowntree found that under 2 per cent of the York population were in poverty in 1950, a ten-fold decline compared with what was found in an earlier survey in the mid-1930s (Glennerster, 2004).

But, even if these figures are correct, and even if we were willing to make the heroic assumption that they are more or less representative of the situation across the UK as a whole, that would not in itself mean that this aspect of the welfare state had worked. For, as Beveridge made clear, the ending of want depended crucially on there being a high level of employment. If the overall level of want was much lower after the war, employment, rather than the welfare state, may have been the reason. A better test of the welfare state's role in abolishing want needs to reflect the specific aspects of the problem that it was designed to deal with, namely to prevent want among those experiencing a loss or interruption of earning power as well as among larger families whose earning power alone is insufficient for that purpose.

Although there is very little data for the 1950s, the Institute for Fiscal Studies has recently published estimates from 1961 onwards of annual poverty rates using the modern measure which counts people as being in poverty if their household income is below a certain fraction of median contemporary disposable equivalised household income in the year in question.[6] Table 1.3 gives the figures for 1961–3 for pensioners, children and working-age adults living in households with incomes below both 60 per cent of median income (the principal modern measure), as well as two lower thresholds, namely 50 per cent and 40 per cent of median income. The pensioner data gives an indication of how far the welfare state had abolished the want that was due to an absence of earnings while comparisons of the data on child and working-age poverty give an indication of how far it had abolished want arising from larger family size.

From the modern perspective, table 1.3 leaves no doubt whatsoever that the welfare state had failed to abolish want in the early 1960s. The principal modern measure is the 60 per cent threshold. Fully 40 per cent of pensioners had incomes below this level, while

Table 1.3: People in households below low-income thresholds, 1961 to 1963[7]

	Pensioners		Children		Working-age adults	
Below 60% of median	40%	2,900,000	14%	1,700,000	8%	2,300,000
Below 50% of median	29%	2,000,000	6%	700,000	4%	1,300,000
Below 40% of median	11%	800,000	3%	300,000	2%	700,000

14 per cent of children – almost twice the proportion for working-age adults – were in this situation too.

But is this – the modern measure of poverty – the right yardstick by which to judge the welfare state? In 1961 and 1962, the pension for a single adult was worth 57s. 6d a week, slightly below (by my reckoning) the value of the 40 per cent income threshold. Table 1.3 shows that some 10 per cent of pensioners had incomes below that threshold – so by no means abolition, but obviously much better. But taking the benefit as the yardstick is a circular argument. What about taking Beveridge's 1942 estimate of 24s. a week and uprating it to 1961? As prices were about twice as high at the start of the 1960s as in 1942, the implied minimum income to avoid want then would have been 48s. Even if the required minimum income were to rise in line with the average standard of living, the figure would be still only be 60s. per week, still close to the 40 per cent threshold.

Ultimately, in the absence of an agreed measure of want, there can be no definitive answer to the question of whether the welfare state succeeded in abolishing it. From the modern perspective, it most certainly did not. By contrast, projecting Beveridge's own standard forward some twenty years suggests a much better performance. Yet, Beveridge's standard, which was after all based on what was deemed necessary subsistence in 1938, may reasonably be thought to be too low, even after uprating, for the early 1960s. Certainly, by the mid-1960s, campaigners were citing the two-thirds of a million children in households with incomes below the national assistance rate and the further 1½ million with incomes only slightly above it as evidence of child poverty. These figures look much more like the modern 60 per cent threshold than the lower 40 per cent one.

Did breaking with Beveridge help?

However well or poorly the welfare state performed relative to its goal of abolishing want, were things better once the constraints of the Beveridge system were abandoned? Figure 1.3 begins with the proportions of children, pensioners and working-age adults who were in poverty in the early 1960s (and which appeared in table 1.3) and extends them all the way up to the present day. With one exception, the answer delivered unequivocally by figure 1.3 is that departures from the Beveridge scheme did not improve things at all; far from it.

Looking at children first, after fluctuating around some 13 per cent in the 1960s and 1970s, child poverty doubled in the 1980s. Despite the high priority attached by the New Labour governments in office since 1997 to reducing it, the fall in the child poverty rate since then, from above 25 per cent to above 20 per cent by 2005–6, looks fairly modest. A return to the levels that so concerned campaigners in the mid-1960s would now be seen as a triumph. The poverty rate among working-age adults, meanwhile, fared even worse. Not only is it, at around 15 per cent, double the levels in the 1960s and 1970s, but there was also no subsequent fall, even a modest one, in the early 2000s.

Figure 1.3: The proportions of children, pensioners and other adults in poverty since 1961[8]

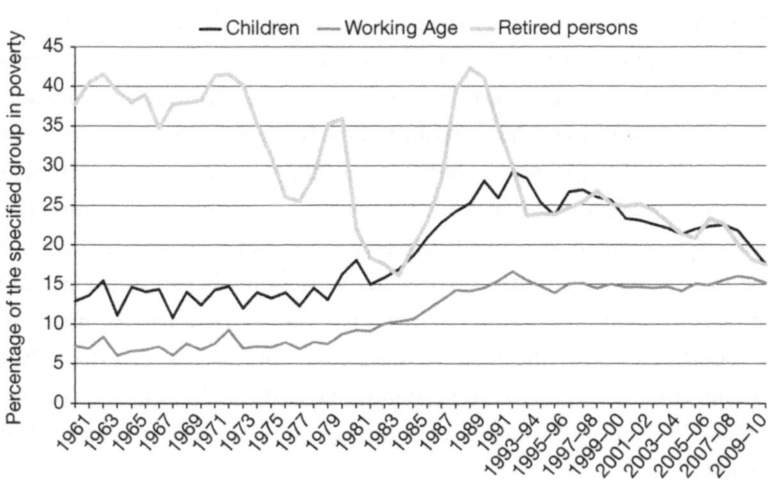

The one exception to the generally negative view of the break with Beveridge, the one clear success in other words, is the substantial fall in the rate of pensioner poverty over the 1970s. It must be said that the reliability of these estimates prior to the mid-1990s is much lower than it is now, which may lie behind the gyrations in the pensioner poverty rate in the early 1980s.[9] Nevertheless, the sense that there was a substantial fall over the 1970s and into the early 1980s is not implausible. The substantial and sustained increase in the state retirement pension (relative to the benefit for working-age people) from 1974 certainly played a role, although this was not the only factor. But while the ending of parity between the benefits for working-age and retired adults was a break with a Beveridge principle, it is fair to say that that principle is only a second-order one. The principle of equality between the two had, after all, been invoked by Beveridge to argue for a higher rate for pensioners than considerations of subsistence alone would have dictated. That it should be higher still (the 1974 argument) is therefore hardly a fundamental challenge.

What should be noted, however, is that (as per figure 1.2), the large fall in pensioner poverty in the 1970s predates the modern preference for relying upon means-tested rather than insurance benefits to bring about falls in pensioner poverty. Beveridge's preference for insurance over the means test was unambiguous. The fact that the fall in pensioner poverty in the 1970s and early 1980s did not rely on means-testing suggests that the one great success of the modern programme of poverty reduction, that is, the fall in pensioner poverty, cannot as such be attributed to the preference for the means-tested benefit (pension credit) over the insurance-based benefit (the state retirement pension).[10] This later experience – not only the subsequent steep rise in all poverty rates but also the subsequent failure to do any better than had been done before (and usually in fact to leave them much worse) – means that earlier negative conclusions about the welfare state must be heavily qualified. For while the Beveridge system could have done better, the record since 1979 shows that without it, things could have been a great deal worse.

The political significance of social insurance

It may be argued that since the great rise in poverty in the 1980s was the result of the return of mass unemployment, Beveridge's scheme could no longer have coped anyway. But even if that is valid, the argument misses the vital point that the return of mass unemployment was not the result of some exogenous 'shock' (as economists like to call such things), but rather the conscious result of political decisions to reject the goals and methods of economic policy which were as integral to the post-war settlement as was the welfare state itself.

It seems to me that it is against this wider background, of the whole post-war settlement, that the welfare state must be seen and judged. Coupled with the commitment to avoid mass unemployment, the institution of the welfare state was not only the means by which want could be abolished, but also, critically, the embodiment of the idea that it was a society-wide responsibility to see to it that it should be abolished. The routine criticism of insurance-based schemes (as well as universal ones, such as family allowances or their modern incarnation, child benefit) is that increasing benefits is 'expensive' because the money is spread thinly across the whole population. By contrast, means-testing, so it said, concentrates the money on 'those who need it most'. Even if this argument makes sense from a narrow accounting point of view,[11] it pays no attention to the need to secure and maintain popular support for the arrangement. Beveridge was not designing his welfare state for the short term. The fact that the scheme was part of the consensus for a quarter of a century is testament to the popular support that it must have enjoyed. Although Beveridge saw himself writing at a revolutionary moment, I suspect that a crucial source of that popular support was the fact that his plan was a consolidation of what had gone before, of the various 'voluntary' schemes for social insurance and allied services that he sought to take over and replicate at a higher, more complete level.

With its goal of abolition within a generation, the modern attempt to end child poverty is not a short-term enterprise either. But unlike Beveridge, it neither has deep roots nor is it in any sense aimed at offering something for everyone.[12] While it would be premature to discount the possibility of reaching a goal whose achievement is set for nine years hence (in 2020), the gradual accumulation of evidence year by year suggests that the prospect is vanishing fast. In broad terms, progress on child poverty ceased in around 2004/5, since then the numbers have once more started to drift up again. As a result, with half of the time gone between the announcement of the goal and the date by which it was due to be achieved, the number of children in poverty in the UK had fallen by only one-eighth (Palmer et al., 2008: 39–40). To reach its goal by the given date, progress thereafter needed to be three times as fast as actual progress up until then – a very tall order indeed.

Could a 'return to Beveridge' play any part in the reinvigoration of the anti-poverty strategy that the crude numbers alone show is urgent? On the face of it, the answer would appear to be an emphatic 'no', for the simple reason that several key assumptions on which Beveridge's scheme depended do not hold. For one thing, the UK has not, for several decades, enjoyed anything that could remotely be described as full employment. Even at its lowest, in 2004 and 2005, unemployment in the first decade of the twenty-first century had still fallen no lower than what were, until then, the record post-war levels of unemployment seen at the end of the 1970s.[13]

For another, half the children in poverty in the UK belong to working families. After a pause in the late 1990s, the number of children in what is called 'in-work poverty' has been rising steadily since at least as long ago as the end of the 1970s (Kenway, 2008: 10–12). For a strategy based on the assertion that 'work is the best route out of poverty', both the extent of in-work poverty and its seemingly inexorable upward trend are potentially fatal. But since Beveridge, too, believed that (larger families excepted) income from work would be sufficient to avoid want, in-work poverty appears to be as much a threat to his approach as to the modern one.

But while a 'return to Beveridge', even if such a thing were possible, could not be the answer, there are elements of his approach that certainly would help. We mention two here. First, the government could follow Beveridge in basing the monetary value of out-of-work benefits on estimates of the amount of money people need in order to be above the poverty line.

This principled approach to setting benefits, in relation to need, would be quite different from the purely pragmatic approach which concerns itself simply with choosing a rule to govern the annual up-rating of benefit, in line with either prices or earnings. In the short term, the difference between these two rules is trivial and it is a sign of how limited the debate about benefits has been that this should be the great dividing line. It is therefore to be hoped that a recently published study from the Rowntree Foundation, on minimum income standards, can provide an authoritative basis on which to resurrect the approach that Beveridge himself took (Bradshaw et al., 2008).

Secondly, the government should consider the role that an improved contribution-based 'job-seeker's allowance' (the relic within the modern system of Beveridge's insurance benefit for the unemployed single working-age man or woman) might play in combating in-work poverty. The explanation for the apparent paradox here, of using an out-of-work benefit to reduce in-work poverty, is that an unemployed person's entitlement to this insurance-based benefit is not in any way diminished by the earnings or other income of their partner. By contrast, the means-tested, income-based job-seeker's allowance depends on family income – and is therefore reduced, pound for pound, by the amount of any partner earnings. As a result, while the means-tested version of the benefit can do nothing to increase the income of 'part-working' families (i.e. where one partner only works), the insurance version does increase it. The reason why this is so relevant is that most in-work poverty is to be found among 'part-working' families (Kenway, 2008: 16)

We stress that this is no panacea: probably only a small minority of non-working partners in part-working families are unemployed. Nevertheless, the modern-day descendant of Beveridge's insurance benefit is ideally suited to addressing short-term unemployment – which, since that is what it was designed for, is not surprising. What may be surprising, though, is that this benefit works so well for couples. There is an irony here: Beveridge is sometimes dismissed as being hopelessly out-of-date because his system was designed for a family in which the man worked and the woman did not. Yet, unlike means-testing, which treats the couple as a single economic entity, Beveridge's approach allows them to pursue independent working lives, offering to support either individually, without harm to the other, in the event of unemployment.

Notes

1. Here and elsewhere in this chapter, the measure of prices used is the Office for National Statistics' 'Long term indicator of prices of consumer goods and services' (series reference CDKO) – an annual series before June 1947 and monthly thereafter.

2. This graph combines three types of data. 1) Three series for the values of selected National Insurance benefits for single adults (unemployment; retirement pension) and for child benefit (before 1977, family allowance) for the second and subsequent children (Institute for Fiscal Studies, 2007). 2) An index of consumer prices (the Office for National Statistics' 'Long term indicator of prices of consumer goods and services', series reference CDKO) which is used to adjust the benefit series for the effects of price inflation. 3) Two series from the Office for National Statistics, on household final consumption expenditure at constant prices (series reference ABPF) and UK resident population (series reference DYAY), used to construct an index of consumption per head. On a technical point, the graph is drawn using monthly data, with the individual figure for each year shown being for the month of July.

3. As noted above, the value of family allowances in 1948 was only 50 per cent of what Beveridge thought necessary. Even after a 70 per cent increase, the value in 1990 was only 85 per cent of what Beveridge judged necessary.

4. It should be stressed here that the references to child benefit here refer to the specific, universal benefit of that name and not to the array of means-tested benefits for children. Child benefit, introduced in 1977, is the direct successor to the family allowance and incorporated child tax allowances.

5. Two lines on this graph, for the state retirement pension and consumption per head are identical to the corresponding series shown in figure 1.1. The other two lines, namely the indices of national assurance benefits are calculated the same way as those in figure 1.1 but using values for 'Income Support' and 'Pension Credit' via Institute of Fiscal Studies (2007).

6. It should be noted that in this procedure, incomes are 'equivalised' – a simple numerical process using standard formulae which is intended to take account of the fact that a single adult living on, say, £200 a week is obviously much better off than a family of four on the same money.

7. Author's calculations based on data on poverty before housing costs from Institute for Fiscal Studies (2007).

8. Author's calculations based on data from Institute for Fiscal Studies (2007). The series graphed are those showing the proportion of people living in households whose income is below 60 per cent of the contemporary (same year) median, before housing costs.

9. From 1994/5 onwards, the poverty estimates have been calculated using a much larger and more reliable survey (the Family Resources Survey) than before.

10. As Liz Lloyd notes correctly, the current value of the state retirement pension is such that anyone who is reliant on this alone for their income will be in poverty and entitled to the means-tested pension credit as a supplementary source of income

11. It should be noted that there is no basis for it in economics for the simple reason that income transfers are not, in themselves, economic costs. Only to the extent that such transfers have adverse effects on economic output can they be said, in economic terms, to incur a cost.

12. Whether a social insurance scheme could be use to abolish poverty among just one group of the population is another moot point. Certainly, Beveridge went to some lengths to try to show how his scheme offered some benefits to all.

13. In 2004 and 2005, 1.43m and 1.47m, compared with 1.47m, 1.45m and 1.43m in 1977, 1978 and 1979 respectively. Source: Office for National Statistics, series MGSC, four quarter seasonally adjusted UK unemployment.

2

DISEASE

Social democracy, health inequalities and the welfare state

Michael Sullivan

> It [social security] is one part only of an attack upon five giant
> evils: upon the physical Want . . . upon Disease, which often
> causes that want and brings many other troubles in its train, upon
> Ignorance which no democracy can afford among its citizens,
> upon Squalor . . . and upon the Idleness which destroys wealth
> and corrupts men.
> (Beveridge, 1942: 170)

> The story combined elements of More's Utopia, Bunyan's
> Pilgrim's Progress and Swift's Gulliver's Travels, with a dash of
> Star Trek thrown in: it urged politicians to boldly go where none
> of their predecessors had dared venture before.
> (Pimlott, 1992)

The National Health Service was established over sixty years ago, an achievement often (and understandably) attributed to the Welsh, working-class, post-war Labour minister of health, Aneurin Bevan. Without that political colossus, the development of socialised medicine, as part of a welfare state, might have been thwarted – or at least delayed – by the posturing of the medical profession and the lukewarm attitude of the Conservative opposition.

Seventy years ago saw the publication of the report of an aristocratic academic cum wartime civil servant, which provided the legitimacy and rationale for the NHS as one of the state institutions which would do battle with disease, one of the 'five giants' associated with unregulated capitalism – and for a welfare state which would civilise capitalism. The Beveridge Report (1942) recommended that a post-war government should establish a social security system to banish 'want'. Alongside health and social security systems, it perceived the need for a meritocratic education system (to fight ignorance), public housing (to tackle squalor) and government intervention to achieve full employment (and thus make 'idleness' a thing of the past). The report was, as Ben Pimlott wittily summarises in the quotation above, a combination of elements from Utopia, *Pilgrim's Progress*, *Gulliver's Travels* and *Star Trek*.

The ex-miner from Tredegar and the Oxbridge don might then be seen as the joint midwives of a quintessentially British revolution. Whether our political inclinations are to nominate the Welsh rhetorician (see Foot, 1973) or the aristocratic 'people's Will' (see Timmins, 2001; chapter 1) as the more significant of the duo, the NHS, vested on 5 July 1948, has come to have a special place in the affection of the British electorate.

Its rationale was both universalistic and targeted. That is to say, the NHS was established effectively to vanquish disease and ill health irrespective of the social standing of the patient (universal services, free at the point of use). But an equally important objective was to see that this occurred by ensuring equal access to healthcare and that the scars of fundamental health inequalities – that had characterised pre-war services – should be healed. This chapter accepts that the NHS has played a part in facilitating the development of curative medical science. It looks in some detail, however, at the development of health policy since the end of the Second World War in order to address whether health policy and the NHS can also tackle inequalities in health.

The creation of the NHS

The NHS has often been seen as the main socialist achievement of the 1945–51 Attlee government. It has been seen not only as a rational means of tackling health problems but also as a health equality machine. This is entirely understandable: the Beveridge Report argued that something had to be done about capitalism. More narrowly, it reflected the view of socially liberal members of all political parties that the economic Depression and social deprivation of the 1930s should not be allowed to recur. At the core of its recommendations for a full-employment welfare state was a conviction that governments have a legitimate moral obligation to intervene in the economy and the social fabric of society. Beveridge envisaged the creation of a welfare-capitalist, post-war society in which government intervened, when necessary, to maintain full employment and established basic state services and rights – to health, education, income maintenance, housing and personal social services. Though it is clear that Beveridge himself saw that such a welfare state would aid both industrial capitalism and the recipients of welfare services (Harris, 1977, 1981) – and despite the seminal contribution of Marshall in locating welfare state development within notions of rights acquisition in welfare capitalist societies (Marshall, 1963, 1972) – some left-wing commentators (Deacon, 1983; Player and Barbour Might, 1988) have seen the NHS as an instrument of socialism.

Powell (1997a) reminds us that this belief in the socialist pedigree of the NHS was reasonably widespread among the political left. In 1950, *Tribune*, the Labour left newspaper, called it 'the most socialist measure to be introduced by the last Parliament' (cited in ibid., 1997a). However, Carpenter (1980) draws the distinction between the socialist ends of the NHS and the non-socialist means used to introduce it – including, though not restricted to, the agreements to allow general practitioners to relate to the service as private contractors and to permit hospital doctors to retain some private practice. Michael Foot (1973) – Bevan's biographer, disciple, friend, successor as MP for Ebbw Vale and leader of the Labour party in the early 1980s – defines it as simply the most socialist achievement of the 1945 Labour government. The last words here should perhaps be left to Bevan. In what Iliffe strangely terms the 'communism' of the NHS – 'from each according to his ability to each according to his need', in Marx's famous phrase (Marx, 1974: 347) – and Bevan sees as the 'collective principle', the post-war minister of health celebrates the fact that

> resources of medical skill and the apparatus of healing shall be
> placed at the disposal of the patient, without charge, when he

> or she needs them; that medical treatment and care should be a
> communal responsibility that should be made available to rich
> and poor alike in accordance with medical need and by no other
> criteria. (Bevan, 1952: 78)

Elsewhere, he elaborated that this '100% principle' was important
to ensure that there was not only universal entitlement to the new
NHS but also as near to complete use of it as possible. It had, *de facto*
as well as *de jure*, to be a universal service. According to Bevan, the
NHS was redistributive as well: 'what more pleasure can a millionaire
have than to know that his taxes will help the sick? The redistributive
aspect of the scheme was one which attracted me almost as much as
the therapeutical' (Bevan, cited in Webster, 1991: 193)

This redistributive principle sees the NHS as being about – and
being capable of – reversing health inequalities. In the late 1970s, for
instance, Julian Tudor Hart – a socialist GP in a south Wales valley
community and the author of the 'inverse care law' (Hart, 1975) –
could still, and despite the evidence he marshals to indicate that those
areas in most need are most under-doctored, describe the NHS as 'an
island of socialism in a sea of capitalism'. This dogged belief in the
socialist pedigree of Bevan's health service presents us with two key
questions: whose victory was the establishment of the NHS and what
are the factors associated with the persistence of health inequalities,
over the period since the welfare state was established?

Whose victory was the establishment of the NHS?

Viewed from one perspective, Hart's (and indeed Bevan's) view
appears sustainable. Introducing the NHS Bill in the Commons in
1946, Bevan presented the service as divorcing the right to receive
the best service from both the ability to pay and geographical location. The NHS would redistribute service and life-chances by making the same standard of health care available to all, irrespective of
income, class or region. On this reading, the establishment of the
NHS can, indeed, be seen as a victory for ordinary people and as
rooted in socialist ideas. Disease – both as the presence of patho-
genic and other disabling agents and in the sense of inequalities in

the access to remedies – is on this reckoning confronted by Labour's health equality machine.

However, this is far from the whole story. For the establishment of the NHS can also be seen as reflecting a sort of rational managerialism rather than the socialist ideas of the health minister. Looked at from this angle, the war-time departmental civil service and the medical profession collaborated to rationalise the complexities and inequalities of the pre-war health service. Thus the principles that guided the emergence of the NHS are seen as having been consensually established during the tenure of the war-time coalition government. Klein's attempt to square this circle is persuasive (1989). He points to the need to appreciate that different policy actors and different political priorities were influential at different stages of the policy debate. During wartime, the civil service worked to create and nurture a consensus on the need for a national health service. They operated within a politics of health care in which the views of the medical profession were acknowledged as key constraints. Bevan, however, chose to move outside these internal politics.

In fact, shared assumptions and common ground were as prominent in the emergence of the NHS as were disagreements and discord. The creation of a universal, free health service represented the mutual political property of the Conservative, Liberal and Labour parties, as did the belief in the capacity of medical science to conquer ill health. At face value, issues of distributional equality failed to separate the political parties. In other words, the goal of establishing a national health system was a consensual goal. Conflict emerged less over ends than it did over means. It was the Labour government's choice of political means that brought policy makers into head-on confrontation with professional interests. This conflict of interests was accompanied by a clash of values. The values that the emergent NHS represented were rationality, efficiency and equity. The NHS was intended to provide health services in a rational, efficient and fair way. It is at this level that Hart's 'island of socialism' analysis is relatively convincing. These values reflected a victory over other values. Chief among these contending arguments about political means was local government's preference for the local administration of the health service and Morrison's promotion of their interests. This view was rooted in a value of localism that prized local accountability above efficiency, difference above uniformity and local government above national and equitable standards of service.

What emerged from these conflicts were contradictions that were built into the structure of the NHS on its establishment. These contradictions have been the focus of policy discussion, and sometimes change, in the sixty-plus years since the establishment of the NHS. Here we consider, particularly, those issues salient to the failure – or incomplete success – of the NHS and government health policy to eliminate health inequalities.

The hardening of inequalities?

Bevan had justified the creation of a centralised NHS on the basis of universalising the best. That is to say, he believed that central control would avoid the problem of richer areas getting better services. However, during the 1950s this seems to have been exactly what happened, at least in relation to bed numbers. This hardening of inequalities stemmed from the Ministry of Health's decision to accept health authority budgets inherited from the period of post-war Labour government, rather than starting from first principles and assessing need. This had the effect of rewarding most those authorities that had been most profligate following the establishment of the service, a point that the Guillebaud Committee in 1956 was quick to see.

> the system favours most the authorities who showed the least degree of financial responsibility in the early years of the service . . . We agree that the main weakness of the present system of allocating revenue funds is the lack of a consistent long-term objective. (HMSO, 1956: 77)

The committee's report provided, however, no motivation for change. This is perhaps because any attempt to help the least well-off authorities would, during a period of zero growth, have meant redistributing resources. The more favoured authorities were well able to resist this suggestion by pointing out that, despite their relatively favoured position, they were unable to meet need adequately. In this context, the principle of giving priority to maintaining unequal provision rather than changing it won through.

On some other indices, the NHS appears to have mitigated health inequalities, however. In general practitioner services, the NHS developed a system of negative controls that were designed to prevent new practitioners moving into already over-doctored (usually financially well off) areas. The effect of this strategy was to reduce the proportion of patients in under-doctored areas (those where the size of lists was exceptionally large) from 51.5 per cent in 1952 to 18.6 per cent in 1958.

The distribution of specialist hospital services also has to be seen as a qualified success though the scope of those services has to be seen as a failure. In other words, although the evidence suggests that a softening of inequalities occurred in this area, significant general shortages pertained throughout the 1950s. These were not the birth pangs of the NHS but the early signs of persistent health inequality.

Health inequalities in a cold political climate

Health inequalities persisted through the 1960s and 1970s, alongside technological and medical advances and despite attempts to plan rationally. In the early 1970s, there was a furious debate on the best way for the NHS to evolve. One of the key moves was to try to match local health authority boundaries with the new boundaries created in local government. A new system of distributing the resources of the health service more evenly was also implemented in 1974, but it soon came under fire for being too complicated and top-heavy with managers. Less than two years later, a Royal Commission was appointed to look into the problem. Major changes were heralded, however, in the developing policies of the Conservative Party.

The NHS was popular. In the words of the journalist, Melanie Phillips:

The NHS . . . rides high in people's affections. Unlike teachers or housing officials, the producers of the service can do little wrong in the eyes of its consumers. The perception is that its faults are caused not by the doctors, nurses or even the hospital administrators but the government. People believe that the health service is not being given enough money. When asked they even say they would happily pay more in taxes to provide more for the NHS. (Phillips, 1987)

Mrs Thatcher's governments were determined to change the nature of the debate about the NHS and to change the institution itself. This was in line with neo-liberal views that the responsibility for welfare in general should be returned to individuals and families, or at least shared between them and the state. In this context, health inequalities, like other inequalities, were inevitable.

> The sense of being self-reliant; of playing a role within the family, owning one's own property, of paying one's way, are all part of the spiritual ballast which maintains responsible citizenship, and provides a solid foundation from which people look around and see what more they might do for others and for themselves. (Thatcher, 1977)

According to the late Robin Cook, what actually occurred was slower in pace than anticipated, 'a succession of Granny's footsteps tiptoeing away from the universal, publicly-funded comprehensive health service hoping that no one [would] be sufficiently alarmed by the noise to ask the questions of principle raised by each step' (Cook, 1988: 6). Change in government policy – away from interventionism and towards the market and greater legitimised inequalities – was clearly afoot.

Marketisation and the NHS: competitive tendering and private practice

Early in Mrs Thatcher's first administration, competitive tendering for the provision of non-medical services was encouraged. The contracting-out strategy was intended, at least in part, as weakening the grip of public sector unions on the NHS. The second Thatcher government moved from persuasion to coercion. In 1983, the newly returned government issued a directive that required health authorities to put cleaning, laundry and catering services out for tender.

More directly, Thatcher governments addressed the issue of private practice in the NHS. After an acrimonious dispute between Barbara Castle (secretary of state for health in the 1974–6 Wilson government) and the doctors, the then Labour government had established a Health Services Board to oversee a phased rundown of private beds. The first Thatcher government set about reversing this move. The Health Services Act (1980) abolished the board and made the secretary of state responsible for ensuring the presence of private beds in NHS hospitals. Though battle was joined with relish, the victory was pyrrhic: the passage of the Act, in fact, coincided with the growth of private hospitals which took increasing numbers from the private patient 'pool'.

The insinuation of private practice into the NHS system was achieved in other ways. In 1980, the government introduced changes to hospital consultants' contracts. These allowed consultants to increase their private practice without jeopardising their NHS practice. The contracts allowed a greater proportion of a consultant's salary to be earned in private practice before forfeiting any of his/her NHS salary. They also reduced the proportion of NHS salary forfeited once the cut-off point had been reached (Higgins, 1988). According to Higgins, the result of this change was that there was a significant increase in the number of consultants who, while working on full-time or maximum part-time contracts for the NHS, engaged in significant private practice. As Higgins notes:

> In a situation where there were so few wholly private practitioners and where the service was so firmly consultant-led the potential for the expansion of private practice was dramatically changed. Although the increase in private health insurance and the availability of new private sector facilities were important factors, their contribution to the changing scene would have been marginal were it not for the radical restructuring of consultants' contracts and consultants' willingness to take on new work. (1988: 87)

Private insurance and private facilities

Along with the growth in private practice came the growth in private insurance schemes and private provision. By 1988 over 10 per cent of the population were covered by private health insurance, double the proportion covered in 1979. This apparently small proportion is, in fact, deceptive because health insurance schemes have tended to exclude older people and those with chronic illnesses and disabilities. This steady growth in private health insurance was accompanied by a growth in the provision of private facilities. Notwithstanding the changes introduced by Conservative governments in the 1980s, the number of private patients treated in NHS hospitals declined continually after 1975. This had less to do with the number of pay beds available in the NHS and more to do with declining rates of occupancy of those beds. Instead private treatment increasingly occurred outside the NHS. Some commentators see the stimulus for this growth of private facilities as stemming from the attempt by the Callaghan government to phase out pay beds. Whatever the reason, the acceleration of provision of private facilities in the 1980s was substantial: 'while in the 1970s around three out of every four private patients were treated in the NHS, the reverse is now the case' (Griffith et al., 1987: 79). This growth in facilities was accomplished through the development of two kinds of hospital facilities: commercial hospitals and those run by not-for-profit organisations.

Notwithstanding the development of an incipient free market in health during the 1980s, the private health sector has grown as a result of its dependence on the NHS as well as its competition with it. In the first place, the NHS increased the potential profitability of private medicine. This was so because it had to treat all patients in need of hospital care. This included the bulk of patients who were not, in any event, able to pay for their treatment and left the private sector to concentrate on the more exotic or more profitable acute cases. Secondly, private hospitals profited during the late 1980s from work diverted to them by district health authorities. This was largely, though not exclusively, the result of central government waiting-list initiatives in 1987 and 1989. In both these years, the Department of Health made extra funds available to district and regional health authorities for the purpose of reducing patient waiting lists (£25 million in 1987 and £33 million in 1989). In many, though not all, cases waiting-list initiative monies were used to contract out work to the private sector. This was particularly the case with relatively uncomplicated minor operations. Thirdly, the NHS increasingly subsidised the private medicine business through its use of 'agency' doctors and nurses in locum capacities. Last, the NHS heavily subsidised the private sector through its training of medical personnel. Doctors and nurses transferring from NHS to private hospitals bear no responsibility to repay the NHS for their training nor is there any expectation that their new employers will be involved in reimbursement. None of these developments was facilitative, in terms of achieving equality of health service provision.

The NHS reforms

Throughout the 1980s, the purchasing power of the NHS had barely increased above the rate of inflation. But, despite this relative standstill, demands on the service were increasing. One source of demand was demographic, with the proportion of the population above sixty-five years growing at about 1 per cent per year in the late 1980s. If we take into account the disproportionate use of the NHS by older people, then the amount of resources available for each member of the population fell during the 1980s. The political fallout from this saw the government on the defensive. It announced a review of the NHS in 1988 which led to the publication in 1989 of two White Papers (*Working for People* and *Caring for Patients*). At the heart of both was the idea of an internal market.

The NHS and internal markets

In the end, the review recommended a compromise solution. Methods analogous to a private corporation were to be introduced into the NHS but it was to remain publicly funded. Of most significance, perhaps, was the creation of what has come to be known as an internal market. The internal market idea was a brainchild of the right wing of the Conservative Party and found favour with the prime minister. It was promoted in the late 1980s by an ultra-right-wing group of MPs known as the No Turning Back Group (which had been established to protect the radical right ideas that had informed the policy making of government during most of the 1980s) in the following way:

> Particular hospitals and particular areas should be able to specialise, with patients being referred to whichever can provide the cheapest or best service. Excess capacity should be traded across district boundaries instead of having empty places in one location accompanied by shortage in another. (No Turning Back Group, 1988: 20)

This move exposed clear political and ideological preferences. First, it increased competition in the service, with hospitals competing with each other to secure contracts. Secondly, it was seen as improving efficiency in the service. Efficient hospitals with lower unit costs would reap the reward of more contractual work. This would not only have consequences for them but would also act as an incentive to less efficient hospitals to improve efficiency levels and avoid the financial penalties that such a marketplace in health creates. Here, then, we see the ideological assumptions of the Conservative government: competition and efficiency are inseparable bedfellows. The post-war NHS had been inefficient because it did not operate in a health marketplace. Monopoly provision had bred waste and the introduction of both external competitors and internal competition was intended to create a service more responsive to consumers and more efficient in its activities.

Papering over the White Paper cracks

It is well documented that the prime minister insisted on White Papers that would underline the review committee's preferences. This was policy making on the hoof par excellence for the document, suggesting bold departures, left the detail to be worked out as the process unfolded. It created the most tremendous furore. Health service managers were fearful that they would be left with the task of implementing policy without adequate guidance. The Labour Party thundered that the proposals meant the privatisation of the health service. The British Medical Association, which had opposed Bevan's publicly funded NHS, now argued against the reforms and supported the NHS as it was. Though Kenneth Clarke, the secretary of state for health, stuck out against the opposition and saw the legislation through virtually unchanged, the government was rattled. It slowed down the pace of reform and told health managers to do as little as possible about the reforms before the next election. And indeed, it increased spending on the NHS substantially. More than this the language of commerce gave way once more to the language of the public service.

> In retrospect . . . it is clear that as Mrs. Thatcher's grip on office began to weaken, so ministers and their officials began to distance themselves from the stance they had been taking . . . 'Buyers' became 'purchasers' and then 'commissioners'. 'Sellers' became 'providers'. GP budgets became 'funds' and 'marketing' became 'needs assessment'. (Butler, 1992: 136)

The persistence of health inequalities

When the NHS was founded, over sixty years ago, it was believed that providing health services 'free at the point of use' would make services accessible to all and result in the narrowing of inequalities in health. This did not happen. The NHS helped dramatically to improve the health of the population as a whole – both overall mortality and morbidity rates have consistently declined over the years – but the gaps in health between 'rich' and 'poor' people and between 'rich' and 'poor' areas have widened. The health of the rich has improved at a much faster rate than the health of those living in poverty.

Substantial and consistent differences

According to a major review of the evidence (Whitehead and Drever, 1997), health inequalities remained substantial and consistent in the fifty years following the establishment of the NHS. Using several sources – including cross-sectional data from the census and the full national deaths data; a 1 per cent representative sample of the population of England and Wales followed up in the Office for National Statistics (ONS) Longitudinal Study; linked records on births and infant deaths, and morbidity from household interview surveys – the reviewers argue that they have the ability to examine the phenomenon from a variety of angles. Although there is some variation in the absolute rates calculated from these different sources, the socio-economic patterns of health are, they report, remarkably consistent. All the sources show a marked socio-economic gradient in mortality and morbidity persisting into the 1990s. For example, using the full national deaths data, in 1991–3 the all cause Standardised Morality Ratio (SMR) for men aged 20–64 was almost three times higher among unskilled manual workers in social class V than among professional men in social class I.

Furthermore, substantial differentials were not confined to the extremes of the social scale, but showed a step-wise increase with decreasing social class – men from class III and IV, for example, had nearly double the mortality of class I. The Longitudinal Study, for the slightly earlier period of 1986–9 and for the wider age range of 15–64, had reported a two and a half-fold difference in SMR between class I and V, and a similar graded mortality across class I. In absolute terms, the standardised death rates for men aged 20–64 in 1991–3, calculated using the full national deaths data, ranged from about 290 deaths per 100,000 in classes I and II to over 800 deaths per 100,000 in class V. From the ONS analysis of the latest period covering 1986–92, an older age range (from age 35–64) was studied; so the two analyses are not directly comparable. However, what can be compared is the general pattern and this gave a consistent picture. In the LS, male death rates increased with declining social class, ranging from 455 deaths per 100,000 in class I/II to 764 deaths per 100,000 in classes IV/V. The social class gradient in the mortality of women was slightly shallower than that for men, but still evident. Women's death rates ranged from 270 to 418 per 100,000 from classes I/II to IV/V.

More recent evidence suggests that the problem of relative inequalities in health might have further worsened over the last ten years or so. So, looking at life expectancy, we find that although it increased for all social groups in the UK between 1972–6 and 2002–5, health inequalities – gaps in life expectancy between social groups – have persisted. More than this, since the baseline period from which the previous Labour government began to measure progress towards its target to reduce health inequalities (1995–7), the gap between the 'routine and manual' groups and the population as a whole has widened. The gap in men's life expectancy in the period 2005–7 was 4 per cent wider than the baseline period, while for women this gap was 11 per cent wider. From 2005–7, infant mortality in routine and manual groups was 16 per cent higher than in the population as a whole, compared to 13 per cent in the baseline period (House of Commons Health Committee, 2009).

To this, we can add the evidence that in the ten years to 2003 the absolute difference in life expectancy between the top and bottom social groups in the UK has increased to more than four years and that the difference between local authority areas with the highest and lowest life expectancies (Kensington and Chelsea and Glasgow City) had risen to 9.4 years by 2001–3 (Shaw, Davey-Smith and Dorling, 2005: 1017–18).

Widening of relative differences

There also appears to be evidence of a widening of relative differences. For instance, infant mortality rates for all social classes declined in the 1980s and continued to decline in the 1990s. However, there is a more negative picture when other age groups are examined. There appear to be indications of deterioration in the relative position of adults in manual social classes: the gap in life expectancy between classes I/II and the other classes is seen to widen between the late 1970s and the late 1980s. And so we could go on – but the message is clear.

There is widespread agreement (although also some recent scepticism, to which we will return) that the causes of these inequalities in health and early death are embedded in poverty and inequality in material well-being. In 1980, the Black Committee on Inequalities in Health (DHSS, 1980) concluded that while the health service could play a significant part in reducing inequalities in health, measures to reduce differences in material standards of living at work, in the home and in everyday social and community life are of even greater importance. This understanding was not lost on Beveridge, of course, almost forty years earlier. In his final report as the chief medical officer for England, commissioned in 1997 by the incoming Prime Minister Tony Blair, Sir Donald Acheson argued that the strongest determinants of ill health were low income, unhealthy behaviour and poor environmental and housing conditions (Acheson, 1998). Poverty, as it had been in the Black Report ten years earlier, was the major culprit in the crime of health inequalities.

These were, or might have been, calls from the political wilderness. The Black Report, published in the year after the election of a Conservative government (headed by Margaret Thatcher and more committed than any post-war government to the politics of individual responsibility) was released on a Friday afternoon before a holiday, following a very restricted print run.

Report followed report. On a global scale, the 1995 *World Health Report* (World Health Organisation, 1995) argued that poverty had become

> the world's most ruthless killer and the greatest cause of suffering on earth. Poverty is the main reason why babies are not vaccinated, clean water and sanitation are not provided, curative drugs and other treatments are unavailable and why mothers die in childbirth. Poverty is the main cause of reduced life expectancy, of handicap and disability and of starvation. Poverty is a major contributor to mental illness, stress, suicide, family disintegration and substance abuse.

At the national level, too, poverty research has consistently suggested that poverty is related to worse health outcomes. For example, the 1990 Breadline Britain Survey (Gordon, Middleton and Bradshaw, 2002) found that poor people were 1.6 times more likely to suffer from long-standing illness, 5.4 times more likely to suffer from feeling isolated and 5.5 times more likely to feel depressed. The health gap is even larger if the intensity and history of poverty among survey respondents is taken into account. At an area level there is a very close relationship between high rates of poverty and high rates of premature mortality. This evidence is bolstered by the study carried out by a multidisciplinary team of epidemiologists and social geographers which found that 'the relative index of inequality for mortality increased steadily' during the 1990s (Davey-Smith, Dorling, Mitchell and Shaw, 2002: 434–5).

The links between poverty in children and worse health outcomes are well documented. For example, babies born to poor families are at much greater risk of prematurity, low birth weight and infant mortality, illness and disability, injury and accidents. Changes in the socio-economic profile of Britain in the past two decades have had a particular impact: households with children, the proportion of lone parent households, children in families with no earner and the proportion of households with children living in poverty have all increased. The *Poverty and Social Exclusion Survey of Britain* (Gordon et al., 2000) showed that 18 per cent of British children were suffering from multiple deprivations. The links between poverty and child health are extensive, strong and pervasive – virtually all aspects of health are worst among children living in poverty than among children from affluent families. The report of the Academy for Learned Societies in Social Sciences (Forbes, 2001) adds to the weight of evidence to support these conclusions. We have already mentioned the findings of Sir Donald Acheson's independent report on the problems associated with ill health, which supported a socio-economic explanation of health inequalities (Acheson, 1998). In this model, ill health is the result of such determinants as income, education and employment as well as the material environment and lifestyle.

And, perhaps most momentously, in 2010 came the Marmot Report, *Fair Society, Healthy Lives*: the culmination of a major review of health inequalities in England led by Sir Michael Marmot, president of the British Medical Association. In corroboration of those previous findings it found clear evidence of wide-ranging health inequalities and that – in line with the traditional social democratic analysis – these result from social inequalities (rather than from the self-generated lifestyle choices of individuals). It concluded that reducing such inequalities 'is a matter of fairness and social justice' (Marmot, 2010: 9).

A change in the style and substance of the debate?

Against this backcloth, what appears to have happened since 1997 is, at first blush, bewildering but also explicable. Put crudely, at the level of UK (or should it be English?) policy and policy discourse, concern with eradicating health inequalities became meshed with an account of their aetiology which saw their victims as their cause. In other words, lifestyle and behaviour issues – obesity, smoking, alcohol and other abuse – came once more to be conceptualised as a cause of health inequalities, rather than one aspect of them. I return to this below.

At the same time, however, health became one of the key areas of differentiated policy between England and the devolved administrations, following the introduction of political devolution in the UK in 1999. Initially, both Wales and Scotland seem to have retained a more 'Labourist' understanding of inequalities in health than has been the case at UK government level. By the middle of the second terms for the Scottish parliament and the Welsh assembly, these understandings appeared to have shifted substantially, however.

From 1997 onwards, policies in England, Wales and Scotland consistently emphasised the need to tackle health inequalities and all three countries focused on health differences between socioeconomic groups and geographic areas. England was the first to introduce quantifiable national targets for reducing health inequalities, doing so in 2001. Scotland also introduced quantifiable national targets for reducing health inequalities in 2004. Wales did not introduce quantifiable national targets for reducing health inequalities, opting instead for qualitative statements about the direction of travel. Indeed, much of the language in Welsh policy documents suggests that Welsh policy makers were less concerned with targets than their colleagues in England and Scotland. An expert group, headed by Professor Peter Townsend, was established in 2001 and advised against setting specific, national health inequalities targets. Instead, members suggested that avoiding short- or medium-term targets would facilitate a longer-term (and more effective) approach to the issue by allowing policy makers to focus on the wider social determinants of health.

What we find subsequently, however, is that emphases on 'wider' determinants of health and health inequalities (such as social exclusion, poor housing and inequalities of opportunity), as well as underlining the need to address differential patterns of lifestyle behaviour (the former often being articulated as a key cause of the latter), give way to policy convergence of a different kind. By 2005, statements in all three countries placed increasing emphasis on the need to tackle lifestyle behaviours (smoking, diet, alcohol consumption, etc.), the responsibility of individuals, and clinical priorities and the role of the NHS (Harrington et al., 2009).

So what has happened?

For more than sixty post-war years, government health policy and the NHS have been focused, inter alia, on the possibility and legitimacy of abolishing, or mitigating, health inequalities. There have been disagreements about how this might be achieved and failures to achieve it. During the 1980s and 1990s, right-wing Conservative governments questioned the legitimacy of using government policy as a health equality machine. But, for most of the period, Liberals and social democrats held fast to the tradition of Beveridge: that government not only had the right to intervene economically and socially but also was morally obliged to do so. The objective of that intervention was the amelioration of inequalities.

I have argued elsewhere (Sullivan, 2000) that the 'third way' approach of the Blair administrations (Blair, 1998; Giddens, 1998, 2000) was much more than the inchoate rationale for welfare reform that some had taken it for. Though lacking the richness, sophistication and sheer intellectual power of the post-war social democratic settlement, it may well have marked a further secular shift in the politics of social democrats, if not of social democracy. The Blair approach emphasised the responsibilities of citizenship as equally, if not more, important than the rights which old social democracy had conferred and had the effect of eclipsing a rights or entitlement-based welfare regime in favour of one that changes the balance between rights and responsibilities.

Julian Le Grand, a one-time social democrat of the old type, represents this shift in his 2007 Beveridge Memorial Lecture (Le Grand, 2007). Here he argues that Beveridge's five giants have been diminished to be replaced by the giants of excess. Those giants are the creatures not so much of the social or economic structure – except inasmuch as they are the malaise of plenty – but rather of individual excess. Health challenges of the twenty-first century, such as heart disease, diabetes and cancers, are not seen by the new social democrats (in whose number we might presumably now count Le Grand) as reflections of health inequalities. They are often seen as the outcomes of individually chosen patterns of behavioural excess, though they are still disproportionately concentrated at the lower end of the social structure. Dealing with them is a matter, therefore, for individually focused behavioural change rather than for large government programmes. In an elegantly penned article published two years later, Le Grand widens the argument and appears partly to be arguing not only that our major illnesses are often a result of choice – and, therefore, to use Fleurbaey and Schokkaert's categorisation, 'legitimate' health inequalities (2009: 73–4) – but also that their remedy is best delivered by a health service based on the principles of choice and competition (Le Grand, 2009: 483–4). Though this sort of argument is supported by the political right and some health economists, its claim to be evidence-based is roundly debunked by others. Chief among its current critics is Durham's professor of health policy and management, David Hunter. Hunter's argument is that the bulk of the evidence is that health inequalities are caused by social and economic inequalities. Amelioration of these inequalities is rarely achieved by the intervention of choice and the market (2009: 490). In this context, he puzzles as to why, when Wales and Scotland have apparently chosen a different trajectory (Greer, 2008), English New Labour ministers have taken choice and competition as their policy mantra. While, as I have suggested above, it is simplistic to argue that health policy in Wales and Scotland takes a completely different route from that in England, there is enough truth in Hunter's claim to warrant further explanation. Wales and Scotland have responded, or so it seems, to persuasive international evidence not only that levels of material inequality are causally related to health inequality, but also that policy regimes drawing on political ideologies which justify inequality lead to widening health gaps between the rich and the poor. Conversely, according to much of the contemporary international research literature, social democratic policy regimes are associated, over and above narrower income disparities in society, with amelioration of health inequalities (see Coburn, 2004; Mitchell, Shaw and Dorling, 2000; Deaton, 2001; Navarro and Shi, 2001). Wales's early post-devolution decision to craft a health service based on preventive, public health principles and Wales's and Scotland's decision to avoid market-oriented targets are reflections of a wider commitment to social democratic aspirations to ameliorate poverty, inequalities and the health gap (Sullivan, 2000). Not for the first time we find that, in Greer's words, 'Wales is radical and under-reported' (2004: 128). This judgement incorporates an appreciation of a health policy prospectus aimed at diminishing health inequalities via preventive services, the restructuring of funding based on health need and the use of the unique Welsh Health Survey to mine the depths of citizens' perceptions of their health status. Guided by classic Labour values for the most part, it has also unfolded in the context of financial restraint, administrative lethargy and, at times, political opposition (Drakeford, 2006).

Perhaps then, Hunter's puzzle is solved. Le Grand's theses on both the causes of, and solutions to, health inequality are quintessentially New Labour. They move it from a problem which we seemed unable to abolish to one that we should, at the level of government, no longer worry about. The New Labour writ failed entirely to penetrate the 'Celtic social democracies' in the first decade of devolved governance. With the election of a Conservative-led coalition government in the UK in 2010, the next decade presents different challenges.

3

IGNORANCE

Combating ignorance: education, social opportunity and citizenship in Wales

Gareth Rees

Education in the welfare state

Education has occupied a somewhat ambiguous role in the post-war development of the welfare state, both in Wales and across the UK more widely. Certainly, it was identified as one of Beveridge's 'five giants' in his famous report, which laid the foundations for many aspects of the welfare state during much of the second half of the twentieth century. However, Beveridge had nothing to say about the actual provision of educational services, and education was semi-detached from his mainstream concerns with income support, health insurance, pensions and so forth. Nevertheless, there can be little doubt that educational opportunities have come to be seen as a key element of social policy provision over the period since the publication of the Beveridge Report. Successive governments have accepted that individuals are entitled to have access to education provision, simply by virtue of their being citizens. Indeed, some of the most controversial aspects of social policy during this period have revolved around the nature and extent of citizenship entitlements to educational opportunities (Timmins, 2001).

Underpinning this acceptance of the citizen's entitlement to education, there has been a complexity of different rationales. All of these emerged from long-standing debates that stretched back well before the middle of the twentieth century. However, as with other aspects of the welfare state, the decades around the Second World War did mark a significant watershed in the development of educational provision. In a real sense, then, what emerged at this time was an educational system that has persisted, at least in many of its key features, until the present day.

Beveridge himself articulated one of these underpinning rationales: for him, 'ignorance' was something that 'no democracy can afford among its citizens' (Beveridge, 1942: 7). Here, the emphasis is on providing citizens with access to the knowledge, skills and understanding necessary for them to participate fully in society. What is important to understand in this context is that, up until the earlier decades of the twentieth century, access to anything beyond the most basic educational provision was widely held to be necessary only for those who were destined to become the 'leaders' of society; education beyond elementary schooling was deemed unnecessary for the bulk of the population. With the extension of democratic political rights and the wider restructuring of the social hierarchy through the later nineteenth and early twentieth centuries, this view of education's purpose as essentially a moral preparation of society's elites became increasingly untenable. Concerns came to be expressed that educational opportunities needed to be extended in order to provide the intellectual basis for democratic participation by the citizenry as a whole. More generally, it was ever more widely acknowledged that the social and cultural fabric of the national society could not be sustained without a more inclusive educational system (McCulloch, 1991). What followed from this, therefore, was an impetus to extend educational opportunities for all beyond elementary schooling to embrace secondary schooling and even access to further and higher education. What remained controversial, however, were the exact ways in which this could be achieved.

A second rationale underpinning the citizen's entitlement to education is embodied in the notion of economic efficiency. The essential argument here is that the nation cannot afford to forego any of the human capital potentially available in its population; wasting talent needs to be avoided at all costs. Hence, everyone should have the opportunity to equip themselves with the knowledge and skills necessary for them to participate effectively in the labour market. Again, these sorts of arguments are long established. However, as technologies developed and, perhaps more importantly, Britain's pre-eminent position within the world economy came to be increasingly challenged through the latter part of the nineteenth century, so the economic significance of education became an increasingly controversial matter: what was seen to be Britain's relative economic failure was attributed increasingly to the failures of the education system (for example, Barnett, 1996).

In part, this too boiled down to a debate about how much education should be provided to citizens. However, in this case, the critical focus was also on the forms of education that should be provided: in what ways could the education system meet the needs of the economy most effectively? Here, the balance between general education, on the one hand, and vocational preparation, on the other, has been a key issue, especially in secondary, further and higher education (even if, in reality, this sort of distinction is very difficult to sustain convincingly). Moreover, these debates have intensified in recent decades, as the 'knowledge economy', based on new and ever-changing technologies, has come to be seen as making increasing demands on the knowledge and skills of workers of all kinds. Indeed, it has been argued that economic efficiency has come to be the overriding rationale for the provision of education and the ways in which this is organised (Ball, 2008).

A further – and in some ways the most familiar – rationale for sustaining access to educational opportunities as a right of citizenship is that of social justice. Especially since the middle decades of the twentieth century, education has been conceived by many as providing a means through which individuals can escape from the disadvantages of their social backgrounds. Educational achievement, on this view, provides a route to social mobility and, potentially, access to desirable jobs and careers. Citizens should be able to attain the highest level of educational achievement of which they are capable, irrespective of the social and economic disadvantages into which they are born.

What this implies, in turn, is that the education system should be organised in ways which does not discriminate against individuals on the basis of their social backgrounds. Each should have the opportunity to fulfil his or her talent, or, as Michael Young put it in his satirical account of 'meritocracy', 'merit = IQ + effort' (Young, 1958: xiii). This has been a principal preoccupation of later twentieth-century educational reformers, who have been especially concerned over the principles on which access to educational opportunities – especially for secondary schooling and, more latterly, higher education – are organised. Equally, the internal organisation of the education system – the curriculum, forms of teaching and assessment methods – has been evaluated in terms of its 'fairness' to different groups of children and young people. Interestingly – at least until very recently – much less concern has been expressed about the relationship between educational achievement and subsequent jobs and careers. However, this too is crucial if the educational system is to achieve the 'meritocratic' ideal which has increasingly been espoused for it (Ball, 2008).

The debates around these rationales and their implications have largely shaped the controversies over educational policy, certainly since the middle decades of the twentieth century. This has been true within Wales, as it has elsewhere in the UK (and, indeed, more widely too). In Wales, however, the general arguments have been given particular inflections, shaped largely by the specific ways in which education has been located within the wider political and ideological currents of Welsh society.

This is certainly not to suggest that positions within the educational debates can be mapped easily on to party political differences. Nevertheless, it does appear to be the case that the inheritance left by the religious nonconformism and liberalism that dominated Wales during the late nineteenth and early twentieth centuries is at least partly reflected in the importance attached to providing the widest possible access to educational opportunities for the whole population of Wales. And these opportunities were extensively defined in terms of the perceived intellectual, civic and cultural virtues of a general, liberal education (Jones and Roderick, 2003).

This emphasis, in turn, has sometimes conflicted with the notions held by some sections of Welsh society about what forms of education would provide the most appropriate vocational preparation. This was especially the case where the jobs for which this vocational preparation was undertaken were largely restricted to the traditional economy based on coal, metal manufacture, transport and agriculture. Even as that traditional economy has been swept away during the latter decades of the twentieth century, the relationship between educational provision and the economy and its needs in Wales has remained one of balancing legitimate educational aspirations against the limitations of the economic reality. Quite simply, tying the educational system to the perceived needs of a poor economy can be seen as unduly restricting educational potential (Istance and Rees, 1994).

Perhaps most strikingly, however, Welsh education has been affected by the idea that it offers the opportunity to improve one's social circumstances. The popular perception of the sons and – albeit less frequently – the daughters of miners or farm labourers using educational success to move into middle-class occupations (stereotypically, as teachers or clergy) has been a powerful one, irrespective of its accuracy as an historical account of changes in the Welsh class structure. Not least, it has exerted a marked influence on the ways in which educational policies have been shaped in Wales, perhaps especially since the advent of parliamentary devolution, with the establishment of the National Assembly for Wales in 1999. In short, 'equality of opportunity' has been embedded in educational provision in Wales in ways that are seen to distinguish Welsh education, especially from that in England.

The welfare state and policies for educational provision

These complex ambitions for educational provision have been reflected in the development of an extensive system of educational provision that has grown significantly since the middle decades of the twentieth century. The state has come to be the dominant provider of educational opportunities for its citizens, in a way that would be unrecognisable to those who lived earlier in the twentieth century, let alone in the nineteenth. For much of the period during which education has been largely provided through the welfare state, patterns of educational provision in Wales have followed very closely those in England. Whilst there were Welsh inflections, educational policy essentially conformed to an 'England and Wales' model

(Jones, 1997). This began to change during the 1970s and 1980s and, following the establishment of the National Assembly for Wales in 1999, the development of educational provision (in just about all its forms) became a devolved responsibility, with the Welsh Assembly Government having the powers to shape the character of the educational system in Wales. For the first time, it begins to make sense to think in terms of a 'national system of education' in Wales (Rees, 2005: 28ff).

What is striking, however, is that, in both Wales and England and as with other aspects of welfare state provision, the story of the second half of the twentieth century is one of expansion: of increasing numbers of citizens engaging with education, in an increasingly diverse pattern of provision (Aldrich, 2002). So much so, that, currently, the education system provides opportunities for citizens across the course of their lives, literally from cradle to grave. Educational institutions – nurseries, schools, colleges, universities and so forth – have increased significantly in number to deliver these extended educational opportunities. The numbers of people employed in the education system have grown correspondingly. Increasingly, too, the importance of the learning that takes place in settings that are not devoted solely to education has been recognised; policies have been developed to influence learning within families, work places and other social settings (Ball, 2008). Not surprisingly, therefore, the amount of public expenditure devoted to education has also increased very substantially in real terms, reflecting this huge expansion in the state's involvement in educational provision.

The question remains, however, as to how far this undisputed expansion in educational provision has achieved the aims which provide its justification. Here, a careful examination of the impacts of educational policy reveals that – in Wales, as in England – there remains a great deal to be done if the aspirations that have underpinned policy developments are to be wholly fulfilled. In part, of course, this can be explained in terms of the shortcomings of policy implementation. More fundamentally, however, it reflects the extent to which the expectations that have been espoused for education are themselves unrealistic.

Extending educational opportunities

All three of the rationales underpinning the provision of education through the welfare state implied extending educational opportunities more widely to the population as a whole. By the middle decades of the twentieth century, when Beveridge affirmed the need to combat ignorance, this entailed the need to expand the scope of secondary education. The nineteenth century had witnessed the progressive extension of access to elementary education. Thus, by the early decades of the twentieth century, the bulk of the population had access to a basic education, notionally at least, until they were fourteen years old. However, proceeding beyond this basic level remained overwhelmingly the preserve of those who were fortunate enough to be born into families that could afford the fees payable in the independent and grammar schools and that recognised the advantages which could accrue to those who followed this path (Banks, 1955). In Wales, the creation of the intermediate schools during the 1890s had alleviated this picture somewhat; nevertheless, the basic pattern of universal access only to elementary education applied here too (Jones, 1982).

The 1944 Education Act was designed to transform this situation. By abolishing fees in state schools and making attendance compulsory until the age of fifteen, it hugely extended the educational opportunities available to the bulk of the population. For the first time, all children were entitled to an education from the time they were five until they reached school-leaving age. However, the post-1944 system remained one that was socially divided; the educational entitlement available to children from different social backgrounds remained highly differentiated.

A significant proportion of children remained outside the state sector and, in general, benefited significantly from the superior resources available in the fee-paying, independent schools (although this was much more of an issue in England than in Wales). Moreover, within the state sector, most local authorities adopted a tripartite division of secondary schooling into grammar, secondary technical and secondary modern schools, which were intended to cater for different types of aptitude amongst pupils. Allocation to the different types of secondary school was on the basis of children's performance in the 11-plus examination. All of this reflected the dominant educational thinking of the time, as expressed, for example, in the Hadow Report of 1926, the Spens Report of 1938 and the Norwood Report of 1943 (Fitz et al., 2006).

Despite the official aspiration to achieve parity of esteem between the different types of school, it soon became apparent that the grammar schools were pre-eminent, with significantly higher levels of resources than the secondary modern schools (in reality, very few secondary technical schools were created). Not surprisingly, the bulk of pupils left their secondary modern schools without attaining any recognised educational qualifications (McCulloch, 1998). Moreover, the critics of the tripartite system (in Wales and elsewhere) came to emphasise that allocation to the different schools through the 11-plus discriminated against children from working-class backgrounds, who were, accordingly, over-represented in the secondary modern schools (for example, Floud et al., 1956). Not only was this seen to be socially unjust, but it also led to an enormous wastage of talent.

At least partly in response to such concerns, some local authorities began to move away from tripartite provision during the later 1950s and early 1960s, establishing what came to be known as comprehensive schools, catering for the bulk of young people in a given local area. In 1965, the then Labour government issued its famous Circular 10/65, which invited all local authorities to abolish the 11-plus and to institute comprehensive secondary schooling across the country. In many parts of England, this was met with stiff opposition. However, this was not so in Wales. Here, under the tripartite system, a much higher proportion of the age group (some 40 per cent) were allocated to grammar schools than in England, and a correspondingly smaller proportion went to the secondary moderns (Jones, 1990). Accordingly, the shift to a comprehensive system required less upheaval and the Welsh local authorities responded enthusiastically to the Circular. Certainly, by the 1970s, nearly all young people in Wales were attending comprehensive schools (Benn and Chitty, 1996).

Even with this further reform of secondary schooling, however, educational entitlements remain significantly differentiated by pupils' social backgrounds. Certainly, critics have contended that comprehensives, in effect, recreate equivalent inequalities to the tripartite system as a result of the internal organisation of schools. Hence, it is argued, there are systematic relationships between pupils' social backgrounds and factors such as streaming and the management of curriculum choice (for example, Ball, 1981). More generally, others have identified a wider 'hidden curriculum' which devalues and antagonises young people from less advantaged backgrounds. For whatever reasons, it is clearly the case that comprehensive schools differ starkly according to the social characteristics of the areas from which they draw their pupils. Dramatic stories of failing comprehensives in inner-city areas or disadvantaged peripheral estates have become a media commonplace. And it undoubtedly is the case that levels of educational attainment – in all its forms – continue to reflect the social backgrounds of pupils as clearly in the comprehensive schools as they did in the grammar and secondary modern schools that they replaced (for example, Kerchoff et al., 1996).

In England, criticisms have crystallised around the notion that comprehensive schools have failed to nurture the talents of students (especially the most able ones), irrespective of their social backgrounds, thereby contributing to a more general decline in educational standards. Under the Conservatives during the 1980s and 1990s and New Labour since then, a characteristic response to this criticism has been to use the power of parental choice of school to drive up attainment standards across the board. A necessary condition of this has been the diversification of secondary schooling, giving parents a range of types of school from which to choose. Indeed, an almost bewildering variety of new types of secondary school has been created during this period – city technology colleges, specialist schools, foundation schools, faith schools, academies, trust schools – and some of these have already disappeared. However, how far this strategy has been successful in improving academic standards, let alone producing a less socially divided education system, remains a matter of considerable doubt (Ball, 2008).

These perturbations have almost wholly passed Wales by. The Welsh Assembly Government and the National Assembly have remained wedded to the provision of secondary schooling through state comprehensives that serve the needs of 'their' local communities. In contrast with what has been happening in England, this approach is seen as especially attuned to Welsh circumstances (Phillips, 2003). Indeed, for some observers and rightly or wrongly, this emphasis on community comprehensives reflects a Welsh tradition of equality of opportunity that extends back at least to the intermediate schools (Jones, 1997).

However, here too, legitimate questions remain as to how far secondary schooling remains divided. Certainly, in overall terms – and as in England – young people are now far more likely to achieve good levels of educational qualifications and to stay on in education beyond the minimum school-leaving age than used to be the case. Yet – and again as in England – these rising trends mask very sharp differences in the performance of schools in different areas and with pupils drawn from different social backgrounds. To take only one, frequently quoted indicator, in 2007–8, of the young people taking GCSEs (or vocational equivalents), in Powys 65 per cent achieved five or more passes graded A*–C; in Merthyr Tydfil, the equivalent figure was 40 per cent and in Blaenau Gwent 45 per cent. Moreover, it is somewhat ironic that, despite what is argued to be a greater commitment to 'equality of opportunity', some of the deepest concerns about Welsh secondary schooling – both under the tripartite and comprehensive systems – have been voiced about its failure to make adequate provision for those pupils who are the academically least able (for example, Istance and Rees, 1994).

Education as a preparation for employment
Some of the consequences of this socially divided secondary education are apparent if attention shifts to what happens after compulsory schooling. Indeed, the provision of post-compulsory educational opportunities has been, in many ways, even more starkly unequal, precisely because the citizen's entitlement – at least until the very recent initiative to extend participation in education and training

until eighteen years of age – has ended with the completion of secondary education. Hence, on the one hand, for those who wished to continue in education and who met the academic requirements, there has been a clearly defined route to higher education. Welfare state provision has extended not only to advanced secondary education, but also to the heavy subsidy of universities and other higher education institutions, both directly and through the financial support of full-time students (especially after the 1960s). Even following the changes to arrangements for student finance during recent years, these elements of subsidy remain, albeit in different forms. And this is despite the fact that those going into higher education have been drawn disproportionately from middle-class families (Rees and Stroud, 2001).

On the other hand, for those who pursue alternative pathways nothing like the equivalent level of support has been available, even though they are far more likely to be drawn from a less advantaged background than their higher education peers. Hence, for example, students who progressed – in ever increasing numbers, again especially after the 1960s – from secondary school to further education college have very largely been left to support themselves both in full- and part-time study (Ainley and Bailey, 1997). For those entering the labour market, their access to further education and training has essentially been prescribed by their employer, with provision ranging from high-quality apprenticeships to the most minimal and instrumental on-the-job training. Indeed, only with the growth of youth unemployment during the 1970s, did the welfare state become engaged in training provision; here, the quality of what was made available through programmes such as youth training was highly variable (Bates and Riseborough, 1993).

Of course, it was not intended to be like this. As we have seen, the 1944 Act was intended to create a secondary system that would draw on the widest pool of talent, including those in the secondary technical and secondary modern schools, as much as the grammar schools. At this time, it was envisaged that only a small minority would proceed to higher education. However, the Act did provide for the creation of a system of 'county colleges', which were intended to provide continuing education for workers between the ages of fifteen and eighteen (they would be entitled to attend for one day per week), as well as adult leisure-time classes and the vocational programmes that had been offered by the technical and commercial colleges since the nineteenth century. Much of the latter was associated with the apprenticeships that continued to thrive in substantial sectors of industry (at least for men) (Bailey, 2002).

In the decades immediately following the 1944 Act, this system was not adequately developed, largely for financial reasons. Indeed, it was not really until the 1960s that the further education sector began to develop significantly. In part, this reflected a substantial – but largely unplanned – growth in the numbers of students who wished to take, or re-take, academic qualifications. It also resulted from the growth in demand for intermediate technical qualifications, as the industrial structure of both England and Wales began to shift appreciably as the long post-war boom came to an end. However, it was not until the 1990s that further education finally shed its image as the 'Cinderella' of the education system: the colleges were made independent of the local education authorities; investment increased significantly (particularly in England), and student numbers grew exponentially (there are now far more students in further education colleges than school sixth forms) (Ainley and Bailey, 1997).

What was crucial to this shift was an increasingly dominant perception – not least on the part of central government – that the emergence of a knowledge-based economy required not only improved standards of general education, but also the development of more effective vocational preparation. What this was seen to imply, in turn, was a shift to lifelong learning, enabling individuals to acquire essential knowledge and skills through their general education and initial vocational programmes, as well as to renew them throughout their careers. Inevitably, this recasting of education as lifelong learning – albeit in especially instrumental forms – has had implications for all sectors of education, not just post-compulsory provision (Ball, 2008). However, further education has been a particular beneficiary of this instrumental focus on economic efficiency, in Wales and, especially, in England.

Nevertheless, there are considerable doubts as to the effectiveness of viewing education in these narrow terms. At one level, it is not at all clear that the economic changes taking place actually add up to the emergence of a knowledge-based economy. The decline of traditional manual employment in primary and manufacturing industries has been partially counter-balanced by a growth of professional, managerial and scientific jobs in the services sector of the economy. However, it is equally the case that much of the employment growth in services is accounted for by low-wage jobs that would conventionally be regarded as low skilled and requiring very little by way of education and training (Wolf, 2002).

Indeed, this is especially true of economies such as Wales's. Here, the collapse of the traditional economy based on coal, metal manufacture, transport and agriculture has been paralleled by a diversification of manufacturing and the growth of jobs in services, especially in the public sector. However, whilst these changes have expanded opportunities in some respects, especially for women, there is little indication that there has been a transformation in terms of the demand for skills in the Welsh economy and, certainly, levels of qualifications amongst the Welsh workforce remain persistently low (Felstead et al., 2007). There is a long way to go before the Welsh economy can meaningfully be described as knowledge-based.

Critically, there is also very little evidence to suggest that a strategy – essentially the one pursued by successive governments – of increasing the supply of skills through the expansion and restructuring of educational provision will bring about economic growth. Quite simply, unless employers adopt production strategies that utilise skills effectively, they will not look to recruit skilled workers. In these circumstances, the impact of increasing skill levels through education and training is likely to be minimal. And again, the Welsh economy provides an instructive example; indeed, the effect of producing more highly qualified and skilled individuals is likely to be the increase of the numbers leaving Wales to seek more rewarding employment in other parts of Britain (and more widely).

Neither is it the case that the development of the knowledge-based economy as the leitmotif for education policy has significantly mitigated the socially divided character of educational provision. In particular, it is undoubtedly the case that the expansion of further education and other aspects of post-compulsory provision has resulted in a widening of access to educational opportunities, especially for those who do not reach the highest levels of academic achievement and who, in a previous era, 'were pushed off the plank [of school], straight into the job market' (Barnett, 1996: 201). However, it remains the case that the nature and extent of such access reflects the social backgrounds from which people are drawn; even at the most basic level, those born into more advantaged families and who have the better jobs are far more likely to gain the lion's share of post-compulsory education and training (Gorard and Rees, 2002).

Education and social mobility
Despite these reservations about the relationships between education and economic development, it remains the case that, for the individual, educational achievement and progression to the higher levels of the educational system provide the most effective route to securing a well-paid and fulfilling job. If one adopts a long-term perspective, then it is undoubtedly the case that those in the upper echelons of the occupational hierarchy today are far more likely to have been selected on the basis of merit – including their educational attainments – than was the case when the modern welfare state was established in the middle of the twentieth century. There is also no doubt that there has been a significant amount of upward social mobility, at least in part as a consequence of the expansion of education opportunities (Paterson and Iannelli, 2007a). Nevertheless, there are good reasons to doubt that educational provision through the welfare state has fulfilled the ambition of at least some of its progenitors to create a wholly meritocratic system.

This can be seen initially in the socially divided nature of the education system itself. For reasons that have been touched upon already, an individual's social background continues to exert a determining influence on access to the higher levels of education (which, more often than not, is necessary to enter higher-level jobs) (Paterson and Iannelli, 2007b). This can be illustrated by reference to the enormous expansion in higher education that has taken place in England and in Wales since the 1960s and, more particularly, since the later 1980s.

As well as the creation of new higher education institutions, the number of students admitted to established universities and colleges has increased enormously. Hence, over the past forty years or so, there has been more than a five-fold increase in the number of students in British higher education. As both Wales and England have moved to a mass system of higher education, 'going to uni' has become a much more 'normal' social experience, certainly than it was at the inception of the post-war welfare state. One sort of reflection of this has been that gender differences in higher education participation have been transformed, with more women now attending university than men. Similarly, many ethnic minorities are no longer disadvantaged with respect to higher education (Rees and Stroud, 2001). However, social class inequalities appear to be much more intractable.

It is true that far more people from working-class backgrounds now go to university, but it is also the case that far more people from middle-class backgrounds go to university too. As a result, the gap between levels of participation in higher education between the two groups remains disturbingly wide, in spite of university expansion and the specific initiatives targeted at raising working-class participation. Moreover, this suggests that the reasons for the gap are rather deeply embedded in the educational experiences of working-class people and, indeed, in their wider social lives. This, in turn, suggests that even the effects of changes in student finance – with the introduction of tuition fees and dramatic restructuring of maintenance support – may be more complex than has often been suggested (Rees and Stroud, 2001).

Not only is there a continuing relationship between social class and progress through the educational system, but also patterns of social mobility cannot be accounted for simply by educational change. Hence, the increases in upward social mobility that were characteristic of the second half of the twentieth century were principally attributable to the expansion of non-manual jobs, the decline of manufacturing and the general up-skilling that was characteristic of this period. Similarly, more recently, as the expansion of middle-class jobs has slowed, so upward social mobility has decreased and downward mobility grown. There is also some evidence to suggest that as the top-end of the labour market has tightened, employers have increasingly adopted recruitment criteria that emphasise qualities which cannot be acquired through the education system (Brown and Hesketh, 2004). In short, whilst people have clearly experienced changing patterns of absolute social mobility, there has been relatively little change in the relative inequalities of opportunity experienced by people born into different social classes (Paterson and Iannelli, 2007a).

Moreover, there is also strong evidence that, irrespective of the continuing inequalities of access to education, there remains a direct influence between the social class into which people are born and the social class they attain in adulthood (Breen, 2004). This too indicates that expanding educational provision and even opening up the opportunities for educational progression are not themselves sufficient conditions of a greater equality of opportunity between the social classes. This is not to suggest, of course, that the latter can be achieved without reference to the educational system. Rather, what it implies is that educational reform needs to be a part of a wider restructuring that entails a greater equality of social and economic conditions more widely (Paterson and Iannelli, 2007a).

This is especially apposite to the case of Wales. As we have seen, the Welsh education system has been somewhat more open to forms of educational reform that have emphasised equality of opportunity than the English system. This is reflected not only in the characteristic organisation of secondary schooling, but also in the long-established emphasis on pre-school provision through the welfare state. At the other end of the educational system, adult education has been accorded greater significance, whilst access to higher education, since its inception during the nineteenth century, has been somewhat more open than in other parts of the UK (Rees and Taylor, 2006). However, there is little indication that this relatively 'democratic' education system has resulted in a more fluid society in Wales.

Recent analysis suggests that the relative chances of people moving from one class to another have changed relatively little over time;

the pattern in Wales is broadly equivalent to that in England and Scotland. Moreover, contrary to popular perception, there is less absolute movement between the classes in Wales than there is in the other countries (Paterson and Iannelli, 2007a). Explaining this pattern is complex and is likely to reflect the specificities of the recent transformations of the Welsh labour market and the latter's relationship to other parts of the UK. What is clear, however, is that the emphasis within the Welsh educational system on equality of opportunity has not been translated into actual social mobility or a greater fluidity in Welsh society.

Education and the future welfare state in Wales

There can be no doubt, then, that since the middle decades of the twentieth century, the welfare state – in Wales and elsewhere in the UK – has provided the context for an enormous expansion of educational opportunities. A state education system has come to dominate the ways in which most people gain access to the knowledge, skills and understanding that allow them to function as independent adults within society. The 1944 Education Act addressed what was at that time the key issue with regard to access to education: the extension of secondary schooling to embrace the whole of the population (with the exception of those who opted out of the state system). More recently, attention has shifted to the questions of how far and in what ways the citizen's entitlement extends to higher education and other forms of post-compulsory provision.

Despite this massive achievement, however – as we have seen – the education system has fallen short of the ambitions that have been espoused for it. Access to educational opportunities remains stubbornly divided according to people's social backgrounds. Moreover, changes in the organisation of educational provision – whether in Wales or in England – appear to have had real, but limited, impacts on these inequalities. Whatever the individual benefits that accrue to the acquisition of educational qualifications, it is clear that simply expanding the education system to increase the total stock of human capital does not provide a 'silver bullet' strategy that guarantees national economic success. In Wales, in particular, it is perhaps surprising that policy makers have been rather slow in acknowledging the limitations of tying the education system too closely to an economy that currently performs over 20 per cent below the UK average (on conventional measures). It is equally clear that the reform of educational provision cannot of itself achieve the sort of fluid society in which people are enabled to attain the occupations that their abilities and efforts warrant; social mobility – in all its forms – reflects the wider inequalities in society, not simply the educational ones. In Wales, again, its relatively open and 'democratic' educational system has not been matched in its characteristic patterns of social mobility.

If this is the story so far of education in the welfare state, what of the future? How should the education system be shaped during the twenty-first century? This is a question which, of course, now resonates powerfully in Wales. For the first time, the responsibility for determining the nation's educational future lies very substantially in Welsh hands, given the devolution of powers with respect to education to the National Assembly for Wales. Already, there is clear evidence that the detailed characteristics of educational provision in Wales are diverging significantly from those elsewhere in the UK; although the limitations of the devolution settlement and its financial aspects, in particular, are an important constraining influence here (Rees, 2004).

This is not the place to provide a detailed blueprint for future development. However, at least one clear – albeit rather modest – principle emerges from an analysis of educational provision since the middle decades of the twentieth century: policy makers should adopt a realistic view of what can and, more importantly, what cannot be achieved through educational reform. Some forty years ago, the eminent sociologist of education, Basil Bernstein, wrote succinctly that 'education cannot compensate for society' (Bernstein, 1970: 344). In other words, educational reform alone should not be portrayed (by and to policy makers) as being capable of achieving the kinds of instrumental changes – economic growth and social justice – that have been espoused for it. This is not to suggest, of course, that education is irrelevant to such objectives, but rather to underline the necessity of embedding a progressive educational system within a wider programme of restructuring economic and social opportunities. A much greater degree of realism and even honesty in this respect is an essential pre-condition of more effective policy making, not only for education, but also for other aspects of welfare state provision too.

Finally, and not a little ironically, in order to think clearly about the future of educational provision in Wales (as elsewhere), it may be helpful to return to the rationale espoused for widening educational opportunities by Beveridge in his famous report (Beveridge, 1942). As we have seen, his ambition was to expand educational provision through the welfare state in order to create a citizenry sufficiently well educated to participate fully in the social, political and cultural life of the nation. However, this kind of rationale has implications not only for the reach and inclusiveness of the education system, but also for its internal organisation: forms of curriculum, pedagogical methods, approaches to assessment and so forth. Whilst certainly not advocating an abandonment of the instrumental aims that have been adopted for education, it would be beneficial to row back from some of the extremes of the commodification of education that have characterised policy approaches, especially during recent decades. Considering educational provision in terms of the need to develop rounded citizens, capable of participating wholeheartedly in society irrespective of their social origins or current occupation, would certainly produce a very different kind of lifelong learning from the one that is currently being pursued.

4

SQUALOR

Shifting boundaries: people, homes and the state since 1945

John Puzey

Introduction

This chapter focuses on the relationship between housing and the state in the UK since the Second World War but with some specific references to developments in Wales. In particular the chapter discusses the changing role of publicly subsidised housing as a means of achieving policy objectives.

The relationship between the provision of homes for people and the welfare state has never been straightforward. Overwhelmingly, most households in Britain have lived in the private sector with the market the main provider. This has left housing, as a public service, operating in a rather ambiguous relationship with the welfare state, indeed described once as its 'wobbly pillar' (Torgersen, 1987).

Nevertheless, ambiguous or not, housing was seen as a key issue in the immediate post-war period, a clear important ally to the development of a new approach to providing essential services. This was not only in recognition that without a decent home other ambitions such as improving health, education and economic prosperity would be undermined, but also an initial belief that housing could address fundamental inequalities. For some this relationship began to be dismantled by the Thatcher governments' housing policies, in particular the impact of right to buy, a process that, it is argued, has continued since as successive governments reduced housing investment and social housing became increasingly residualised.

The degree to which housing became attached to the welfare state, however, is disputed (Malpass, 2004). If the post-war reform agenda is characterised as a fundamental reorganisation of essential services so that they are universal and free at the point of delivery, then housing never had a serious connection. Unlike health, coal, rail and road industries there was to be no nationalisation of the building industry or the private rented sector. The market would still be the key provider for most people living in Britain.

Bringing the argument full circle, it is claimed that there is now greater congruence between welfare services and housing. Recent reforms have meant that other services have 'caught up' with the concepts of 'choice' and market influence that has always been central to the provision of housing.

Finally, the economic downturn has suddenly propelled the issue of how people can find and keep a home as high up the public and political agenda as it was in the immediate post-war period. The role of housing in, once again, precipitating a recession and the apparent return of Keynesian economics using, among other instruments, a possible house-building programme as one of its New Deal infrastructure projects, suggest new relationships may be developing between housing and the state. Alongside this there have been fundamental debates about the role of social housing in the twenty-first century, its relationship with economic inactivity and the so-called 'dependency culture'.

The post-war position

In the grim context of 1945, it is not surprising that housing people was seen as a major priority. About a third of all housing in Britain had been damaged in the war, during which there had been practically no building. Over 200,000 homes had been completely destroyed and another 500,000 were either seriously damaged or uninhabitable (Foot, 1973: 63). In addition, no one was prepared for the sudden increase in marriages and births, which grew by 11 per cent and 33 per cent respectively, in the immediate post-war period. As Michael Foot put it, 'the population of Britain was squeezed into some 700,000 fewer houses than six years before' (ibid.).

The need for more homes was not a party political point. Both main parties recognised the urgency of a rapid building programme, summed up simply and succinctly in a Labour Party election poster, 'Let's build the houses – quick', but it was the how and why that would divide Labour from the Conservatives. Both parties recognised that building council housing would be the main form of provision, at least initially, but Labour wanted local councils themselves to be the developers. The Conservative approach, had they won the 1945 election, would have been to extend subsidies to private developers – Churchill's 'Building Machine' – which had produced so many homes in the interwar years. But critics noted that the free enterprise building boom had only occurred in the 1930s as a result of the slump and the availability of cheap labour and materials. Moreover, much of the provision was for middle-class ownership and what was built for poorer people was 'sub-standard' of which 'a lot were only of minimum standard, a lot are ugly beyond belief' (Barton, 1963: 27).

Left to itself, it was argued, the market would not deliver. For Nye Bevan, minister both of health and housing in the Atlee government of 1945, being able to plan housing development and ensure that it went to those most in need meant that local councils had to take the lead. The municipal approach was at the heart of Labour's housing policy, but an even more fundamental difference between the parties was the purpose of the new council housing. As John English noted in his essay 'Building for the masses', British political parties have had varied views on the role of council housing since the war, ranging from seeing it as the normal tenure of the working class, to a safety net for the poor and people re-housed from slum clearance (English, 1992: 92). But at this time an even sharper ideological divide was apparent. It was clear that the Conservatives viewed council housing as simply an expedient to get homes built quickly, whereas Labour rhetoric saw it also as a universal tenure for all classes – truly a national housing service.

An important indicator of Bevan's thinking at this time was the removal of the legislative requirement that public provision should only be for the housing of the working class. In an echo of current debates about balanced communities, Bevan is quoted as believing that 'it is essential for the true life of the citizen . . . to see the living tapestry of a mixed community' (Foot, 1973: 76). With, even then, a third of housing in Britain owned, this was never going to be a reality. However, with an initial emphasis on quality and space in the new housing, there was, at least in principle, an attempt to make it an attractive tenure for all the classes.

The growth of council housing

The Conservative Party came to power in 1951 criticising some of the key principles of the welfare state including, as Malpass notes, 'lack of individual choice, the wastefulness of universalism and the heavy burden of welfare on the economy' (2004: 216). Specifically their criticism of housing policy, which they considered had failed, was that the government had wilfully and ideologically shut out the private developers who could have made a significant contribution. 'Private enterprise has been penalised and every section in the community is suffering from the housing shortage' (Conservative Research Department, 1951: 7). It was certainly true that the overwhelming majority of new house building in Britain at that time was council developed and owned. Wales was no exception to this huge development programme. For example, 99 per cent of housing developments in Glyncorrwg, Ogmore and Garw were council housing, over 90 per cent in many other parts of Wales (Fisk, 2000: 31).

What is important to note is that this huge council-led building boom went on through the Conservative governments of the 1950s despite apparent ideological objections. Indeed a good, if dull, pub quiz question might be 'which two years saw the greatest output of council housing in Britain?' The answer? It was 1953 and 1954 under a Conservative government. A time also when that same government instructed local authorities to restart the slum clearance programme, halted before the war, to address some of the worst areas of squalor in Britain.

So, was this a contradiction in the Conservative view of the role of public housing? It is important to note that, although initially council house building increased, it began to fall from the mid-1950s onwards. Subsidies for council house building began to decline, and restrictions on private house building were removed. As Malpass notes, the focus by local authorities on slum clearance with a large element of council house provision used to rehouse people from poor housing, moved them away from competition with private interest. In addition, local authorities were increasingly required to raise rents and focus on assisting lower income households through means-tested assistance (Malpass, 2004: 217).

The policy and ideological context for housing is crucial in understanding why, as Malpass notes Noel Whiteside has stated about the welfare state in general at that time, there was a fundamental redefinition of its purpose (Malpass, 2004: 216). No longer would council housing be, or at least attempt to be, a universal tenure. Now the policy agenda was driven by seeing such provision as largely for poorer families unable to buy. Council housing was to become a safety net, the residulisation of social housing, which is now more than ever a key housing policy issue, began at this time.

The new ideology: ownership

By the time Labour was returned to power in 1964 the rhetoric of universalism was gone. The 1965 housing White Paper sought a balance between ownership and council tenures, but the paper notes 'once the country has overcome its huge social problem of slumdom and obsolescence . . . the programme of subsidised housing should decrease'. The expansion of public housing initially proposed by Labour was to meet 'exceptional needs'. Significantly, the White Paper then spells out a new Labour view of housing: 'the expansion of building for owner occupation on the other hand is normal; it reflects long-term social advance' (English, 1992: 96). The 1970s saw little difference between the attitudes of both main political parties to owner occupation as the 'normal' tenure and the one to be encouraged. The Heath government of 1970–4 encouraged local authorities to sell council homes to sitting tenants but resisted legislating to speed it up. Labour, back in power in 1974, did not oppose sales in principle but restricted it to areas of high demand – a policy, at the time of writing, now being pursued again by the Welsh assembly coalition government.

For many the election of the Conservative government in 1979 was seen as a watershed for the idea of housing for social ends. However, the economic crisis of the late 1970s had already seen significant public expenditure reductions in housing before the Conservatives came to power. And, as English notes, 'the 1980 Housing Act was largely a rerun of an abortive bill introduced by Labour shortly before they lost office, with the addition of the Right to Buy' (English, 1992: 98). Malpass, for example, quotes Richard Titmuss in 1978 predicting that the introduction of the right to buy would lead to a 'residual welfare council sector' juxtaposing this approach (the residual minimalist model) with the more 'comprehensive and inclusive redistributive model' (Malpass, 2004: 211). But this is to suppose that the 'redistributive model' existed other than, for a time, in the rhetoric of the post-war left. It is true that council tenancies were much sought after in the post-war period, and that such tenancies did not have the stigma that some now associate with them. But the trajectory of council housing was set firmly in the 1950s. As slums were cleared and private landlords sold up, council housing provided homes for those who largely could not afford to buy. Those who could, did.

One clear change, that can be mapped from the 1980s onwards, is the gradual move of the provision of subsidised rented housing from local authorities to housing associations. These charities, trusts and societies had been around for many years and had provided mainly highly localised limited provision for specific groups of people. Now they were to become the increasingly preferred provider of social rented housing. No longer the primary provider of housing, local authorities were expected to become the strategic enablers. Another trend was the continuous and dramatic fall in public investment for housing. It was, as Malpass notes, 'at the forefront of attempts to reduce and restructure public spending in a way designed to residualize the public sector while boosting the market'. It was calculated that between 1981 and 2001, while main welfare programmes grew, housing investment was cut by 64 per cent (Malpass, 2004: 221).

As a percentage of government spending, investment in housing since the 1980s has been low. Never over 4 per cent on a UK level, it fell to below 3 per cent in 1993–4 and remained at between 1.4 per cent and 2 per cent between 1996/7 and 2003/4, with only marginal increases of just over 2 per cent in the years up to 2006/7 (Wilcox,

2008). The shift between council provision and that of housing associations would be slow through new build alone. However, a new impetus was provided in the 1980s with legal frameworks that allowed the transfer of whole estates to housing association type companies. The advantages of this approach was that such companies would be able to raise significant private funding for renovation and improvements denied to local authorities by Government Public Sector Borrowing Requirement rules. Transfers proceeded apace in England but Wales largely held back. When, however, it became clear that the new Labour government of 1997 was only going to make resources available through this route, and when the National Assembly for Wales itself signalled that stock transfer was really the only show in town, more Large Scale Voluntary Transfers in Wales began to occur.

This shift between the proportion of publicly subsidised homes provided by local authorities to housing associations was dwarfed by the much greater one between the proportion of households in public/social rented housing to those in owner occupation. In Britain as a whole, owner occupation rose from 43 per cent of all households in 1961 to 69 per cent in 2000. In Wales by 2006/7 73 per cent of all households were owner occupiers. Council tenancies in Wales fell from 24 per cent in 1961 to 12 per cent in 2006/7 (Local Government Data Unit, 2008).

The financial deregulation of the 1980s, tax relief for owner-occupiers paying mortgages and the right to buy led to a profound change in the British tenure profile – a shift underpinned by an ideology of individual responsibility, an acceptance of inequality (characterised by an increasingly residulalised social rented sector) and linked to housing as a means of accruing personal wealth. It also carried with it risks, as any economic disturbances or large-scale unemployment would clearly put the ownership model in jeopardy.

What is the legacy of the ideology of ownership? First, it must be said that there has been and continues to be a clear desire by most people to own a home, though often the consequences and costs of ownership are not always fully understood. But the growth of ownership has had other clear broader consequences. The huge increase in house prices, fuelled by demand which in turn was fuelled by high value to income loans, has created significant economic instability, a term that might now be considered a bit of an understatement. The move to ownership has also led to an unprecedented growth in the wealth gap between those who own and those who do not. A report in 2004, commentating on the potential impact on social mobility of housing wealth noted:

> a child will not be able to earn their way out of their social position in the future. A social position that will be increasingly determined by their parents' housing wealth, that wealth determined partly by who their parents are, but mainly by where they happen to live: a postcode lottery to life writ large. (Thomas and Dorling, 2004: 5)

Contemporary debate

More recent debates about the future of subsidised housing continue to juxtapose a model, which, it is claimed, perpetuates dependency and inactivity, with one of enabling choice and personal responsibility.

The old 'welfarist' model, it is argued, is no longer appropriate in the twenty-first century. As a recent introduction to a number of essays on the reform of social housing states:

> current social housing policies and practices were first established on post war welfarist foundations. Whilst entirely appropriate in the 1950s and 1960s, the last three decades have seen a plethora of tweaks and changes, with gradually increasing frequency, to try to update policy to meet changes in society. However the basic welfarist approach has been left untouched. (Dwelly, 2006: 4)

It would be interesting to speculate to what welfarist foundations the author refers. Welfarism here is equated with dependence and the residulisation of social housing, never a part of the lofty ideals expressed by Nye Bevan. The editor of these essays concludes with a set of radical proposals including the ending of the life-time social housing tenancy, the dismantling of estates, ending the link between homelessness duties and social tenancies and ending single tenancy social housing schemes. The last proposal, ironically, is an echo of the socially mixed communities that Bevan wanted.

The UK government-commissioned Hills Report, on the future of social housing in England, continued to explore the concept that the lifetime social housing tenure itself has created a dependency culture. It noted that more than half of all social tenants were without paid work (Hills, 2007). It questioned whether this could simply be an obvious result of residulisation or a product of the tenure itself. Hills concludes that, although the concentration of social tenants among the poorer in society may partly be a product of how social housing is allocated, comparing households with similar disadvantages to other tenures still shows a disproportionate number of social housing tenants failing to improve their living standards. Hills lays out a number of possible ways forward, concentrating on encouraging social mobility and once again highlighting the need to develop mixed-income communities. More recently, and following on from Hills, the (Westminster) housing and planning minister has raised, in an address to the Fabian Society, the question of whether those accessing social housing should sign commitment contracts agreeing to actively seek work and has encouraged speculation over how social tenants can acquire some level of assets from buying a stake in their home (Ryan and Sparrow, 2008; Wintour, 2008).

There are a number of important points to make about these views, which now have so much currency. The first is to be clear about the impact of a home on lives. A decent home is fundamental to a person's health, well-being and life chances. It is also critical to the well-being of the community as a whole. It has been said that of all the forms of deprivation, housing deprivation is the worst as who you are and where you live are so intimately connected (Lloyd, 2007). But a decent home alone, though fundamental, will not be enough. Poverty, lack of education and life chances will still limit what a household can achieve. It is impossible to isolate the tenure of households from other inequalities, although often tenure and postcode will equate to poorer services. Moreover, many people in social housing will not necessarily be living in quality homes or well-designed estates anyway. Focusing on tenure as part of the problem without acknowledging other impacts is short-sighted. Similarly, some commentators contest the benefits of the mixed communities approach, promoted by almost everyone as incontestable facts. Indeed, a number of significant academic studies into attempted mixed communities have suggested that the benefits are more intuitive than actually evidenced. That again, broader structural issues are far more significant factors in the life chances of households than tenure or community.[1]

It is also worth noting that much of the current debate is largely unconcerned with how the broader market has impacted on social housing. The shortage of affordable housing over recent years has placed a dual pressure on social housing. More people who have been unable to afford to buy have joined social housing waiting lists, and tenants themselves have found it difficult to move given the prevailing market conditions. Of course the right to buy (RTB) has provided some opportunities for tenants to move into ownership but, with most of the sought-after stock purchased and little new builds by councils, RTB has been flat lining for some time. Basically with turnover almost at a standstill ambitions to move on and move out are unrealistic.

Finally, it is worth pointing out that since 1997 housing has been a devolved function. The radical ideas circulating social housing in England appeared to have left the administrations in the devolved countries unimpressed. In Wales the focus continues to be on improving social housing through achieving the Welsh Housing Quality Standard by 2012, and neighbourhood regeneration schemes such as Communities First.

In fact, Wales has fundamentally tried to plot an alternative course to the market-driven, choice-based and individualised ways of improving public services seen in England. The Welsh Citizen Centred concept, articulated by Sir Jeremy Beecham in *Beyond Boundaries*, seeks to create a continuous critical learning loop between people and the services that impact on them so that those services become increasingly sensitised to need (Beecham, 2006). The extent to which such a concept is operational yet is questionable, but the intent and direction is clear.

An early indication of this is the Welsh government's approach to stock transfer and its development of the Community Housing Mutual Model with the focus on giving more power to tenants and the community. The model aims to give residents a constitutional stake and a stronger input into management and ownership of the housing and, therefore, to encourage participation as opposed to the housing being transferred to a remote or unaccountable organisation. *Better Homes for People in Wales* facilitates 'a real sense of participation and involvement by the tenants. It also avoids any sense of some remote or unaccountable organisation owning and running the properties' (National Assembly for Wales, 2001).

Full circle?

In 2004, the UK government commissioned the economist Kate Barker to examine why the housing market did not behave like a market should. Rising prices and increasing demand, according to the classic supply and demand models, should bring in new providers, which in turn helps drive prices down. This patently was not happening. The Barker review concluded that continuing the current rate of building was not a realistic option – it simply was not meeting current, let alone future, demand. It noted that in 2001 the construction of homes in England and Wales was the lowest since the Second World War (Barker, 2004). Barker recognised that significant investment was needed as well as the allocation of more land for development. The extraordinary hike in land prices in the UK is a significant factor in both the cost and relative scarcity of housing. But a crucial conclusion of the report was that the weak supply in housing meant a less stable economy. The problem of the lack of affordable housing was being recognised but government responses were slow. The under-provision of social rented housing in Wales led to a proposed social homes target in 2003 of the order of 3,500 a year (Holmans, 2003). In fact, the number of social rented homes completed has never exceeded 500 in any of the years up to 2006–7 (Local Government Data Unit, 2008), leading to a growing backlog of housing need.

This lack of affordable rented homes, combined with high house prices has meant that many households, even those working and with incomes above benefit levels, could not afford to buy even the cheapest homes on the market, putting increased pressure on the social rented sector (Wilcox, 2006). A growing recognition that many households were caught between two largely non-viable options – buying a house which was often both too expensive and unaffordable to sustain, or finding a very rare, reasonable quality, affordable rented home – has seen an increased emphasis on intermediate housing developments such as Homebuy and section 106 planning agreements, which may better suit the circumstances of the household. Although much discussed, there are currently only a few options between outright ownership and outright renting.

Even before the 2008 recession, all the UK governments had begun to recognise, to some extent, the need for the state to take a much closer interest in the provision of housing and that publicly subsidised housing was not only essential to meet increasing demand, but could also help to stabilise economic fluctuations and help iron out the damaging inflationary impact of the recent growth in house prices. These things were being recognised but the urgency of the response and the level of resources necessary to make an impact were not. All the indications were that something in the housing world was going to give. It is perhaps not surprising that a major contributor to the current economic downturn was the extraordinary level of unsustainable lending to low-income households to buy homes. House price inflation, in the late 1980s and early 1990s, fuelled the last British recession. This one, however, starting in the US and infecting the whole banking system, is clearly bigger and more significant.

If this wasn't already bad enough, the new economic realities are likely to make the provision of affordable housing even more difficult. The Welsh Assembly Government of 2007 set out a target of 6,500 new affordable homes by 2011 (Welsh Assembly Government, 2007). This was a modest enough target given that some estimates put the need at 14,000 new affordable homes (Shelter Cymru, 2007), but is at least an increase over previous levels. The Essex review followed up the commitment with a blueprint to achieve this target (Essex et al., 2008). Fate conspired that the blueprint, relying heavily as it did on 'planning gain' arrangements with private developers, was launched just as the economy was nose-diving, taking private housing developments down with it.

But could the economic crisis, like the Second World War, be another turning point in the relationship between the state and people's homes? The political, social and economic fall out of the impact of the recession on people's ability to access and keep decent homes will be significant. Repossessions are increasing and homelessness is likely to grow as well, and not only as a result of defaulting borrowers, but as any form of affordable home becomes scarce. However, perhaps we will see a growing recognition that housing programmes can stimulate local economies and ancillary services, in other words contribute to ways out of the recession. Certainly governments in the UK seem to be taking more decisive actions around housing than have been seen for decades.

Additional capital funding has been found to purchase unfinished private developments for social housing. Future social housing grant allocations have been brought forward to accelerate the social housing programme to respond to current needs. Government-backed mortgage rescue funds have been made available to allow housing associations to buy or part buy homes from struggling borrowers while allowing them to remain as tenants or in shared equity schemes. It is possible to exaggerate the response, of course, and housing investment levels are still only a small proportion of those spent on health, social services and education. Overwhelmingly most people live, and will continue to live, in private housing and much of the focus of government interventions in the banks has been to get them to lend again to stimulate the mortgage market. Private solutions still dominate.

Of course, the apparently new Keynesian approach that began to be deployed to minimise the effects of the economic downturn was brought to an abrupt end in 2010 when the coalition government came to power.

This chapter has only hinted at some of the more recent changes to housing policy in England being introduced by the UK coalition government, but as a final postscript to the relationship between people's homes and the state, the impact of public expenditure cuts and welfare reform cannot be ignored. Briefly cuts to housing benefit and other welfare support payments will have a profound impact on the ability of people to live in decent homes in the places in which they want to live. Cuts to public expenditure make a new, growth-stimulating, house-building programme even more remote. In Wales, the new Welsh government will need to innovate if it is to respond to growing housing need. New programmes, like the Empty Homes initiative launched in 2012, show a willingness to look at any options to provide more affordable homes. Utilising the private rented sector and identifying ways in which new private finance can be encouraged to support affordable housing developments are crucial as homelessness and housing waiting lists rise.

These disparate, relatively low volume and pragmatic responses to the growing housing crisis seem a long way from the post-war house-building programmes which responded to the emergency situation following the war. The state as provider is now replaced by the state as facilitator trying to operate as best it can in the market. The very purpose and future of social housing is now also being debated in Wales, and in the UK at large. Who is it for? How long should people remain in it? Should it be means-tested? Shouldn't the focus no longer be on subsidising bricks and mortar but on people – and how they are supported into different types of homes and tenures according to the different needs they have at different points in their lives? The debate moves on: perhaps the 'Citizen Centred' principles, articulated by the Welsh Government, are ultimately a new expression of Bevan's vision – but citizens still need somewhere to live.

Note

1. See St Andrews University Centre for Housing Research, Publications: Mixing Tenures, Social Balance and Neighbourhood Change.

5

IDLENESS

'No longer a problem of industry'? Principles, practice and policy in the early twenty-first century

David Byrne

> The Report which I now present is a sequel to my earlier Report, in that is concerned with one of the assumptions of Social Security: the assumption that employment is maintained and mass unemployment prevented. But it is more than a sequel. Maintenance of employment is wanted for its own sake and not simply to make a Plan for Social Security work more easily. The new Report takes as its aim freedom from Idleness and sets out a Policy for Full Employment to achieve that aim.
>
> (Beveridge, 1944: 17)

> Idleness is not the same as Want, but a separate evil, which men do not escape by having an income. They must also have the chance of rendering useful service and of feeling that they are doing so. This means that employment is not wanted for the sake of employment, irrespective of what it produces.
>
> (ibid.: 20)

It was quickly evident in the wake of the 1997 election that Labour's approach to welfare reform and the labour market was different to that of any of its predecessors. A dependence on macroeconomic policy to achieve full employment would remain a thing of the past, although Labour would not rely exclusively on private enterprise and market forces. Instead, the benefit system would be turned from a passive provider of financial support into a tool to promote labour market engagement (Fothergill and Wilson, 2007: 1007). This chapter considers the legacy of this approach.

When William Beveridge wrote *Full Employment in a Free Society*, his assertion that the maintenance of full employment was the central task of a capitalist democratic state, and endorsement of Keynesian methods for macroeconomic management as the mean to achieving this end, he laid out the programme for United Kingdom social democracy for some fifty years. It is true that he paid some fairly minimal attention in his earlier *Social Insurance and Allied Services Report* (1942) to the problems of being rendered unfit for employment which derived from prolonged separation from work. Here he revived the idea, around since the 1890s, of 'resettlement' processes to restore the culture and habits of work to those who had lost it. However, this was a footnote at best to the great project of ensuring that adequate decent work was available to all and that by ensuring that the demand for labour always exceeded the supply of it, the state would modify the relationship between workers and employers to the considerable advantage of the former. I venture to think that he would have been surprised to find that nearly seventy years later a Labour government would develop a set of policies founded in large part on a merchant banker's[1] report on the future of welfare which focused exclusively on the resettlement aspect of his approach (see Freud, 2007).[2]

In December 2007, the government published a command paper *Ready for Work: Full Employment in Our Generation* (Department for Work and Pensions, 2007b). This delineation of principles was translated into a document for 'public consultation' on the actual way in which the principles will be implemented: *No One Written Off: Reforming Welfare to Reward Responsibility* (ibid., 2008a). This has been followed up by *Raising Expectations and Increasing Support: Reforming Welfare for the Future* (ibid., 2008b), which takes things towards legislation. The Beveridge Report (1942) was also a command paper of the old style, in that it comprised analytical and descriptive text. It sold 100,000 copies within a month and combined sales of the full report and a summary exceeded 650,000 copies. The 2007 and 2008 reports are downloadable, full of pretty pictures and essentially assertive rather than analytical. The first lays out its cards very plainly:

Starting with the introduction of the New Deal in 1998, the Government has demonstrated a determination to move towards full employment – and to apply the concept in a modern setting. A new definition of 'Full Employment in the 21st century' was set out in Gordon Brown's speech to the 1999 Labour Party Conference – high and stable levels of employment with employment opportunity for all. This aim of maximising employment opportunity for all continues to be one of the key aims of this Government. *What this means in practice is our long-term aspiration of an employment rate of 80 per cent, up from 74 per cent, with employment opportunity open to all.*

This means above all ensuring that all aspects of the benefits system support the welfare-to-work agenda. In our modern world, work is a realistic option, or a realistic aspiration, for most people and we need a modern benefits system which reflects this. Most people should work: it is good for them, their families and society, and key to tackling child poverty. For most people, out-of-work benefits should be a temporary solution to a temporary problem – not a way of life. (Department for Work and Pensions, 2007b: 98; emphasis in the original)

This document has set out how we are responding to our long-term aspirations of an 80 per cent employment rate and world-class skills. We will bring more inactive people into work than ever before, and ensure people have the skills and attitudes they need to progress in work. We will increasingly look to *move people from being passive recipients of benefits to jobseekers* actively seeking and preparing for work, and then progressing in work. (Ibid.: 103; emphasis in the original)

If the 2007 document was a statement of principle, the 2008 follow up is about implementation. Following the intervening consultation document, which attracted a deal of informed criticism, the government commissioned an 'independent review' from Professor Paul Gregg of Bristol University's Centre for Market and Public

Organisation: *Realising Potential* (2008). Normally such an independent review would take the form of a more-or-less systematic review in which all available evidence is assembled and then a disinterested summary of the balance and contradictions of that evidence is presented for consideration. Gregg concluded:

> The evidence presented here and emerging across many different welfare reforms is clear that movements into work are largely beneficial for the claimant and their dependents, that the use of conditionality is effective in changing behaviour, and that the support services onto which people are placed are effective. (2008: 6)

There is some qualified agreement across a range of studies that the first statement here is correct. People are often better off in work, although as Gregg notes there is 'the possibility that conditionality leads to people being directed to inappropriate courses or jobs' (ibid.). That can mean in the United States grossly exploitative employment at low minimum wages with high job-related costs in transport and childcare. However, there is certainly not general agreement either that conditionality works or that agencies based on conditionality are effective. Studies by Millar (2003, based on work commissioned for the Department for Work and Pensions (DWP) itself) and Osborne (2007) are much more sceptical. Osborne is not cited in Gregg's bibliography nor is Millar's worked-up study. The content of two DWP reports by Hosain and Breen (2007) and Thomas (2007), which are cited by Gregg, cannot easily be interpreted as supporting the notion that support services are inherently effective. Nor does Gregg review the evidence on regional differences presented by Sunley et al. (2001). Gregg has a view but it is one that can be and has been contested. His location in a centre which has a fundamental logic of supporting private engagement in public services and emphasising incentives might be considered to have coloured his perspective. For those with a historical sense we might say that Nassau Senior[3] lives on. In particular, Gregg's report singularly underplays a point made in a submission by Adrian Sinfield in response to the consultative document: 'there is clear evidence and widespread acknowledgement, that child poverty would have fallen much faster if getting into work had more often succeeded in lifting families out of poverty rather than trapping them in working poverty' (Sinfield, 2008: 7).

So, we now have a policy that addresses not what Beveridge understood as idleness and its causes in the untrammelled operations of a market capitalist economy, but rather 'dependency' understood in much the same way as it was by those who framed the New Poor Law of 1834. *Ready for Work: Full Employment in Our Generation* (2007b) laid out the way in which James Purnell, the very 'New Labour' Secretary of State for Work and Pensions was thinking. We will return to the detailed content of these proposals towards the end of this chapter.

First, let us examine the nature of 'idleness' in the United Kingdom in the early years of the twenty-first century. To do this we need to consider the changing nature of social conditions and especially the emergence of both single parenthood and long-term illness/disability among those of working age, as sources of 'dependency'. However, we also need to examine the changing nature of understandings of the origins of that dependency and in particular the way in which the blame for that condition has, in the best tradition of 'possessive individualism', been reassigned to those who are dependent. We also have to examine how we have revived a practice abandoned in 1834 of subsidising low wages from taxes. And we need to think about the nature not only of macroeconomic policies since the election of the Thatcher government in 1979 which, Tory and Labour alike, have prioritised the interests of finance capital over manufacturing capital and have thus led to a greater decline in the significance of industrial employment in the UK than in any other 'advanced' industrial country. This has had profound meso-economic consequences for the space economy of the UK as a whole with a massive decline in the previously core industrial regions. It is a particular irony that Labour's safest bastion heartland, the north-east of England, has suffered most severely from the combination of these processes and has in consequence the highest dependency levels of any mainland British region.

This chapter will review in order the scale and nature of 'idleness' in the contemporary UK; the endorsement by New 'Labour' of a US-derived understanding of non-employment – the difference between non- and unemployment will be established momentarily – which assigns the causes of that status to deficiencies in those outwith the labour force and not to the nature of the macro- and meso-economic policies that have led to an especially severe deindustrialisation of the UK and devastation of the employment base of its industrial heartlands which, coupled with one of Europe's weakest job protection regimes, has pushed the marginally employable to the wall; the re-emergence of Speenhamland-style subsidies to low paid work; the actual character of the contemporary 'idle', and the form of employment promoting policies that represent in important respects the coercive principle of less eligibility expressed in true 'third way' fashion with a smiley face. At the end of it neo-liberalism and classical liberalism look very much alike and neither has much to do with the social liberalism of Beveridge and Keynes and still less to do with social democracy as that term would have been understood by their Labour contemporaries.

Contemporary non-employment

'Unemployment is a count of jobless people who want to work, are available to work, and are actively seeking employment' (International Labour Organization definition used by the UK Office for National Statistics in that agency's official definition of unemployment). In the UK this has to be distinguished from the claimant count of unemployed which is the total number of people claiming job-seeker's allowance (JSA), which was 1.23 million in January 2009, whereas the survey established unemployment total was 1.97 million (63 per cent). The 'inactivity rate plus unemployment rate' for people of working age was 26 per cent which meant that 7.9 million people of working age were economically inactive in addition to the nearly 2 million unemployed. The term non-employed does not have an official definition but we can see it as composed of those who are economically active but unemployed, and of those among the non-employed who are not students and if looking after the home and family are not single parents dependent on state benefits. Those are the groups targeted as dependent by Freud and the component groups are:

- 2.0 million people of working age inactive due to long-term sickness or disability with the focus on the 2.4 million in receipt of incapacity benefits as of August 2008 – here the benefit receipt figure exceeds the labour force survey figure;
- lone parents with the focus on the 745,000 in receipt of income support;
- those on JSA, i.e. 1.23 million who are claimants;
- 1.3 million 16–24 year olds who were not in employment, education or training – NEETs for short – although this term is applied particularly to those aged 16–18 (those over eighteen might also be counted as on JSA or incapacity benefit claimants). (All figures as of late 2008 unless otherwise specified.)

As of November 2007, the proportion of people of working age, that is, between sixteen and the age of sixty-five for men and sixty for women, in employment was 74.7 per cent. Government targets were to raise this to 80 per cent, a figure only exceeded by Iceland at that time. This rate stayed the same until 2009 but the total UK workforce fell over the period. Iceland's economy has of course collapsed. In effect, New Labour counted as non-employed everybody of working age, other than students in full-time education, who is not employed. However, some are exempt from consideration as targets for being 'encouraged' into work. These include some of the disabled and long-term sick, carers and people looking after families or children who are not dependent on state benefits. The government's target is to get all the unemployed and NEETs into work, all single parents on benefit with children over seven – some 250,000 as of August 2008 – and 1 million of those on incapacity benefit (IB). Indeed, under the Gregg review, parents of children over the age of one will be enmeshed in 'progression to work' and those with children over the age of three will be pushed even harder towards employment. The requirement to enter the 'work ready' group will also be extended to the non-working partners of JSA claimants. Only the severely incapacitated and parents of children under one will be in a 'no conditionality group'. Those with milder incapacities and parents of children aged 1–6 will be in a 'progression to work group'.

It is important to reflect on some massive social changes and associated policy changes which have transformed the nature of those dependent on benefit since Beveridge and indeed in effect since the 1970s. The 1970s were the last period when the UK could properly be described as an industrial society. A combination of global tendencies in relation to increasing labour productivity in manufacturing, the relocation of industrial employment to low-wage 'peripheral economies' with UK macroeconomic policies around capital flows and exchange rates that have reinforced all the global pressures have transformed this country into a post-industrial society. The massive growth in the numbers on incapacity benefits derives in large part from a policy response to this. That is to say, throughout the 1980s in effect national government winked at, and in some ways encouraged, the transfer of long-term unemployed ex-industrial workers from time-limited and/or means-tested unemployment benefits to what was originally a non-means-tested insurance benefit payable to those incapable of work by reason of long-term limiting illness or disability. Local officials and medical practitioners in old industrial regions recognised that many ex-industrial workers had no realistic prospect of employment, given their incapacity, although in a full employment local economy they might well have found work, and in effect encouraged such transfers. The effect was to reduce formal unemployment levels but at the same time 'incapacity' became a route towards retirement for many older ex-industrial workers. For men, this reason for economic inactivity increased by 50 per cent from the early 1980s. For women it more than doubled.

It is interesting to examine the extent of deindustrialisation in the UK both in relation to other advanced industrial nations and in terms of the very different regional impacts of this process. Let us deal first with international comparison. The most obvious comparator is Germany, since Germany and the UK were the two most industrialised societies in the 1970s with nearly 50 per cent of all employees in industrial employment. By 2005, the proportions were 30 per cent in Germany but just 22 per cent in the UK. Italy and Spain and even Ireland now have substantially higher proportions of employment in industry than the UK. UK macroeconomic policy in the Thatcher and Major years was founded on the notion that the UK should cease to be an industrial society and focus its efforts on services and in particular financial services. Elliott and Atkinson describe the current nature of the UK economy in forceful terms when commenting on the fact that we are currently running a trade deficit of about 4 per cent of annual GDP:

> But for the past decade the only thing that has made the deficit manageable is that Britain has been earning more money on its investments abroad than foreign investors have made here. One way of looking at Britain is as one offshore hedge fund churning speculators' money while asset-strippers draw up plans for the few remaining factories to be turned into industrial theme parks. (Elliott and Atkinson, 2007: 74)

The consequences of this in relation to employment patterns have not been evenly distributed across the UK. London and the greater south-east (which includes most of the population of the eastern region of England) lost many industrial jobs but these were replaced by service employment, at least until the present crisis. In contrast, the peripheral regions of England – the north-east, north-west and Yorkshire and Humberside, together with Wales – have seen massive employment loss in industry with no equivalent development of new service employment on anything like the south-eastern scale. The consequence is that workless households as a proportion of all households of working age varies from a high of 23 per cent in the north-east of England and Northern Ireland through rates of around 19 per cent in the rest of northern England, Wales and Scotland as well as London within the south-east,[4] to the mid-teens in the English Midlands to rates of around 12 per cent in the east of England, the south-east and the south-west. In other words, 'idleness' has been to a considerable degree a regional issue, and within regions an issue concentrated in formerly industrial urban and coalfield localities.

The collapse of the financial services sector with associated spin off in relation to consumption is of course likely to lead to this pattern becoming more even in the south-east in particular.

We should not, however, ignore neighbourhood effects in apparently prosperous regions. This is most important for old working-class London within the greater south-east. This is by no means just a matter of the loss of dockland and clothing jobs in the East End. David Smith (2005) has described how people living in what were the zones of 1950s and 1960s modern industry in south-west London now live 'on the margins of inclusion'. It is not that they are permanently unemployed or otherwise benefit dependent, although some are, but rather that they move through a series of insecure jobs and periods of benefit dependency. Some of the jobs are regular employment, some are in the cash-in-hand grey economy with varying degrees of legality in the actual work itself. Benefits may be combined with cash-in-hand work. This is a very different world from the if not a job for life then always a regular and usually unionised and reasonably well-paid job available somewhere in the world of industrial south-west London forty years ago.

The other major change has been the growth in the proportions of families with children which are headed by a single parent. This has more than tripled since the early 1970s to more than 24 per cent of all families with children. More than 40 per cent of single parents are dependent on state benefits. Plainly the reasons for this massive increase are complex and multiple but the post-industrial shift and the fragmentation of male work is generally held to be one factor. Previous government attempts to reduce the public cost of benefit dependency by single parents have included a revival of efforts to enforce 'liable relative' status through the Child Support Agency, but that has been notoriously unsuccessful. Ethnographic accounts, like those of David Smith (2005), show how post-industrial flexible labour markets have introduced a level of instability into people's lives and how they have had to abandon family structures based on the assumption of stability in order to cope with them.

Another social change is seldom remarked on. It is plain that Beveridge expected most married women of working age not to work.

In other words, the norm would be to have households dependent on the 'family wage' of an adult male worker. Now most women of working age work. In 2008, 74.2 per cent were economically active compared with 66.4 per cent in 1984. In contrast, the economic activity rate for men of working age has decreased from 88.4 per cent to 83.9 per cent. The full-time housewife, the commonest social role for women in the 1950s, is now less common than both the full-time and part-time working woman. The 'reform' package is plainly predicated on the notion that a non-working partner is a luxury good affordable only for those who are not in any way dependent on direct state benefits, although interestingly the Speenhamland-style subsidies to low wages are likely to go particularly to households with only one earner.

The combined effects of these changes mean that for men of working age formal unemployment is no longer the dominant or even largest reason for being idle. That is long-term sickness. For women, 'looking after home' is the largest reason for economic inactivity[5] at 45 per cent, although long-term sickness is the reason for more than 20 per cent of economically inactive women. As we shall see, in effect contemporary UK policies take the form of moving those on benefits who are not currently classified as unemployed towards that status with a view to moving them off direct cash benefits and into work.

Subsidized employment: the re-emergence of Speenhamland

The interesting question emerges of what kind of work. Whilst we may consider that there was a 'less eligibility' theme to New Labour's policies of labour market engagement, the other foundational principle of the 1834 New Poor Law has been abandoned absolutely. We have had a massive recreation of the Speenhamland system which was done away with in 1834. That is to say we now massively subsidize low wages from taxation revenues either as cash or as allowances against income tax liability which have exactly the same effect. This began with the Conservative government's introduction of family income supplement in 1971, the first modern tax-funded income benefit for which being in work was a condition of receipt. This was a radical departure from Beveridge's principles and from practice since 1834. As Dilnot et al. remarked:

The [1942] Beveridge Report barely discusses the problem of poverty among working households. In this, it is very much a product of the particular time at which it was written . . . for Beveridge it was axiomatic that anyone in employment had resources sufficient to support a wife and one child.[6] (1984: 23)

We have had a massive expansion in the range and cost of benefits for those in low-paid work. The most important of these benefits currently are working tax credit and child tax credit. As of December 2007:

5.9 million families, containing 9.8 million children, were tax credit recipients or were receiving the equivalent child support through benefits; These families comprised:

5.5 million families with children receiving CTC, or the equivalent via benefits;
1.3 million in which no adult was in work;
1.7 million in work receiving the maximum CTC, and also receiving WTC;
0.7 million in work receiving less than the maximum CTC, but more than the family element;
1.8 million in work receiving the family element of CTC;
0.1 million in work receiving less than the family element of CTC;
0.4 million families in work without children, receiving only WTC.
428 thousand families were benefiting from the childcare element of WTC; they were receiving an average of £64 per week help with their childcare costs.
111 thousand families were benefiting from the disabled worker element of WTC.
452 thousand families receiving CTC were benefiting from the baby addition to the family element. (HM Revenue and Customs, 2007)

There were 4.1 million families 'in work' in receipt of one or more means-tested supplements to low incomes. The total cost of all tax credits in 2005–6 was £12.6 billion. All cash social security benefits cost £127.5 billion. Incapacity and related benefits cost £25 billion. Unemployment benefits cost £3.8 billion. Housing benefits, much of which goes as rent and council tax reductions to low-income working households, cost £13.5 billion (HM Treasury, 2006).[7]

The crucial significance of subsidies to low wages mean that dependency among adults of working age on state revenues is no longer a matter of support when unemployed, in Beveridge's terms of being idle. Instead we have an enormous number of adults and their dependents reliant on a combination of necessarily low wages and state subsidies. The significance of this is that transfers from benefit dependency to work are almost invariably to low-paid state-subsidized work.

The idle: a closer look

Who are the idle? Well they are the unemployed, the incapacitated, non-working single parents and the NEETs. Let us look at each group in turn to build up a picture of them in the final months of the New Labour government. We can begin with the unemployed, the category of most significance for Beveridge himself. Figures from the Labour Force Survey for the end of 2008 show that recorded unemployment for both sexes taken together stood at just under 2 million people and a rate of 6.3 per cent. In 1994 the total was 3 million and the rate was 10.2 per cent. The claimant count figures give a total of 1.23 million unemployed but plainly there are people not in receipt of benefit who regard themselves as unemployed. Most unemployed were men and unemployment rates for younger age groups are consistently higher than for older age groups. The rate for 16–17-year-olds was 28.3 per cent at the end of 2008, for 18–24-year-olds it was 14.5 per cent and for those aged over 25 it was below 5 per cent. In what is now, in radical contrast to Beveridge's day,[8] a multi-ethnic society, all ethnic minorities experience higher unemployment rates than white people, and this is particularly true for black and Muslim minorities. Unemployment rates increase 'down' the occupation scale with 'Elementary Occupations' having a rate more than three times that of managers and professionals. Duration of unemployment matters. In 2008, 39 per cent of all the unemployed, 42 per cent of male unemployed and 34 per cent of female unemployed, had been unemployed for over six months and therefore were not part of a pool of frictionally unemployed labour. Long-term unemployment rates rose with age but even for 18–24-year-olds nearly 20 per cent had been unemployed for more than a year. Moreover, many claimants move between short periods of work and longer periods of unemployment. Freud (2007: 4) notes that 250,000 of a recent cohort of new job-seeker's allowance claimants had been on benefits for more than eighteen months in the past two years.

The long-term sick are the largest category of 'idle' persons of working age. For men this is by far the most important category of economically inactive people. Thirty-four per cent of all economically inactive men are in this category and the rate is 37 per cent for those aged between twenty-five and thirty-four and rises to over 50 per cent for older men of working age.[9] For women, 19 per cent of the economically inactive are in this category. However, we have to recognise that there is very considerable movement between the categories of being unemployed and being classified as long-term sick. Bacon, of the Department of Work and Pensions Social Research Branch, examined *Moving between Sickness and Unemployment* in 2002.[10] She used administrative data to show that in the year up to April 1999, 190,000 people left JSA for IB and in the year up to November 2000, 110,000 people moved from IB to JSA. This excellent report showed that:

> benefit clients who experience both unemployment and ill health or disability, and have spells on both Jobseeker's Allowance (JSA) and Incapacity Benefit (IB) as a result – share a number of characteristics that mean they are disadvantaged in the labour market. Survey data showed they were older than other clients, less well qualified, more likely to report problems with basic skills, lacked recent work experience and were less likely to have access to private transport. (Bacon, 2002: 195)

Of those who left IB in 1996 because their claim was disallowed on medical review, only 10 per cent went into employment. Thirty-two per cent moved on to JSA, 15 per cent were unemployed and seeking work but not in receipt of JSA and 44 per cent became economically inactive. Thus, 59 per cent of those leaving IB were removed from state-funded welfare support.

Let us turn to lone parents with dependent children. Not even New Labour was quite impertinent enough to argue that people looking after the home with a working partner have yet to be forced into work but, in line with its US gurus, it has single parents (and the partners of benefit dependents) in its sights. In May 2007, there were 766,000 lone parent claimants down from a figure of 945,000 in August 1999; 730,000 of these were female single parents. In February 2005, 65 per cent of children living in families receiving income-related benefits were living in single parent families. In 18 per cent of these families, the youngest child was aged eleven or more. Thirty-three per cent had a youngest child aged five to eleven years. The rest had a youngest child aged less than five years.

Finally, let us look at NEETs and in particular at young people between sixteen and eighteen years of age who are 'not in education, employment or training'. This term first gained wide currency with the publication of the report *Bridging the Gap* (1999) by central government's Social Exclusion Unit. Provisional figures for 2006 suggest that 22.7 per cent of this age group, that is, some 468,000 young people were in this category. However, we have to be very cautious with this figure. We have already noted that the general state of 'being idle' and all the components of this state are highly dynamic for individual people. Put simply, they move in and out of the condition and move across sub-categories within the condition. This is especially true of NEETs. Ferguson (2004) demonstrated how young adults actually do not follow the patterns laid down for them in the official discourse surrounding discussion of the NEET phenomenon. There are three elements in official discourse – a discourse of social exclusion which has many of the tones of what Levitas (1996) calls the 'moral underclass discourse', a discourse of disaffection and a discourse of marginalisation. All somehow combine in explanations of 'failed transition' to adult life. However, in reality young people move around the statuses of employment, education and unemployment, often combining for example part-time employment either legal or in the grey economy with study. We have a fluid and complex set of trajectories, some of which involve 'refusal' of the demands of New Deal and other inclusionary projects.

So, having identified the idle, what is to be done with them? Let us turn to an examination of New Labour's policies in practice and as proposed in the light of the recommendations of the merchant banker, Freud.

New Deal and beyond

> the Government's attack on worklessness . . . tackles the barriers to work faced by workless households, including low skills, fears about the time lag between benefits and wages, the perverse incentives which discourage people from moving from benefits to work and the lack of affordable childcare. (DSS, 1998: 3)

Unemployment as choice places the emphasis on the individual. The unemployed can find a way into work by demonstrating a willingness to accept lower wages, less attractive working conditions, longer journeys to work or by transferring to other occupations, industries and locations. Insufficient flexibility results in unemployment 'by choice'. The [economics] counter-revolution represents the relationship between employer and employee as remarkably shallow. The loss of job security for an individual, the loss of a way of life for a community are depoliticized and described in a way that minimizes their consequences. Unemployment is seen as a voluntary choice or as the result of government policies that provide incentives to workers to remain unemployed. (MacKay, 1998: 50–1)

The British people can win full employment while remaining free . . . But they have to win it, not wait for it. Full employment, like social security, must be won by a democracy; it cannot be forced on a democracy or given to a democracy. It is not a thing to be promised or not promised by a Government, to be given or withheld from Olympian height. It is something that the British democracy should direct its Government to secure, at all costs save the surrender of the essential liberties. Who can doubt that full employment is worth winning, at any cost less than surrender of those liberties? If full employment is not won and kept, no liberties are secure, for to many they will not seem worthwhile. (Beveridge, 1944: 258)

Beveridge's solution to idleness was full employment. New Labour's solution was an active labour market policy aimed at improving the employability of those who are not employed. In other words, unemployment is no longer 'a problem of industry', of the economic and social system as a whole as Beveridge had it in the title of his first book published in 1909, but is rather a matter of a lack of 'employability' among the non-employed. 'Employability' is not a precise concept but we can see a number of elements which surface in the different ways in which it is employed. First, it refers to deficits in the individual unemployed person. These may be deficits in terms of skill and related capacities and the task for policy is consequently understood as being the rectification of these deficits by training and related programmes to make them fit for work which requires competencies. However, the influential US economist Lawrence Mead (1997) – a key figure in what MacKay describes as the economics counter-revolution – argued that the citizen unemployed are inclined, rationally, to refuse 'poor work' and insist on 'good work' which pays more than available benefits. Refusal to engage with poor work means that people do not acquire a work record and are prone to an internalisation of failure which acts as positive feedback in relation to their non-employability. Mead always, correctly, argued that he was making no moral judgements. He simply was reasserting the utilitarian viewpoint which had informed the New Poor Law but he added carrots of training, job placement and subsidies to low wages to the doctrine of less eligibility in its modern form of administrative hassles and withdrawal of benefit. This would make poor work rational and hence rational people would be willing to engage in it.

New Labour politicians, including the 2007–2010 prime minister, Gordon Brown, were inclined to a rhetoric of the need to prepare the entire population for highly skilled and high knowledge content work in the future. Mead had the honesty to recognise that 'active labour market policies' are primarily about making people take poor jobs.

The concept of 'employability' became extended beyond the characteristics of the non-employed themselves. We find assertions[11] (see, for example, Atkinson 2005) that particular neighbourhoods and social groups are characterised by a culture in which workless-ness has become the norm and is reinforced by cultural expectations. However, the current run of 'active labour market' policies which are largely but not exclusively contained within the overarching New Deal framework are for the moment focused in changing the character and/or behaviour of individuals and are therefore directed at making them employable.

New Deal consists of a set of interrelated programmes targeted at 'young people', 25+, 50+, lone parents, disabled people, partners (of benefit claimants) and musicians. Each is a mixture of sticks and carrots. So New Deal for Young People is compulsory for anybody between the ages of eighteen and twenty-four who has been claiming JSA for six months. 25+ is compulsory for anyone aged over twenty-five who has been claiming JSA for eighteen months or for eighteen out of the past twenty-one months. 50+ is a voluntary scheme for those over fifty or their partners who have been claiming a range of benefits for more than six months, although for those on JSA 25+ compulsion comes into force as above. New Deal for Lone Parents and New Deal for Disabled People have been voluntary programmes. New Deal for Musicians is a specialist version of New Deal for Young People and New Deal 25+ which seems to recognise the crucial historical role of living on benefits in the career trajectories of British rock and pop stars.

There have been a number of studies of the actual experience and impact of New Deal programmes. Of particular interest is that by Sunley et al. (2001). These authors conducted a careful review of the local impact of New Deal and concluded that the programmes had been much less effective in inner urban and depressed industrial labour markets. Those locales saw the kind of churning of people through training, unemployment and poor work which is implied by the French term *chomage d'exclusion*. In other words, New Deal worked less well, if at all, in the areas most affected by the UK's post-industrial transition, in the very areas that are Labour's traditional heartlands.

A lot of New Deal was voluntary, although not for the benefit-claiming unemployed JSA. Lone parents were left only to the voluntary exhortation thus far. In relation to claimants of incapacity benefits the New Labour government waged a war of position through constant hassling in relation to medical entitlement. Although Freud, merchant banker that he is, seems ignorant of these developments believing that an individual's own GP can issue a long-term certification of entitlement to the benefit, there is in fact a 'personal capability assessment' that comes into force after twenty-eight weeks on benefit and there is substantial 'disqualification' at this point. As we have seen above, many disqualified people disappear from the labour market. In effect Freud's proposals had two elements. He wanted more hassle and compulsion for incapacity benefit claimants and for single parents whose youngest child has reached the age of twelve. He also wanted to privatise the process of hassling claimants on best New Labour lines by handing its management and execution over to the corporate sector to run on a for-profit basis.

And so we come to the content of *Ready for Work: Full Employment in Our Generation* and *No One Written Off: Reforming Welfare to Reward Responsibility*. In brutal summary, the first set of proposals in *Ready for Work* would involve lone parents with children over the age of seven being moved onto JSA conditions by October 2010, people on incapacity benefit would be subject to a new test designed not to see if they can work, and certainly not if they can work in their usual occupation, but rather to identify some sort of work that they can do. They would then be coerced towards that work. Incapacity benefits, which already represent a retreat on the insurance-based universal long-term sickness benefits which derived ultimately from Beveridge, would be replaced with a much more conditional 'employment and support allowance'. All other elements would have more stick with a little bit more carrot built into them. There would be schemes focused on neighbourhoods, although a particularly inane proposal by housing minister Caroline Flint to make employment a condition of council housing tenancy was been backed away from in the face of a public outcry. It would have made 'actively seeking work' a condition of obtaining in the first instance a new tenancy but ultimately would have been extended to existing tenants. However, these things have a way of reappearing at a later date. The proposals amount to a more punitive active labour market programme.

No One Written Off takes things further. The proposals contained in it would, if implemented, require not only lone parents but the second parent in a couple where the other partner claims JSA or one set of claimants for the replacement for IB – Employment and Support Allowance (ESA) – to actively seek work when the youngest child reached the age of seven and indeed to start preparing themselves for work when that child starts school at the age of five. Claimants of ESA would be divided into two categories – the work-related activity group who would, in practice, not be distinguishable from those on JSA, and the support group who would pass through the very narrow criteria of a tough work capability assessment and whilst not required to move into the job-seeking category would be encouraged to do so. As *No One Written Off* puts it: 'For the vast majority ESA will be a temporary benefit supporting people until they recover from their health problem or are able to adapt to their new circumstances' (Department for Work and Pensions, 2008a: 15). The nature of 'adapt[ing] to their new circumstances' is not specified.

Towards the end of the Labour government the drive towards 'making the idle work' as opposed to making work available for people who want it was reinforced in a variety of ways. Much media attention was devoted to proposals to require drug addicts and alcoholics to address their addiction problems as a condition of continuing receipt of income maintenance benefits. Far more important is the simple statement that:

> we propose when resources allow, to move to a model where Income Support (the current main means tested benefit for

> non-retired households who receive neither JSA nor Incapacity
> Benefit) is abolished and JSA forms to main out of work benefit
> for people who can work. (Department for Work and Pensions,
> 2008a: 57)

Parents were now to become workers and the role of parent as carer for children was to be abolished. To sweeten this pill it was proposed that gradually all absent parent financial contributions to the maintenance of their children will be exempt from confiscation in relation to receipt of benefits. Other groups targeted included people between the ages of sixty and sixty-five who were certainly not going to be allowed to settle down towards retirement. One way or another, 80 per cent of all adults were going to be in work. The long-term unemployed would, in a return to practices of the nineteenth century, be required to engage in work in return for their benefits.

In neither of the Command Papers was there any mention whatsoever of the role of macroeconomic, industrial or regional factors in the genesis of non-employment. So here we are. New Labour abandoned the notion that non-employment has anything much to do with the organisation of the economy as a whole and has set out to eliminate idleness by deploying 'less eligibility' with a smiley face and by doing so through private corporations operating on a for-profit basis – this in *No One Written Off* is outlined in a chapter entitled: 'Empowerment and devolution'. Not only will Beveridge be turning in his grave but even Jeremy Bentham is likely to jump out of his University-College-London box and do a dance of rage at that latter element. The then Conservative opposition of course merely asserted that New Labour had stolen the Tories' own policies and that when they were elected they would do pretty much exactly what New Labour was proposing. Indeed, the banker Freud defected to them, looking – it was said – for a ministerial post in a probable Tory government.

One thing that should be noted is that two of the UK regions (in statistical terms) which will be severely affected by these developments, Wales and Northern Ireland, and another that contains large areas which will be affected, Scotland, have devolved administrations.

However, social security remains a reserved matter for Westminster governments which have been wholly in hock to the financialisation of the UK economy. It is precisely that financialisation, the massive over-reliance on speculative gains in a phony economy of derivatives, etc., as the source of much of tax revenue, which has rendered the UK so vulnerable to the impact of global recession and the reordering of global power towards the Far East and south Asia. Wales will be almost as badly affected by assaults on incapacity benefit recipients as the north-east and north-west of England. The Welsh government has no authority over social security. This is not an argument against a UK-wide social security system. That a social security system has to be constant in a nation state was recognised by the extension of coverage to Northern Ireland by the 1945 Labour government even though Northern Ireland's Unionist MPs were voting against the scheme. What is an issue is that the London/south-east dominance of the UK economy continues to distort public policy to the massive disadvantage of the old ex-industrial regions, including the ex-industrial parts of London and the south-east as well. It does not look to be a happy prospect for the remnants of the old industrial working class.

If I may be permitted a Geordie turn of phrase, hang on there a minute. 'Oh, Law,' we might say, 'when is this all going to happen?' Just as the world economy sees the massive speculative bubble fuelled and indeed created by merchant bankers like Freud go pop with a very big bang. Recession, major growth in unemployment levels, massive house repossessions, collapse of financial services employment, Northern Wreck in spades: Fantasy Island has blown up like Krakatoa. I take it all back. Plainly, Freud is a most trusted agent of the hidden communist international inserted into the core of the financial and political establishment and now moving position to continue to do his good work. Along with his fellow agents, Flint at housing and Purnell as secretary of state for work and pensions, he was tasked with generating a policy regime that would lead to blood in the streets and the revolutionary overthrow of the capitalist order. With particular flair they propose to overcome the major difficulty those seeking to organise the unemployed have always faced – the isolation of individuals. In a replay of the 1930s they will assemble them together in imposed work to make the task of revolutionaries that crucial bit easier. Impose this in a time of recession and trouble there should be and will be. Idleness is a problem of industry – not of people. It is the task of government to address that reality. Beveridge said so, and it remains true to this day.

The general election of 2010

The establishment of a Conservative/Liberal Democrat government is unlikely to lead to changes in the conceptualisation of 'idleness' by the UK's dominant political class. Liberal Democrat policies in this area have been dominated by the Orange group who are essentially a City-based (where many made their fortunes) group of neo-liberals typified by David Laws, whom many Tories would have liked to see as secretary of state for work and pensions. The commitment to reducing the UK public expenditure deficit will necessarily involve an attack on benefits and in particular on incapacity benefit. It is not that in the face of massive job losses in public sector employment, which provides over a fifth of UK jobs and an even higher proportion in the peripheral regions and nations, there will be much scope for forcing the non-employed marginally employable into work. Rather, by removing the insurance-based non-means-tested entitlement which exists at present, many of those on incapacity benefit will be subject to what is to all intents and purposes a revival of the detested 1930s household means test. Any other income of a partner will be taken into account in relation to benefit receipt as will be assets other than an owner-occupied dwelling. As ever the rich will get the gravy and the poor will get the blame.

Notes

1. In this chapter this term is always employed dualistically, i.e. literally and in its meaning in cockney rhyming slang.
2. He would have been perhaps not so much surprised as utterly confounded to find that much of this report would be concerned with the handing over to 'for profit' corporations of the actual management of the non-employed in complete contradiction of the principle of public delivery of core public

services which he maintained throughout his career. He did allow a limited role for the voluntary sector but expelled the commercial motive entirely from social insurance and would not have tolerated it in the service of 'labour exchanges' and their derivatives which he had created as director before the First World War.

3. An early nineteenth-century economist with a considerable influence on the 1834 commission on the Poor Law and one of the authors of the principle of less eligibility.

4. Worklessness rates are by area of residence and many of London's jobs have gone to commuters from the rest of the greater south-east.

5. It would be utterly inappropriate to say 'being idle'.

6. It was for this reason that Beveridge regarded family allowances as only payable for second and subsequent children, and insisted on their universality regardless of income level or employment status.

7. About 30 per cent of housing benefit recipients are not in receipt of a direct social security payment.

8. Apart, of course, from the Irish who seem invisible in his 1940s writing.

9. The very large number of students under twenty-four distort the overall figures.

10. I cannot locate a citation of this very important study in Freud's report, but then he is a merchant banker.

11. These assertions of 'cultures of worklessness' have no ethnographic foundation. On the contrary careful ethnographic work, for example by MacDonald, 1997, demonstrates that they are a myth.

PART 2

FIVE CHALLENGES

6

GENDER

Continuity and change: gender and welfare

Sandra Shaw

Introduction

This chapter will focus on the way that the concept of an ideal family unit and the sexual division of labour within families has underpinned the welfare state. These basic premises have impacted upon the everyday lives of men and women. The power of ideas about the family not only affects women who are wives and mothers, but other women may be defined in relation to idealised versions of what it means to be a woman. Hence, women may be mothers, become mothers, have been mothers or are women who have made the decision not to have children. In addition, the dominant discourse about appropriate roles for men and women also spilled over into the public world, with certain work seen as more appropriate for women due to their 'innate' caring, nurturing skills.

This discussion will start from the point of view that the welfare state was based on a particular ideal of the family, where men were breadwinners and women carers. Married women were seen as economically dependent on men. Key areas that will be included are feminist analyses of the welfare state; relationships of dependency and interdependency between women and the state; women as clients of the state; gender and citizenship. Some of the social changes that have taken place and their implications will be discussed. The current re-formulation of access to welfare, based on the principle of conditionality, and concomitant reconfiguration of the concept of citizenship also has gendered dimensions which will be considered. Other changes include the process of devolution, which means that social policies are mediated at the local level. At the transnational level, decisions made within the European Union also impact on social policies. The global economic context is also important, and the long-term consequences of the current economic recession are still developing.

Feminist analyses of the welfare state

Feminist analyses of welfare are important in their contribution to our understanding of the way that assumptions about gender informed the setting up of the welfare state, and for exploring its consequences for women. A negative critique of the welfare state highlights how women's unpaid labour was taken for granted, and the way this was exploited by the state. Women, as mothers, have also been the target of social interventions within families. However, women have also benefited from the welfare state, as workers and as clients or users of the welfare state.

From a feminist perspective, women's dependence on the state arose out of traditional and stereotypical views of women's role in society. The Beveridge Report noted that women had 'other duties', that is, those of wife and mother, rather than earning, and married women's entitlement to benefits came via their husband's earnings (Bochel et al., 2005). Policies devised for 'the family' were based on the idea of the heterosexual nuclear family, with a male breadwinner and female carer. Traditional ideas about men's and women's roles, and women's assumed economic dependence on men, left women vulnerable in times of need, for example when a marriage ended (Pateman, 2006).

Women provided unpaid care, which meant that the state did not have to provide or pay for care, for example care of older people or of children (Dale and Foster, 1986). The welfare state was important in 'supporting relations of dependency within families; as putting women into caring roles' (Pascal, 1986: 3). The invalid care allowance, which was introduced in 1975, was initially paid only to men and single women giving up work to look after the disabled or older people, while married women were ineligible (Pateman, 2006). This taken-for-granted approach to women's caring was evident in community care policy and the 1990 NHS and Community Care Act.

The caring work that women undertook across the life course would impact on their capacity to earn money in the paid labour market, and to pay sufficient pension contributions to avoid poverty in old age (Graham, 1987).

Today, there is a greater awareness of the role that carers play, and the long-term impact of a reduced income on their economic futures, though this relates to those that care for older people or disabled people. Women and men are engaged in caring activities, for example, older men care for their spouses. However, the amount of and intensity of caring may still be greater for women, and they have the main responsibility for looking after children, which remains unpaid work. Where women have extended periods of time out of the labour market to look after children, or work part time, their future income will be limited. Furthermore, mothers who are in paid employment often face a 'double-shift', as they are still more likely to take on the responsibility for caring for children.

Dependency and interdependency

While the welfare state depended on women's unpaid caring work (Pateman, 2006), it also offered an opportunity for women to be independent of men, when raising children – whether as never-married mothers, or as divorced and separated mothers. Dependence on the state for money could be preferable to dependence on men, as they had greater control over their income (Millar, 1987; Graham, 1987; Shaw, 1992). However, living in a workless household and being on benefits continues to put families and children at greater risk of poverty (Child Poverty Action Group, 2004, 2008).

In addition, the welfare state has provided paid work for large numbers of women in the public sector, which means that many women are dependent on the welfare state for their income (McIntosh, 2006). This work has been concentrated in areas that have been associated with women's 'natural' capacity for caring, for example, in health care, child care and personal social services (ibid.). Thus, a complex weave of interdependency exists where the state depends on women and women depend on the state, whether as claimants, clients or workers.

Other critiques of the welfare state from the New Right in the 1970s and 1980s focused on the way that the welfare state created dependency and apathy. It has been argued that the welfare state created a 'culture of dependency' (Segal and Marsland, 1989), which is transmitted from one generation to the next. These negative conceptions of the welfare state have been associated with female-headed lone-parent households in particular (ibid.; Murray, 1990). In this way, negative representations of women and motherhood have been used to support wider critiques of the welfare state.

Women as clients of the welfare state

If women continue to take on the primary responsibility for looking after children, then they will come into contact more often with welfare professionals. This applies with regard to health, education, housing, social care and other areas such as the youth justice system. Mothers are held accountable for the behaviour of children and young people within families. Two examples that illustrate this are those of education and housing which are discussed briefly below.

Standing (1999) notes that parental involvement in a child's schooling generally means the involvement of mothers, whether there are two parents or one. As parental involvement in a child's education is promoted, this is likely to mean greater involvement by mothers. The rhetoric of 'parental responsibility and involvement hides the gendered nature of the debate: that it is women, mothers who "parent" . . . who bear the brunt of attacks on inadequate parenting' (ibid.: 481). More recently, New Labour's approach in encouraging parents to work also increased the stress on parents who are struggling to be involved while also earning money to support their children.

In the area of housing, anti-social behaviour is a key area of concern, and Hunter and Nixon (2001) found that households headed by women were over-represented in complaints about anti-social behaviour. What was perceived to be an issue was women's lack of control over the behaviour of other individuals in the household – primarily the behaviour of males (ibid.). Approaches that problematise parenting are likely to penalise mothers, and in particular lone mothers. More broadly, with regard to anti-social behaviour, where parents are the target for social interventions aimed at enforcing their responsibilities for the behaviour of children and young people, it is still women, and often lone mothers, who are seen as 'cause for concern'.

While the welfare state has brought many benefits to women, being the focus of professional interest can be dualistic. Families that are struggling can receive support from social welfare professionals, but parents – generally mothers – are then subject to scrutiny, and potentially more coercive approaches to parenting, associated with the responsibilisation agenda of New Labour (Tisdall, 2006; Garrett, 2007).

Gender and citizenship

Part of a feminist analysis of the welfare state includes an analysis of gender and citizenship. If women's main role is seen to be in the private world of the family, then they are excluded from the public world, which is dominated by men. Contemporary debates about citizenship draw on a long history of theories about citizenship, with the ideas of T. H. Marshall in the twentieth century important for modern conceptualisations of citizenship. Marshall outlined three key elements of citizenship: civil, political and social (cited in Dwyer, 2004: 40) These were associated with the eighteenth, nineteenth and twentieth centuries respectively, but this reflects a male-dominated approach to citizenship that ignores the fact that women's experience has been different. For example, women did not receive the right to vote in elections at the same age as men until 1928 (Lister et al., 2007). In conjunction with rights, individuals are also seen as having responsibilities as citizens, though this also has a gendered dimension.

At the time that the welfare state was established, the formal political participation of women was not as developed as that of men, and decision making was dominated by men. This reflected the patriarchal nature of society, within the family and in the public realm. In the twenty-first century while more women participate politically, it is still the case that the UK Parliament is dominated by men, with women making up 19.4 per cent of members of the House of Commons in 2008 (Government Equalities Office, 2008a). However, there are a higher proportion of female UK Members of the European Parliament (26 per cent) and devolution has provided more opportunities for women's political participation with women constituting 46.7 per cent of Welsh Assembly Members and 34.1 per cent of the Scottish Parliament (ibid.). It would seem that a devolved UK can therefore provide a space for women to have greater input into the shaping of social policies at local level.

The social element of citizenship is strongly linked to the development of the welfare state (see Dwyer, 2004). For example, the welfare state brought with it free access to education and healthcare, which was of general benefit to individuals and to society. Economic participation is connected to social rights, with access to welfare increasingly dependent upon the idea of making a contribution by engaging in paid work. This represents a shift from the recognition of citizenship rights to emphasising the responsibilities associated with citizenship (Pateman, 2006). It also negates the value of caring work undertaken within the family, whether this is provided by men or women (Rummery, 2007).

To address this issue, some authors have argued that the concept of citizenship should be less biased, and recognise the importance of caring work. Fraser (2000, cited in Dwyer, 2010) suggests two models: 'universal breadwinner' and 'caregiver parity'. Both of these represent a move towards greater gender equity, with the universal breadwinner model acknowledging the paid work undertaken by women who do not have children or domestic responsibilities. The caregiver model would acknowledge and support informal care, which could be undertaken by women or by men. As well as addressing gender, it is also important to take account of the fact that experiences differ based on other factors such as sexuality, ethnicity, socio-economic status, disability and age. Lister (1997, cited in Dwyer, 2010) argues for a 'gender pluralist' approach that takes account of these differences.

Social changes

Over the past sixty years or so there have been a number of significant social changes within the UK and in other industrialised countries. These present a challenge to the traditional ideal of the nuclear family and to traditional ideas about men and women's roles in society. They also provide a challenge to national governments providing welfare as some of these changes have added to the costs of welfare. Those considered here include an increase in separation and divorce; increase in lone parenthood; decline in the incidence of marriage; increase in cohabitation; increase in the number of births outside marriage, and an increase in women's labour market participation. These areas will be dealt with briefly in this section.

Marriage and divorce

While the Beveridgean welfare state was founded upon an ideal family unit, organised around heterosexual marriage, there has been a decline in marriage. Marriage is still the most common form of partnership, but it was at a peak in 1972 when there were 480,000 marriages (Office for National Statistics, 2008a: 20). In 2005, there were fewer than 284,000 marriages in the United Kingdom. *Social Trends* (38) indicates that there has been a decline in the 'traditional' couple household with dependent children in the UK. In 1971, this would have been 35 per cent of households, while in 2007 it was 21 per cent of private households (ibid.: 16).

Another change in attitude evident in social policies is a greater acceptance of same-sex relationships. Following the Civil Partnership Act 2004, civil partnerships are now a possibility for same-sex couples. In 2006, 16,000 partnerships were formed; the majority of these in England (90 per cent), with 60 per cent of civil partnerships taking place between males (Office for National Statistics, 2008a: 22).

The number of divorces in Great Britain has increased since the 1960s, with a doubling of divorces between 1958 and 1969, subsequent to legislation that widened the criteria for divorce. It is estimated that over a quarter of children living in married couple families will go through the experience of divorce (Department for Education and Skills, 2007: 3). The increase in separation and divorce, and the increase in lone parent families make these a more usual part of the fabric of modern society. However, lone parent families – the majority headed by women – are seen as a problem for the welfare state, due to a heavy dependence on welfare benefits.

The increase in cohabitation is another noticeable change. By 2006, 24 per cent of men and 25 per cent of women were cohabiting, around double the rates for 1986 (Office for National Statistics, 2008a: 19). While cohabitation indicates a decline in the popularity of marriage, it can still be seen to reflect the dominant ideal of two parents bringing up children together. However, changes in family living and different family formation represent a fundamental shift from the early days of the Beveridgean welfare state, based on the traditional male breadwinner family. The number of births outside marriage has also increased, with the figure at 43.7 per cent in 2006 (ibid.). These may be to couples, but also include lone mothers. Of particular political and public concern recently is the number of young, teenage mothers.

Lone parents
The number of lone-parent households trebled between 1971 and 2007, from 4 per cent to 12 per cent (Office for National Statistics, 2008a: 17). Lone parents have been a concern for successive governments over the past sixty years. They are often seen as representing a breakdown in the moral fabric of society (Murray, 1990) and as a drain on the welfare state due to high levels of dependence on welfare benefits. Historically, the majority of lone parents in the UK have been women who, because of their responsibilities as mothers and their difficulty in finding work with an adequate income, are more likely to be living in poverty (Glendinning and Millar, 1987; Finch and Groves, 1983). The 1991 Child Support Act represents an attempt by a Conservative government to reinforce the financial responsibilities of the non-resident parent – most of whom are men – though this also included a strong moral approach (Rowlingson and McKay, 2002). However, there have been a number of problems with the system, and within the benefits system there has been a low 'disregard' for child support. This meant that only a small amount of child support could be disregarded for the purposes of calculating income and the benefits that a lone parent would be entitled to; any amount above this would be deducted from their benefits. The White Paper *Raising Expectations and Increasing Support: Reforming Welfare*

for the Future (Department for Work and Pensions, 2008b) states that parents on any income-related benefits will keep all the maintenance paid for children, which is a positive move. Today, there are around 1.8 million lone parents of working age in Great Britain and fewer than 170,000 of these are fathers (ibid., 2006a: 52). Lone parenthood is still a gendered experience.

In the past, the state's attitude towards lone mothers was ambivalent and policies did not discourage or encourage their employment. Lone parents could remain on benefits until the youngest child reached the age of sixteen. More recently, in the wider context of encouraging all parents to work, reducing the number of benefit claimants and making access to welfare benefits conditional, this approach has changed (Department for Work and Pensions, 2008b).

Under New Labour, there was a shift in attitude, with a programme of initiatives aimed at encouraging lone parents to work, such as New Deal for Lone Parents. The lone parent employment rate increased, with over 300,000 (57.2 per cent) in employment (Department for Work and Pensions, 2007b: 3). However, the numbers claiming income support are still high, and there was a difference between employment rates for lone mothers and for couple mothers. Towards the end of the New Labour era, there were 787,000 lone parents dependent on income support, and there may be additional reasons why lone parents claim benefits, for example, sickness or disability (ibid., 2006a: 52). There is a clear link between living in a workless household (Hirsch, 2006) and the risk of living in poverty, and children in lone-parent families are still at greater risk of living in poverty (Child Poverty Action Group, 2004, 2008) and all the adverse consequences that this can bring. There is evidence that poverty is related to poor health outcomes and disadvantage in later life (Underdown, 2007: Griggs and Walker, 2008). Hence, part of the wider strategy for reducing child poverty is to encourage parents to work, and this has the added advantage of reducing welfare state expenditure. However, where lone parents do move from welfare benefits to paid employment, they are more likely to be in low-paid, part-time work, and can end up on low incomes (Hoggart and Vegeris, 2008). 'Want' or poverty was not ended with the establishment of the welfare state. Interestingly, poverty is still strongly linked to women's experiences, whether as older women or, in this instance, lone parents. The health and well-being of children is affected by poverty in the present and the future, and this again connects with gender, as lone mothers are among the poorest in society.

Conditional access to welfare

The White Paper *Raising Expectations and Increasing Support: Reforming Welfare for the Future* (Department for Work and Pensions, 2008b) set out the Labour government's agenda for extending conditional access to welfare. This has affected all claimants, but has impacted heavily on lone parents – and as noted the majority of these are women. The welfare to work approach and the attachment of conditionality to access to welfare benefits reflects a change in attitude towards the welfare state, with the dominance of an 'adult-worker' model of citizenship and a move away from a more idealised notion of universal and unconditional access to welfare rights.

With a recent target to achieve a figure of 70 per cent of lone parents in employment (Department for Work and Pensions, 2006a), policies are in place to encourage their engagement with the paid labour market, including mandatory work-focused interviews and the New Deal for lone parents. Lone parents are responsible for seeking work, with clear targets set related to the age of the youngest child. For example, from October 2007, those with a youngest child aged seven or over should be actively seeking work. The White Paper (ibid., 2008b) includes lone parents with younger children in the 'progression to work' group. The 'no conditionality' group includes lone parents with young children, but no age is specified. However, the White Paper states that 'we should not wait until the youngest child is seven before engaging with parents' (ibid.: 14), and parents with children aged between three and six years could be included in those 'supported' into employment. This emphasis on getting lone parents into employment does not recognise the importance of parenting (Levitas, 2005: 145).

The principle of conditionality with regard to access to welfare clearly represents a change in ideas about the welfare state, and the welfare subject, with ideas about 'active' citizenship, predicated upon making a contribution to society – primarily by working in the paid labour market. Thus, the caring work taking place within the family remains undervalued. It also reflects a change of emphasis with responsibilities prioritised above rights. While welfare claimants can be coerced into employment, other parents not on welfare benefits, particularly wealthier parents, may have a choice as to whether or not one or both parents work. Thus, socio-economic status is important in determining the choices that parents make.

The European Union and the United Kingdom
Employment
In the current policy context, it is important to remember that the welfare state is no longer only a national enterprise. Membership of the European Union means that social policies are also affected by decisions made at the transnational level. The pressure for parents to work is not only a national one, but part of the policy of the European Union, where an economic focus means that social policies have developed in relation to labour market participation (Hantrais, 2007). This has shaped the development of social policies within the UK, as well as other European countries. Within member-states, the EU aims to increase women's labour market participation and increase the number of childcare places.

In 2000, the Lisbon European Council agreed an aim to achieve an overall working-age employment rate in the EU of 70 per cent, with a female employment rate of more than 60 per cent by 2010 (Office for National Statistics, 2008a). Across the EU27, the target rate for women in employment was reached in 2006, and the UK had the fifth highest employment rate (66 per cent) (ibid.: 51). While these rates show women's employment, rather than mothers, they indicate a greater potential for women to support themselves economically, and to benefit in the short and the long term from benefits that are associated with labour market participation.

With regard to mothers in employment, figures for the second quarter of 2008 in the UK showed that two-thirds of working-age women with dependent children (68 per cent) were in employment, compared to 73 per cent of women without children (Office for National Statistics, 2008b). However, women are more likely than men to work part time, particularly if they have dependent children, which means they are likely to earn less money. A smaller proportion of lone mothers were in employment – 56 per cent compared with 72 per cent of married or cohabiting women with dependent children (ibid.), indicating that it is still more difficult for a lone parent to gain access to the paid labour market and balance this with caring responsibilities.

Childcare

The *National Childcare Strategy* (Department for Education and Skills, 1998) aimed to provide affordable childcare, and separate policy documents have been published for Scotland, Northern Ireland and Wales. *Meeting the Childcare Challenge: A Childcare Strategy for Scotland* (Her Majesty's Stationery Office, 1998) is aimed at raising the quality of childcare for 0–14-year-olds, as well as increasing places and ensuring that childcare is affordable and available for parents. *Children First: The Northern Ireland Childcare Strategy* was published in September 1999 with the aim of providing high-quality childcare for children 0–14 years – and was reviewed in 2005 (Department of Health, Social Services and Public Safety, 2005). *Childcare is for Children* (Welsh Assembly Government, 2005) sets out the Welsh approach. *Choice for Parents, the Best Start for Children: A Ten Year Strategy for Childcare* (HM Treasury et al., 2004) sets out the agenda for childcare in the UK. Responsibility for delivery of the strategy is shared between the UK government and the devolved administrations.

In England all 3- and 4-year-olds are now entitled to a free part-time early education place for 12.5 hours per week (Office for National Statistics, 2008a: 30). From 2010, the aim is to extend this to fifteen hours a week (Government Equalities Office, 2008b). There has been an increase in participation rates for 3- and 4-year-olds in maintained nursery and primary schools (Office for National Statistics, 2008a: 30). Since 1997, the number of registered childcare places has doubled to over 1.29 million, with a registered place now available for one in four children under eight (Government Equalities Office,

2008b). This increase in provision is allied to policies aimed to encourage paid labour market participation by parents, but the figures indicate that there is still a significant shortfall in childcare places.

In reality, childcare is not always available to parents when and as they need it, and the flexibility of working time is not matched by the same flexibility in childcare provision. The costs of childcare will also influence decisions made by two-parent families as to whether one or both parents should be in the paid labour market, and could be prohibitive for lone parents.

Childcare policy within the United Kingdom reflects policy aims within the European Union, with the 'Barcelona Objectives' to increase childcare provision. By 2010, 'at least 90% of children between 3 years old and the mandatory school age and at least 33% of children under 3 years of age' should be provided with childcare (Commission of the European Communities, 2008: 2). Again, this provision is linked with giving parents choice over work, and enabling them to balance work and family life. The lack of affordable childcare has historically been seen as a barrier to lone mothers' labour market employment (see Bradshaw and Millar, 1991). Expanding provision may enable more mothers to remain in or enter the paid labour market. The dual policies of increasing women's labour market participation and increasing childcare provision represents a change in attitude, so that working mothers come to be seen as 'the norm' rather than the exception.

Parental leave schemes are another dimension of this approach to supporting working parents. The member-states of the EU 'provide a statutory right to maternity and parental leave with a job guarantee', meaning that parents can return to work at the end of this (Lister et al., 2007: 121). The longest maternity leave of fifty-two weeks is in the UK (OECD, 2008). However, paternity leave is not as generous, meaning that traditional gender roles are reinforced (Lister et al., 2007) as fathers cannot spend the same amount of time at home with their children, without this impacting on the family income. While men and women may aspire to share parenting duties more equally, the reality is that it is still women who do most of this work. This again limits their capacity to be in full-time employment throughout their working lives. In turn, this impacts on women's ability to build up sufficient pension funds to ensure that they have a reasonable standard of living in old age and means that women are more likely to be dependent on the welfare state for basic income support in later life.

Parents and employment

The emphasis on working applies to all parents, as the economic well-being of families is prioritised above other dimensions of well-being or, alternatively, work is presented as the solution to all problems. This means increased pressure on parents as they seek to achieve work–life balance. If women continue to retain primary responsibility for children, this will impact more heavily on them. However, the structure of working systems and practices means that it is more difficult for men to take time out of work to look after children. Where men's wages remain higher than women's wages, this makes it more difficult for role diversity to develop. Balancing work and family life is important and may prove difficult and not operate equally between men and women (Kilkey, 2006), as gender roles within society and within the family often change more slowly than social policies would suggest.

A range of policies are in place to support working families in the UK, including working families tax credits (Clarke, 2007), the National Childcare Strategy (HM Treasury et al., 2004) and Extended Schools (Department for Education and Skills, 2005). An important fact to note is that if parents are working, then other people are caring for their children. Increasingly, more children will be cared for by others, within the state, voluntary and private care sectors. This suggests a move towards seeing children as a 'collective resource', freeing up parents from childcare, and where women have had the main responsibility for this could mean more economic and social freedom for mothers. An extension of childcare places results in the commodification of childcare (Lister et al., 2007). Where professional childcare is largely provided by other women on a paid basis, this still perpetuates the sexual division of labour embedded in the welfare state. In addition, the absence of universal childcare provision results in what is referred to as a 'care deficit' (ibid.).

Gender and parenting

Every Parent Matters (Department for Education and Skills, 2007) is a policy document that looks at the roles and responsibilities of parents. Mothers are not referred to directly, which might imply that parenting has been de-gendered despite the fact that women's lives are linked to the well-being of their children (Lister, 2006). However, while mothers are absent, fathers are clearly present, with their role in parenting highlighted. It is seen as important to involve fathers in families and in policy initiatives like Sure Start Children's Centres (Department for Education and Skills, 2007: 10). This means changing an 'overtly female focus and culture amongst staff and service users' which may put fathers off (ibid.). It is also suggested in *Every Parent Matters* that services need to be designed for men, and some 'traditional male interests' might provide a 'basis for engaging with fathers' (ibid.: 16). These are interesting points, which perpetuate stereotypical differences between men and women, and the roles of mothers and fathers.

While it is the case that fathers can have a significant impact on children's well-being and early development, removing mothers, or subsuming mothers within the category of 'parent' fails to recognise the fact that they still play a central role in children's lives. In addition, policies that seek to include fathers may be symbolic, rather than embedded in the 'actual division of labour between mothers and fathers' (Lammi-Taskula, 2006: 95). There is also a lack of recognition that not all families have fathers, for example, lesbian mothers or lone mothers choosing to have a child alone; for some families, there can be valid reasons why a father is absent from a child's life, for example, where abuse or domestic violence has occurred.

Conclusion

This reflection on the welfare state more than sixty years on, in the aftermath of the New Labour era, is based on a perspective which draws on feminist analyses of the welfare state, with a focus on assumptions about men and women's roles in society, which informed the welfare state. In the twenty-first century, discussion of these ideas still seems relevant as women continue to take on the main responsibility for caring work within UK society. This is particularly the case when looking at the care of children. However, it is no longer the case that mothers are expected to stay within the home to look after children, as all parents are encouraged to do paid work, though whether this is in the best interests of children is questionable. Concerns about the costs of the welfare state are one of the drivers for this approach, as is the aim to reduce or end child poverty.

The welfare state remains an important source of support for many women as claimants, and also as clients or users of services, whether they are mothers, disabled women or older women. Poverty continues to affect women across the life course, as their caring work affects their capacity to earn as much as men. Large numbers of women are still workers within the welfare state, often in the 'caring' professions and therefore are dependent on the state for their income. The complex relationship between the welfare state and women still exists. Clearly, there are social changes over the longer term that could have an impact on some of the areas discussed. With more women, including mothers in the paid labour market, there is a greater potential for women to be economically independent and for them to avoid extreme poverty in old age. However, increasing the number of women in employment does not necessarily mean that caring responsibilities within the home have changed, and it is still more difficult to envisage an equal division of caring work between men and women. Where there is only one parent, this is still more likely to be a mother who is dependent on welfare benefits.

With regard to the welfare state, New Labour policies reshaped the way that access to welfare is regarded. The element of conditionality that is attached to claiming welfare benefits is evidence of this. Access to welfare ceases to be a universal 'ideal', and relates to the individual's ability to contribute to society by being in paid work. This will have the greatest impact on the most disadvantaged in society, including sick and disabled people, and lone parents. These impacts will be intensified by the post-2010 coalition government's further reforms to welfare provision.

7

RACE

A very 'British' welfare state? 'Race' and racism

Charlotte Williams

Introduction

The establishment of the British welfare state coincided with the beginning of what would be the largest mass migration of citizens from the Commonwealth countries. Britain was to be gradually transformed by a presence it had neither anticipated nor prepared for. Policy makers engaged in the project of rebuilding the post-war nation did not, or chose not to, foresee the implications of what has been aptly called *'The Irresistible Rise of British Multiculturalism'* (Phillips and Phillips, 1998). The British welfare state was not designed with diversity in mind and its institutions reflected a service philosophy that would ultimately prove ineffective in responding to the needs of the changing population. The transformed demographic profile of Britain would ultimately be a major factor in the unsettling of this grand enterprise, a factor that remains a challenge to the notion of state-provided universalist services. More than sixty years on, the relationship between ethnic minority groups and state welfare is still a very troubled one. There is evidence of persistent and longstanding inequality from cradle to grave (Walby et al., 2008; Winckler, 2009). According to the Commission for Racial Equality (CRE), an ethnic minority British baby born on an NHS ward today is still more likely to go on 'to receive poor quality education, be paid less, live in substandard housing, be in poor health and be discriminated against in other ways than his or her white contemporaries' (2007: 1) Ethnicity remains a major determinant of life chances and key to an understanding of poor access to public services for most ethnic minority groups. The principles of universalism and equal access for all, fundamental to the British welfare state, have failed to serve the needs of ethnic minority groups and social policies and professional practices continue to operate in ways that perpetuate poor outcomes for Britain's ethnic minorities. In addition, those from minority backgrounds who have been engaged in the provision of state services have found it equally dispiriting, experiencing exploitation, discrimination and overt racisms (Parmar, 1982; Parekh, 2000).

There is little room for nostalgia. In examining the response of the British welfare apparatus at any level – its policy making, its institutional framework and its practices – it is not difficult to suggest that it is at best ambivalent towards immigrants and racialised minorities, and at worst, racist (Craig, 2007). Anxiety and moral panic about the interplay between immigration and domestic welfare provision has characterised the political discourse on 'race' and welfare from the inception of the welfare state to the present day. Kathleen Paul (1997: 116) argues that the image of 'foreign parasites remained the stereotypical prism through which both Labour and Conservative administrations viewed colonial immigrants' in the post-war period. In contemporary debate David Goodhart (2006b) has pointed to the dilemma raised by the tension between the progressive liberal ideal of multicultural society and populist fears that immigrants are a drain on the resource base of welfare provision and undermine the sense of British solidarity so fundamental to a risk-pooling welfare state. New Labour, Goodhart argues, 'has found itself squeezed between its liberal supporters and its anxious ones' (ibid.: 30). These anxieties and unresolved tensions have meant a failure to develop a coherent strategy for a multicultural welfare. The nation's minorities continue to be seen as 'outsiders' draining welfare resources and as a threat to the solidarities and reciprocities that underpin the collectivism of the welfare state. For this reason the concept of 'welfare' embodied in 'welfare state' has become somewhat conditional for many ethnic minorities. It is possible to argue that this state of affairs is not simply the product of the rather on the hoof policy making of the post-war era in response to an unanticipated set of events, but more accurately, as both Paul (1997) and more recently Craig (2007) have suggested, the product of an identifiable political tendency driven by a fundamentally racist sentiment.

This chapter aims to capture something of the experience of ethnic minorities within the traditional welfare state and to chart the failures of an assimilationist politics that shaped the post-war welfare response. It notes parallel welfare movements emerging from the grass roots that challenge the nature and direction of mainstream welfare delivery. It argues that transformations to the traditional welfare state under the neo-liberal mantle have brought new considerations and new challenges for equality and diversity strategies, not least those thrown up by devolution in Scotland, Wales and Northern Ireland.

'The Windrush moment': the historical legacy

If Aldwyn 'Lord Kitchener' Roberts was right when he coined the words to his calypso on board the *SS Empire Windrush*, 'London is the place to be, London is the place for me', he reflected a shared optimism in the mother country of these new Commonwealth migrants (see Phillips and Phillips, 1998). News clippings of the period tell us one of the calypso player's compatriots mused on arrival of the ship at Tilbury dock: 'If this is Englan', I like it' (*Guardian*, 1948). Severe labour shortages in post-war Britain were answered by the readily available supply of workers from the British colonies, and the 492 Jamaicans who set sail for Britain on the *SS Empire Windrush* have come to symbolise the opening of a distinctive chapter of British immigration history. This was to be the first wave of mass migration in the post-war period and it would be followed by several others. The statistics of this migration wave are interesting in particular when compared with contemporary labour migrations from the Eastern European countries since 2005. Between 1948 and 1953 about 2,000 West Indians migrated to Britain in each year (Paul, 1997: 119) in a steady but small trickle. By 1951, the figure was 30,000 and at its peak in 1961 the Commonwealth migration totalled 400,000. By contrast in just four years since the accession of the A8 countries the figure for migration from the new Europe is currently running at about 650,000 (Commission for Rural Communities, 2007). Whatever the implications for welfare services of both these migrations, it is clear that the threat posed by the former was not simply a numbers issue. The Commonwealth migration was a very visible one, impacting on very specific parts of Britain, namely the metropolitan areas and was accompanied by an overtly racialised political discourse.

The response to the post-war migration is well documented. Kathleen Paul's (1997) detailed account of the response of civil servants and politicians of all persuasions indicates bedrock racism underpinning the decision making. Whilst these migrants were officially British subjects under the terms of the 1948 immigration legislation and whilst Britain desperately needed their labour, the incursion these individuals made into deep-seated notions of British identity evoked intense feelings of hostility. 'By moving from periphery to the centre, these 492 Jamaicans were challenging the imperial system' (Paul, 1997: 121), a long-established system that was marked by biological hierarchies of race which, on the basis of physical features, conferred white-skinned superiority and black-skinned inferiority.

> When we came here we swore we were English because Guyana was British Guiana. We were brought up under the colonial rule ... When you come here you discover it's a different thing. If you're English, you have to be white. (Oral testimony in Webster, 1998: 44)

The affront the 'coloured' migrants posed to constructions of British national identity, to white British domestic space and to notions of community solidarity was manifest at every level of society. The everyday animosities that characterised the reception of this increasingly racialised group of British subjects are described in a range of literature. In a wonderful synthesis of humanities and social science we have the elements of the story. Academically it has been recorded by writers such as Wendy Webster (1998), Bryan, Dadzie and Scafe (1992) and Fiona Williams (1989). Experientially rich personal accounts appear in, for example, Beryl Gilroy's *Black Teacher* (1976), and Phillips and Phillips' *Windrush* (1998), and the narrative has an identifiable place in British literature, two examples being

Sam Selvon's *Lonely Londoners* (1979) and Andrea Levy's *Small Island* (2004).

The upshot is clear: no provision had been made to respond to the welfare needs of these migrants and neither did state policy wish to respond. They lived, in the words of one contemporaneous social commentator (Elspeth Huxley), in the 'hugger mugger' of London rooming houses (Webster, 1998: 45), their convivial lifestyles counterpoised against the landscape of true Englishness, the privet hedge and the net-curtained parlour. They faced hostile landlords and landladies who refused to let rooms to 'blacks'. They were deskilled and ghettoised in the lowest paid jobs in the labour market and their lifestyles were pathologised as problematic by a range of public servants charged with responding to need. On the front line of the services of the welfare state they faced not simply exclusions and neglect but structured racism within it. As one commentator has said they 'were acceptable as cleaners, porters, kitchen staff, even nurses and doctors but never wholeheartedly as patients. They could build council houses but were not expected to live in them' (Jacobs, 1985: 13).

The immediate post-war period is characterised by a distinctly laissez-faire approach both in terms of domestic politics and in terms of immigration. The policy assumption was that those who did arrive on British shores would quickly settle down and fit in. However, this was to change rapidly. The liberal immigration of the 1940s and 1950s gave way to increasingly restrictive measures from the mid-1960s onwards, thinly veiling a biased and racist policy trajectory designed to produce a hierarchy of citizenship (Paul, 1997). At each legislative turn, immigration policy introduced new categories of eligibility linked to differentiated rights of access to welfare. 'Race' in this way became shackled to state policy.

Welfare policy from the 1950s onward focused on a twin strategy of assimilation for those 'at home' and ever increasing strategies of punitive immigration control to those seeking entry. The immigrant within was expected to relinquish aspects of their lifestyle and culture in order to fit into the so-called 'British' way of life. At the same time those seeking to enter and settle or join relatives in Britain found themselves subject to rigorous scrutiny aimed at keeping them out. The exclusionary force of immigration policies resulted in harsh immigration practices such as virginity testing, voucher systems and the 'primary purpose ruling' which provided no recourse to public funds for the dependents of migrants (Parmar, 1982: 245). These degrading practices and rigorously applied penalties produced widespread hardships for migrating families, including the break up of families and their supportive family networks. As new waves of migration occurred, for example from the Vietnamese boat people and the Ugandan Asians in the late 1970s, so national anxieties were hyped up in successive political regimes. Most notable amongst inflammatory political posturing were Enoch Powell's 'Rivers of Blood' speech in the 1960s and Margararet Thatcher's 'swamped by alien cultures' speech of the early 1980s (see Parmar, 1982). Such political proclamations readily fuelled populist fears of immigrant scroungers.

If on arrival the passengers of the *SS Windrush* viewed 'Inglan' with warm anticipation, by the late 1970s Linton Kwesi Johnson, the Jamaican poet, coined his iconic ditty: 'Inglan is a Bitch' to reflect the widespread sentiment of discontent and unrest amongst Britain's black population. Treatment at the hands of the police on Britain's streets provided the focus for unrest in the public sphere but it was matched by shoddy and punitive treatment at the hands of welfare professionals behind the closed doors of welfare institutions and in the private spaces of family and community (Bryan et al., 1992). In that span of time from Lord Kitchener to Kwesi-Johnson, the British welfare state had both flourished and been undermined. The processes of multiculturalism had served to unsettle the bedrock assumptions and approach of the British welfare state and British welfare policy had been exposed as neglectful of the needs of a critical wedge of its population. The principle of universalism that underpinned welfare provision was both unsustainable and unworkable on several fronts, and the retreat from high state intervention in matters of welfare for British citizens had begun. As the neo-liberal agenda of the Thatcher administration began to radically dismantle the social democratic underpinnings of the universalist welfare state in the early 1980s, the 'race' policy instruments shifted from laissez-faire assimilationism to a reluctant multiculturalism. Policy interventions in this era were effectively a mix of weak, add-on and minimalist special measures for ethnic minority groups coupled with overtly punitive controls of black communities largely aimed at quelling discontent (Williams, 1989; Lewis et al., 2000). At the same time the autonomy of more progressive left-wing local authorities who had been initiating change in response to the multicultural realities was reined in.

The legacy of this story is far-reaching in as much as setting a new course for welfare policy that is accommodative of difference and diversity has proved all too illusive (Craig, 2007). The Windrush narrative, as it can be called, illustrates clearly a welfare template in use that failed to fit the changing realities of an increasingly multicultural Britain. The 'one size fits all' universalism based on the assumption of assimilation into a particular notion of Britishness and British ways of life would necessarily lead to unmet needs and discriminations of all types for black and ethnic minorities. In addition the policy trajectory was infused with racist ideologies that permeated both policy discourses and welfare practices. Ideologies that pathologised and inferiorised lifestyles that failed to adhere to the prevailing norms are exposed in the detail of this narrative (Williams, 1989). Social workers, housing officers, health visitors and the range of public servants were positioned as key actors in effecting containment, control and censorship of the 'undesired' aspects of black domestic life. The resultant experiential hardship of these exclusions and discriminations resulted in the politicisation of groups in the welfare arena and there exists a rich account of the mobilisation of welfare organisations and self help at community level and the concomitant mobilisation of dissent (Parmar, 1982; Bryan, Dadzie and Scafe, 1992; Bhavnani and Bhavnani, 1985; Sivanandan, 1990). In the face of adversity minority groups found their own means of survival. The development of alternative welfare provisioning beyond the mainstream – such as the sickle cell movement, the black housing movement, the Saturday school movement (Rex and Tomlinson, 1979; Mirza and Reay, 2000) and the development of faith-based welfare organisations offers a parallel story to the evolution of the British welfare state. What is apparent is that this sector – the realm of non-governmental organisations, voluntary organisations and informal provisioning – offered the potential for a more finely tuned response to the welfare needs of ethnic minorities but was largely ignored in policy directives of state-orchestrated welfare. For decades activities at this level did not form part of any systematic effort to design a robust strategy that could be responsive to ethnic minority need, nor were adequate resources made available to support and sustain efforts at this level.

The plight of ethnic minority workers as producers of welfare in the emerging welfare state was equally problematic (Parmar, 1982; Ahmad, 1993; Parekh, 2000). Setting up the whole welfare apparatus of the National Health Service in particular relied heavily on the exploitation of cheap labour from the Commonwealth. Ethnic minorities were, and are, highly represented amongst those who mop and slop this great institution of the welfare state. Research evidence tells us that the care industry would be unsustainable were it not for the vast army of migrant labour (Rawles, 2008).

The summation of this narrative of 'race' and welfare – the Windrush story – is the establishment of an explicit hierarchy of negatively differentiated citizenship rights linked to the nation-building project of post-war Britain (Lewis et al., 2000; McLaughlin and Boucher, 2007). This was a welfare project built on the idea of a bounded and homogenous national community to which 'outsiders', however defined, would only ever have limited rights of access. But the definition of 'outsiders' was essentially racially proscribed, against exclusive notions of national identity. This has contributed significantly to deep and entrenched inequalities for the majority of the 4.6 million (8.1 per cent) non-white ethnic minorities in contemporary Britain. In all the major areas of welfare – health, housing, education, social services and social security (Craig, 2007; Ratcliffe, 2004; Parekh, 2000) – there is longstanding evidence of the neglect of rights, discrimination and racism. A few sobering examples across the life course illustrate the breadth and extent of the impact of this neglectful welfare state. A child of a Pakistani or Caribbean mother born today is twice as likely to die in the first year of life than the rest of the population (Commission for Racial Equality, 2007). The same Pakistani or Caribbean family will be at disproportionate risk of poverty. Nearly 70 per cent of Pakistani and Bangladeshi children and 41 per cent of Caribbean children live in poverty (compared with 30 per cent of white children). In youth, people from ethnic minority groups are more likely to suffer mental health problems, more likely to be found in the social care system and if in care stay in the system longer than white children. They are more likely to be NEETS (not in education, employment or training) than teenagers of a more generalised category. The educational chances of ethnic minorities, whilst varied by ethnic group, indicate that those of Pakistani and Bangladeshi origin fall below the national average at all key stages. Poverty in childhood casts a long shadow and in adult life general deprivation in housing, poverty and worklessness take their toll on health. About 40 per cent of Caribbean, Pakistani and Bangladeshis have poor health and a person of black or of mixed parentage is three times more likely to experience an admission to a mental health institution (for all figures see Equalities Review, 2007; Commission for Racial Equality, 2007). In older age the pattern persists with poverty linked to limited access to private pensions and factors of deprivation. Whilst such factors of inequality are the product of a broad spectrum of causal factors, it is this dynamic that indicates patterns of need to which state services must respond. Welfare-based measures are crucial to reducing such inequalities (Parekh, 2000; Pilkington, 2003; Walby et al., 2008) and such measures require a positively differentiated approach rather than one based on the principle of universalism.

> Since citizens have differing needs, equal treatment requires full account to be taken of their differences. When equality ignores relevant differences and insists on uniformity of treatment, it leads to injustice and inequality; when differences ignore the demands of equality, they result in discrimination. (Parekh, 2000: ix)

The failures of the traditional welfare state are encapsulated in the Windrush narrative. However, whilst the Windrush story must represent the master narrative describing the legacy of issues at the interface of the British welfare system and Britain's ethnic minority populations, it should be remembered that this is only part of a much more complex picture. It is possible to open up a number of more detailed perspectives in order to understand the dimensions of the patterning of welfare neglect. The state-centric and metropolitan focus of the Windrush analysis masks to a certain extent the parallel story of change produced by the agency of black and ethnic minority individuals and groups on the front line of welfare provision and as actors within state services. Accounts from elsewhere, such as Ken Little's 1947 study of Cardiff in the interwar period, illustrate that the local state was well versed in the crafty devices of containment and control of ethnic minorities long before the arrival of the Windrush migrants and provides evidence of a delicate web of welfare reciprocities and provisioning as practised within the black and ethnic minority communities (Little, 1947). The master narrative also belies a complex differentiation across the nations of the UK. Accounts such as those provided by Fiona Williams (1989), Gail Lewis et al. (2000) and Kathleen Paul (1997) appropriately highlight the centrality of ideologies of nation to the exclusions experienced by ethnic minorities. However, in such analysis the organising concept of nation itself has been limited by the undifferentiated account within a four country UK. Accordingly, for 'British' we have been obliged to read 'English'. The conflation of British with English goes a long way to explain the policy neglect of these issues at the level of the sub-nations, Wales, Scotland and the sub-state Northern Ireland. In particular the ways in which within these national contexts an apparent disassociation from the notion of multicultural welfare provision has held sway (Williams, 1995; Williams and Johnson, 2010). It is also apparent, however, that the post-war events crystallised the debates on British race relations in very particular ways and led to the development of a form of state multiculturalist policy making that has been increasingly subject to criticism from a range of quarters (Alibhai-Brown, 2000).

The shape of multiculturalist policy making that developed from this master discourse on race relations to some extent subsumed analysis and accordingly development in 'elsewhere places' more particularly rural, sub-urban and sub-national regions where concentrations of minorities may be low. Much of the contemporary critique has focused on a construction of multiculturalism as a number of bounded and static ethnic groupings that have become increasingly self-serving and segregated. This particular conceptualisation, however, has barely been applicable beyond the metropolitan areas. In several respects the 'problem of immigration' and 'the problem of ethnic minorities' had become associated with the city, frustrating efforts to develop provisioning for minorities beyond the metropolis (Henderson and Kaur, 1999; Williams, 2007). This has had a particular impact on forging a race equality agenda at the level of the devolved nations (Williams and De Lima, 2006).

In 2000, the publication of the Parekh Report signalled 'a turning point', highlighting a number of new directions that would forge, as a minimum, a changing debate on 'race' and welfare (2000: 2). Perhaps the ill-conceived concept it proposed of Britain as 'a community of communities' failed to convince but the report was nonetheless important in its acknowledgement of a territorially diverse Britain, as well as powerfully advancing a challenge to conceptions of Britishness that did not accommodate the multi-ethnic, multi-racial and multi-faith nature of society. It signalled the need to move from 'multicultural drift' to a purposeful process of change' (ibid.: 11). It made a number of recommendations on social welfare directed to the administrations at Cardiff, Holyrood and Westminster at the same time acknowledging the limitations of relying solely on state-generated reform.

Ideology and intervention

Several writers have posited reasons for the failure of the welfare state in addressing the needs of ethnic minorities as lying in a fundamentally racist ideology underpinning policy thinking. Fiona Williams (1989), for example, has detailed particular ideologies in what she identifies as three distinct epochs of welfare history. She traces exclusionary policies of the nineteenth and early twentieth century such as the Alien's Order of 1905 which reflected particular notions of national unity and British cultural supremacy and was aimed at limiting the migration and settlement of people. She notes the influence of Eugenicist thinking in the interwar years which constructed certain groups as deficient and pathological, including racialised groups and she documents the fears about the loss of empire and preoccupation with the degeneration of the 'British race' as shaping policy and practice in the post-war period (ibid.). Others have suggested the issue of racism in welfare cannot be fully addressed without attention to deeply embedded and widespread culture of racism in British society (Craig, 2007). Craig rallies against successive governments' failure to challenge racism, pointing to ineffectual legal enforcement of anti-discriminatory law and failure to rein in inflammatory discourses perpetrated by a racist media that fuel populist fears and moral panics on issues such as asylum, immigration and terrorism. He suggests that repressive immigration policy has been coupled with a welfare policy aimed at containment of the domestic race relations problem rather than real concern for enhancing the well-being of minorities and concludes 'there are relatively few convincing signs of embedded and sustainable action against racism in welfare provision' (ibid.: 606).

An understanding of this realm of ideas and beliefs in shaping welfare policy is critical to an understanding of the limitations of the traditional welfare state. However, I would suggest two important caveats. First, however compelling this account of the role of ideology is, and there is consistent evidence to suggest that the powerful instrument of state policy may orchestrate or be orchestrated by such widespread belief systems, it is also true to say that ideologies are rarely evenly influential. They are subject to counter-movements and counter-ideologies that emerge at specific moments or are subject to the exigencies of place and context. Pilkington (2003) speaks of the two-pronged strategy of government policy which includes both racism and liberalism sometimes working in tandem, sometimes in contradiction. Whilst immigration policies have reflected racist ideologies, domestic anti-discrimination legislation he suggests, in some eras, are based on much more liberal and inclusive assumptions (ibid.). What, for example, did the role of the abolitionists play in countering racist ideologies in the eighteenth and nineteenth centuries and ultimately forging new citizenship rights for non-white minorities in Britain? Why did race relations legislation emerge at all in the British context? How can we understand the welfare system that emerged in areas such as Butetown in Cardiff in the interwar period which crossed ethnic and racial lines locally and operated well beyond the boundary of nation? What role did counter-national belief systems such as prevailing ideas about Welsh national identity or Scottish national identity play in their interpretations of racist ideologies and the treatment of minorities? This type of analysis may lead to more intricate and detailed ways of understanding the interplay of factors at local and sub-national levels as well as actions or inactions that emanate from the central state.

The second observation relates to the role of pragmatism and ineptitude and unanticipated consequences in policy making. With any new or emergent social phenomenon, civil servants, policy makers and practitioners, as well as welfare recipients, begin by working things out as they go along. If the post-war welfare state set off on a misguided, neglectful or actively discriminatory course in relation to ethnic minority well-being, it is also fair to say that even in its own terms it would inevitably have been exposed as an unwieldy and unsustainable instrument in responding to diverse and particularist needs in a changing society. It was in one respect laudable and indeed radical in its ambitions to provide universalist services but how do you at the same time as ensuring minimum standards offer responses tailored to individual or group differences? Perhaps some of the greatest sins of the traditional welfare state therefore lie not in its original architecture or ambitions but in its failure to learn lessons from the past in resetting the compass for future travel; in essence the lack of any coherent, systematic or developmental approach to responding to the emergent needs of a changing society. The unhappy conclusion is that this political ineptitude reflected the perennial assumption that ethnic minorities would ultimately 'go home' or just plain 'fit in'.

The new context of welfare delivery

A plethora of new challenges and questions emerge in the contemporary era. What can be said of the direction of travel in twenty-first-century Britain and hopes of a more responsive welfare system in terms of diversity? The welfare state was designed in an era of closed borders and particular ideologies about national solidarity both of which have been undermined by far-reaching social, economic and demographic changes. Globalisation, transnationalism, changing identities and changing social attitudes have evoked new realities and demanded a redesigned and dynamic welfare framework built on more sophisticated and differentiated responses to diversity of need. Economic constraints demand the involvement of welfare sectors beyond state provision. We can no longer afford the assumption of state-provided welfare and this has led to a reconfiguration of the relationship between the state, the individual and welfare. In the wake of such widespread change new and old anxieties prevail at the nexus of 'race' and welfare – concerns about rights of citizenship and establishing entitlements amongst increasingly diverse groups, concerns about the undermining of solidarities necessary to sustain investment in a collective welfare state, concerns about risk and national security.

In several respects the New Labour regime offers a number of continuities with the neo-liberal project of Thatcher. The overriding strategy of neo-liberal politics has been the policing of national borders, both real and imagined, and careful 'management' of diversity. However, there are some identifiable shifts in relation to the treatment of 'race' in New Labour welfare politics. A number of key trends can be identified that mark out the parameters of the contemporary approach to race and welfare:

- the emphasis on an inclusive 'British' national ideology embracing more civic as opposed to ethnic conceptions of 'Britishness' as the overarching glue which will forge solidarity in an increasingly diverse society;
- increased managerialism in the delivery of public services which includes clear duties imposed on public bodies and performance measures for achieving race equality;
- a clear departure from the old language of race relations towards the more neutral terminology of equality, cohesion and inclusion in policy speak and documentation;
- the shift to governance rather than government, opening up opportunities for greater involvement in decision making and more visible close-to-home solidarities. This includes the devolution project;

- the increased reliance on social capital and co-option of the organs of civil society to advance fine-tuned and responsive welfare delivery and to develop community cohesion;
- the forging of the links between rights and responsibilities coupled with the mobilisation of active citizenship;
- the management of key risks, such as unfettered immigration, asylum and ethnic terrorism.

This refreshed approach perhaps indicates the deep tensions and contradictions at the heart of a policy trajectory that is simultaneously trying to display liberal intent whilst at the same time trying to garner widespread popular appeal within a culture deeply caught up with racist anxieties. A few examples illustrate these contradictory trends.

New Labour political rhetoric deployed the institutions of welfare, and in particular the NHS, to represent the beacon of the 'shared values' of Britishness. 'Shared values' replace ethnic ties as the essential glue of solidarity.

> Britishness is defined not on ethnic and exclusive grounds – but through our shared values, our history of tolerance, of openness and internationalism, our commitment to democracy and liberty, to civic duty and the public space. These values, embodied in our great institutions – such as the NHS, the BBC, the Open University – tell a national story that is open to all British Citizens. (Blunkett, 2005: 4)

Citizenship tests and citizenship ceremonies have been established to act as symbols of a new and inclusive Britishness and politicians continue to moot flag waving Britishness public holidays. At the same time traditional formulations of the concept of multiculturalism have been undermined in political speeches and by key academics (Alibhai-Brown, 2000) in order to reduce the risks posed by ethnic exclusivity and segregation, particularly in the wake of the riots in northern towns in 2001. Thus, 'community' when applied to ethnic minority association has now become a point of suspicion and anxiety and there has been a distinctive shift away from the language of race relations in policy speak (Worley, 2005). Accordingly, many might argue that this new styled authoritarian assimilationism is but a variant on its post-war predecessor.

New Labour has taken significant steps to strengthen the equalities framework and make public services more effective. Following the Stephen Lawrence Inquiry (McPherson, 1998), the twenty-first century opened with the Labour government setting a new course in relation to public services with the far-reaching requirements under the Race Relations (Amendment) Act 2000 and, more recently, it has undertaken a comprehensive Equalities Review (2007) to target persistent inequalities more effectively. The government is building a framework under the Equality Act (2006) for enforcement of equality legislation and for building a pro-active agenda on tackling discrimination, moving away from race-specific legislation to a generic approach to equalities (see Williams and Johnson, 2010). Such steps could be interpreted as a shift away from a forthright positioning on race equality and as the language of race is diluted in policy discourse so might be the political constituency and clout of the 'race' lobby. It could also be argued that the increased focus on technical and bureaucratic approaches to race incorporates and thus effectively depoliticises the issues and that the ever growing co-option of the black voluntary sector bodies into the machinery of government has a similarly stultifying effect. Despite these forthright steps to galvanise the efforts of public bodies the overall evaluation shows that organisations are slow to change. As the Commission for Racial Equality closed its doors in 2007, opportunity to review the efficacy of such approaches over the thirty years of its existence indicated public authorities across the board systematically failing to meet statutory requirements (Commission for Racial Equality, 2006).

Many of the contemporary shifts in welfare policy are aimed at increasing agency, voice, active participation and engagement of ethnic minorities in the machinery of welfare delivery. The government has signalled its intention to promote the role of the 'third sector' in delivering public services launching its *Community Empowerment* White Paper in 2008. This may serve to strengthen the position of what has been a largely under-funded and barely sustainable black voluntary sector in meeting specific need and generating alternatives to mainstream methodologies (McCleod et al., 2001). There is room for scepticism. Funding streams to voluntary sector organisations have discernibly shifted towards the privileging of activities related to the government's cohesion agenda under New Labour and since 2010, over the rights and race equality agendas that were more prominently profiled in the 1980s and 1990s (Worley, 2005). This may well be seen as a method of increasing the arm of state surveillance and social control, in particular of newly perceived risks associated with Muslim communities. Research suggests this sector is little able to resist the force of wholesale co-option by the state and experiences the curtailment of its autonomy in working to government agendas (Williams, 2006). That said, the focus on voice and choice are potentially more promising ways forward for enhancing responsiveness to minority well-being. To this end the championing of devolution is significant to the contemporary understanding of multicultural welfare delivery.

From welfare state to welfare societies?

> Back then, Britain still thought of itself as a monocultural, even a mono-national society constructed on the twin anvils of warfare and welfare: especially with the experience of total war a mere generation previously and the homogenising function of the Welfare State. Back then, the British thought of themselves as a single, largely white society born and brought up in these islands. (McCrone, in Commission for Racial Equality, 2006: 63)

As has been illustrated in this chapter, much of the discourse on race and welfare has been conducted with an exclusive construction of the 'British' nation and a construction of a 'British' welfare state that belies considerable variation across the UK. There have always been differences across the UK in terms of localised policy directives, cultures and 'ways of life' that impinge on the social relations of welfare. Contemporary developments have seen challenges not only to notions of 'British' and 'Britishness' but to the hegemony of ideas about the 'welfare' in the architecture of the welfare state. In the context of devolution the framework for delivering welfare is being shaped by increasingly divergent policies and philosophies of approach across a four country UK (Mooney and Williams, 2007). Attempts to promote more civic and inclusive interpretations of nation and to maximise engagement and inclusive policy making are being tested in the newly devolved nations with varying results (Williams and De Lima, 2007). The devolved nations have in place robust equality duties in addition to the requirements of the Race Relations (Amendment) Act and are forging new agendas on issues of redistribution, inclusion, cohesion and race equality. They are producing alternatives to mainstream thinking on welfare and involving new policy actors in welfare delivery. In Scotland, for example, more liberal approaches to immigration are signalled by schemes such as the Fresh Talent Initiative which encourages immigration to Scotland for those with skills and expertise. In Wales, experiments in 'progressive universalism', a citizen-focused rather than a service-oriented approach to welfare (Drakeford, 2007a) reflecting high citizen involvement and bolstered collaboration and partnership working between public bodies and the voluntary sector are being rolled out, and have the potential for more effective and responsive service delivery to minority groups.

These are new beginnings and require considerable political effort and no small amount of skill and capacity building to become workable and sustainable in terms of inclusivity. Efforts to secure more effective public engagement through consultation with, and the participation of, minority groups in decision making and to incorporate the political lobby of these constituencies is being embraced in welfare frameworks across the UK and beyond. Whilst devolution was never intended to produce differentiated citizenship it will inevitably produce different experiences in the social relations of welfare and necessarily different outcomes: in this sense it represents the antipathy of the ambitions of the traditional welfare state model. Whilst such frameworks must reject traditional one-size-fits-all universalism, a new universalism based on ensuring standards, laying down principles of care and care values, mediating equitable outcomes and ensuring the capacity for responsible governance will be increasingly important.

There is no one welfare state, but more accurately states of welfare in newly evolving welfare societies. More inclusive societies are critical to the enhancement of ethnic minority well-being and are clearly not the preserve of state policies alone. State strategies, legislation and policy are inevitably only part of the story in which wider collective commitment is essential to the creation of truly welfare societies.

Conclusions

The British welfare state was built on a particular conception of Britishness that ring-fenced eligibility to services around a narrowly specified national collective. This would inevitably result in exclusions and discriminatory treatment. In addition it proved to be an unwieldy instrument in responding to the fine-tuned and ever changing needs of a diverse society. The evidenced limitations of centralised collective state provision in meeting minority needs means looking to the refreshed welfare frameworks that are emerging across the UK and the potentials they hold for equality, trust and engagement in securing welfare outcomes. Self-determination and empowerment at neighbourhood/local level, bolstered by capacity-building strategies offer a way forward and policy learning and policy exchange are important to the development of these welfare frameworks. More effort needs to be made by both policy makers and academic researchers to understand and capture multicultural welfare practices beyond the state – at the level of user-led services, within the intricate web of reciprocities and exchange at local, national and transnational level and to secure the sustainability of good practices in this arena. More needs to be understood about the ways in which various minority groups access and utilise services in different contexts and mobilise to fill gaps in provision. It should be remembered, however, that in the new welfare mix and in the new networks of governance ethnic minority groups remain weak partners and that racism as an ideology remains deeply embedded in social relations at the level of everyday exchanges and within powerful institutions like the media, politics as well as welfare institutions.

8

DISABILITY

What rights for disabled people in a welfare state? Need-fulfilment versus identity-assertion and the 'problem of dependency'

Steven R. Smith

Introduction

Tracing aspects of British welfare state history since its post-war inception, this chapter will explore ways in which conceptions of rights have changed during this period in relation to disabled people – reflecting, in turn, different views of the welfare state. On the one hand, we find the welfare state presented as a benign provider of resources for those who are defined as 'vulnerable' and 'dependent', with a right to have their needs met. Yet, we also encounter a more ambivalent attitude towards state provision in which, as well as supporting disabled people's rights to 'independent living' via paid work and other forms of 'active citizenship', it is seen as a potential threat to the achievement of these goals.

As we will see, the former view can be said to reflect the 'medical model' of disability. There is an assumption that 'rights to welfare' can be understood monolithically, as a single unproblematised entitlement to state resources, and as an alternative to charity for those defined as 'vulnerable' and 'dependent'. The latter view, meanwhile, reflects a different conception of rights, with its origins in the Disability Rights Movement (DRM). This conception shifts the political discourse from the monolithic conception to a more pluralistic alternative, based on the 'social model' of disability. It invokes not only a resource-based understanding of rights to need-fulfilment, but another very different conception of rights relating to 'identity-assertion' and notions of 'personal empowerment' – conceiving a disabled person as an autonomous and independent chooser, who is able to take control of his or her life as an active and equal participator within society. An acknowledgement of this latter type of identity-right underpins much of the ambivalence towards the welfare state outlined above. For the DRM, 'the state' is often seen as a powerful force undermining rights to individual choice, autonomy and 'independent living'. However, this ambivalence raises questions as to the extent to which rights to having disabled people's needs met may readily co-exist with disabled people's rights to identity-assertion and the achievement of independent living. As I will argue, problems emerge in the promotion of both kinds of right when this involves the promulgation as an ideal of what I have called the myth of independent living. So, even if financial independence is secured for disabled people through paid work (often seen as a hallmark of independent living), this so-called independence is reliant on highly mutually supportive and interdependent relations being maintained in a complex post-industrial society.

My argument in this chapter is that both notions of rights (to identity-assertion/independent living and to need-fulfilment) are problematic, and should be rejected. Instead, a more reciprocal understanding of rights is recommended, establishing that all persons, disabled or not, have something valuable to contribute to wider society. That we all have a right to this contribution being facilitated through various state-administered systems and services not only underpins and promotes the value of interdependence, but also establishes a notion of universal citizenship which is active and empowering for disabled and non-disabled people alike.

Rights, disability and the contrast between medical and social models

What is a right? First, a right allows a person or group to claim something as a matter of entitlement. This claim can be made directly by the person or group themselves, or indirectly through a third party; either way, it entails that obligations are placed on others who are duty-bound to protect these rights (Heywood, 2004: 185–97). Some of these duties are negative, requiring another individual or group to refrain from actions – as in the case of not preventing a person from doing or saying something, thus allowing the right to free movement and free speech. Others are positive, requiring an individual or group to commit an action, such as providing state services to protect a right to have needs met (ibid.: 197; Goodin, 1985: 110–11).

Secondly, the fulfilment of a right is not a matter of charity, where the individual or group is gratefully beholden to the willing generosity of a benefactor. Rather, the entitlement status of a right means that the right-holder makes a claim on others independently of those others' attitudes or predispositions – that is, whether or not they are willing or generous towards the individual or group concerned (Heywood, 2004: 196–7; Blakemore, 2003: 34–5). Given this claim, rights are often asserted before they are fulfilled in institutional practices, and as such provide a robust platform for political demands based on principles of justice. Thus, an individual or group can claim that if a particular right remains unfulfilled in any society, then that society is not conforming to acceptable standards of treatment for its citizens (Heywood, 2004: 204–13). From this position others may argue that the basic structure of society is not being properly maintained, as just institutional rules between citizens are undermined because rights are not being respected (Rawls, 2001: 10–11).

But how do rights relate to welfare state provision generally and the promotion of paid work and notions of citizenship specifically? It is perhaps accepted wisdom that post-1945 'welfare state Britain' was created on the principle that citizens should no longer depend on charity or family support for fulfilling their needs, but that the state has a duty to meet these needs as a matter of entitlement (Goodin, 1988: 11–12). Whether concerning housing, income support, social services or health, post-war citizens were seen as possessing 'social rights' to need-fulfilment, especially perhaps when these needs cannot be met by independent means and/or paid work (Blakemore, 2003: 34–5). Yet, this principle of entitlement has been viewed ambivalently by the DRM. In large part this is due to the way the medical and social models of disability are juxtaposed in the analysis offered by the DRM – with the former model associated with institutional practices that, while fulfilling the above social rights, are also deemed oppressive.

As understandings of disability, the medical and social models represent two extremes, with others occupying the middle ground (Shakespeare, 2006). Given this polarity, they offer helpful bearings in exploring the significance of the different types of right so far outlined, and how they might be variously promoted. So, the medical model is seen by the DRM as an inaccurate description of disability, forming the basis of oppressive and exploitative relationships between the non-disabled and disabled – including those between non-disabled professionals employed by the welfare state and disabled 'service-users' (Swain, French and Cameron, 2003; Oliver and Barnes, 1998; also see my arguments in Smith, 2001a, 2001b, 2005).

A key proposition is that in focusing on individual medical conditions as the causes of disability, the medical model incorrectly defines disability as a fixed condition related to the severity of a medical impairment. It also incorrectly assumes that it is this medical condition – often defined as 'handicap' – which inevitably causes a relation of 'dependency' between disabled and non-disabled people. So, according to Barnes, the medical model links the term 'handicapped' with 'individually-based functional limitations', which in turn falsely implies that 'the impairment is permanent and that [the handicapped] will almost certainly remain dependent throughout their lives' (Barnes, 1991: 2).

Against this, the 'social model' for the DRM offers an understanding of disability in which the causes of disability are located in the social domain. Here, rather than being reduced to a fixed medical state relating to the severity of a particular medical impairment, the experience of disability or handicap stems from how society is organised and structured in relation to particular medical conditions. For example, according to Liachowitz, 'Disability exemplifies a continuous relationship between physically impaired individuals and their social environments, so that they are disabled at some times and under some conditions, but are able to function as ordinary citizens at other times and other conditions' (1988: 2). Thus, the focus for the DRM is on active citizenship, inclusion and the problems of accessibility and discriminatory barriers to participation (Swain, French and Cameron, 2003; Oliver, 1996: 63–77). Rather than recommending policies based on medical treatment or rehabilitation – aimed at 'adjusting' the individual condition to conform to standards of non-disabled normality – attention is directed toward changing the social environment. The social environment is perceived as unfairly discriminatory. It requires restructuring – both physically and in relation to dominant beliefs and attitudes – in order to enable individuals with certain medical conditions to function and be perceived as actively participating 'ordinary citizens'. Here, the DRM will deploy an important distinction between 'impairment' on the one hand and 'disability' on the other. Impairment is a physical or mental characteristic associated with a particular medical condition. Impairment may or may not lead to a 'disability': the latter condition arising from the various social restrictions imposed upon that impairment.

For the DRM, as well as being an inadequate account of what disability is, the medical model also promotes negative images of disabled people, portrayed as 'tragic victims', 'suffering' from 'deficiencies', etc., as distinct and 'other' from 'the normal' and able-bodied population. Disabled people, as a result of their impairment, are regarded as unable to conform to standards of 'normality' which in turn are associated with what is defined as 'ideal' and 'best' (Swain, French and Cameron, 2003; Shakespeare, 2006). This legitimates policy strategies in which the non-disabled professional, as guardian of this normalisation process, is assumed to be the 'expert' in relation both to the condition of the disabled individual and the gauging of what is in their interests. In short, policies based on the medical model of disability, according to the DRM, render disabled people as passive and powerless targets of state intervention in the face of non-disabled expertise and in the process reduces the person and their experience to the 'abnormal' and 'deficient' medical condition.

Indeed, it has been argued that this type of 'reductionism' was particularly prevalent in the two or three decades after the Second World War. In this period, welfare legislation in Britain and throughout the industrialised world explicitly invoked a medical approach to disability, defining individuals as medically 'deficient', 'sub-normal' and other similar terminology (see my arguments in Smith 2001a, 2001b, 2005). As a result, policies of segregation and 'medical treatment' were legitimated under which disabled people, being individually 'deficient', were automatically categorised as unable to function 'normally' and therefore as requiring separated and 'special' care. Subsequently, these very explicit forms of the medical model have been rejected by later policy makers and have been replaced by more social and integrated models of disability. Nevertheless, for those within the DRM, there are still strong echoes of the medical model found in the way in which disabled people are treated by non-disabled professionals. For example, according to Morris:

> Academics and professionals play a key role in influencing the meanings which non-disabled people give to disability and in determining the policies and services which affect our lives. The models of disability that most commonly inform this role are the 'personal tragedy' or medical models of disability. Those who subscribe . . . to these models view disabled people as individuals whose experience is determined by their medical or physical condition. Someone who is blind is thus viewed as experiencing a 'personal tragedy' and it is the role of the professional to mitigate the difficulties caused by not being able to see . . . The medical and 'personal tragedy' models of disability and the attitudes which go with them are a very important part of the powerlessness experienced by disabled people in their relationship with those professions whose role is so important to the quality and nature of our daily lives. (1991: 180)

Therefore, so the argument goes, policies are still recommended that in general either involve non-disabled experts tackling the individualised 'deficient/tragic' condition through medical intervention and/or providing rehabilitation programmes for individual adjustment (physical and/or psychological) to that condition. The point for the DRM is that despite the good intentions behind them – and even in cases involving considerable redistribution of resources from non-disabled to disabled people – these policies have usually served to reinforce the exclusion of, and discrimination against, disabled people. Consequently, intervention strategies based around the meeting of 'needs' (defined by the non-disabled experts), whilst justified on the grounds of providing care and enhancing welfare as a matter of right and entitlement, function as mechanisms of social control and serve to undermine the autonomy and decision-making power of disabled people. For example, according to Oliver, community care policy implemented since the 1980s in Britain has made:

> [N]eeds led assessment the linchpin of service delivery . . . however, above all else assessment of need is an exercise of power, as even the language we use to talk about the exercise shows . . . The professional assesses the need of the client or 'user', as they have now come to be called . . . [Yet] various studies show that professionals have distorted or defined their needs . . . The new reforms do not change this balance of power at all. (1996: 70)

So, what are identity-assertion rights and how do they reflect the social model outlined above?

First, the promotion of identity-assertion rights involves the creation, as a matter of entitlement, of some kind of space in which a person might express who they are (their personality, character, opinions and so on) and what they want (their desires, aspirations and goals) (Swain, French and Cameron, 2003). This space can come in a number of forms, but all are based on the assumption that a person has a voice or a perspective on their life which demands respect, and towards which social relations, policies and practices ought to be sensitive. Secondly, following from this assumption, other identity-assertion rights are often promoted as a correlate, such as the right to independent living where individual choice or autonomy allows a person to plan for their own life, rather than having their life planned for them, which in turn 'empowers' that person as they are viewed as an 'active citizen' who is able to take control of their life.

How, then, are these identity-assertion rights reflected in the demands of the DRM and how does it see these rights relating to other rights to the state meeting needs explored previously?

The DRM often promotes individual rights to choice-making as a separate moral category to meeting individual needs. For example, many within the DRM have asserted that meeting 'special needs' in policy and practice often overrides disabled people's capacity for making choices (Oliver and Barnes, 1998; Oliver, 1996; Morris, 1991; also see my arguments in Smith, 2005). Substantial conceptions of need are defined by non-disabled professionals who exert power over disabled people by imposing state-driven categories of need on their clients or service-users, which then undermines a disabled person's ability to control or have power over their own life. Again, according to Oliver:

> Professionalised service provision within a needs-based system of welfare has added to existing forms of discrimination ... based upon invasions of privacy as well as creating a language of paternalism which can only enhance discriminatory practices ... institutional discrimination is embedded in the work of welfare institutions when they deny disabled people the right to live autonomously. (1996: 75–7)

In the terms developed in this chapter, the link Oliver makes between anti-paternalism and a disabled person's right to live autonomously is in effect promoting rights to identity-assertion. However, the resulting commitment to autonomy, free choice and personal empowerment can be interpreted in various ways, particularly in respect to redistributive state policies. For example, one interpretation might be to consistently advocate meeting needs via state provision as a right, if (and only if) representatives of the state can show that they first respect rights to individual autonomy and self-determination. Here, these rights are effectively being placed in a priority ordering, where the right to define one's own needs is promoted first (reflecting identity-assertion rights) before these needs are then met by the state (reflecting need-fulfilment rights). Consequently, there is no conflict between these rights provided that they are ordered correctly. Indeed, this move is allowed in Oliver's position above, despite his initial stance against state meeting of needs: 'It is nonetheless right to appropriate welfare services to meet their own self-defined needs that disabled people are demanding, not to have their needs defined and met by others' (1996: 7). Moreover, it is through this latter conception of rights that 'active' (as opposed to 'passive') conceptions of citizenship are also promoted. For Oliver, passive conceptions of citizenship are rooted in post-war justifications of welfare state provision, which view disabled people as dependent recipients of pre-defined welfare services. Whereas active conceptions of citizenship assume that disabled people can participate in society on the same bases as non-disabled people, and that this provides a proper rationale for state intervention (ibid.: 63–77).

However, another interpretation of identity-assertion rights is much more sceptical about the positive role of state intervention, and about the easy co-existence between identity-assertion rights and rights to have one's needs met by the state. In short, this latter interpretation assumes that the ideal of independent living involves being independent of any state support, and other forms of professional intervention, all seen as potential threats to individual choice, autonomy and personal empowerment. For example, although notions of empowerment and individual autonomy are promoted in social work codes of ethics, and other forms of state welfare practice, Oliver and Barnes have severely critiqued the pretensions of social and voluntary workers who aim to empower disabled people:

> There are numerous texts advising on how to empower . . . and conferences where the powerful talk endlessly about how to empower the disempowered. The contradiction in all this is that empowerment is only something that people can do for themselves because, ultimately, deciding to empower someone else, whether they want it or not, is the most disempowering thing that can be done to them. (1998: 10)

In other words, empowerment is not about providing a given set of 'empowerment rules' to be accessed by anyone (including non-disabled professionals and other welfare state representatives) and implemented accordingly. Rather, it is about a person creating for herself a perspective on personal empowerment, to be used against those who seek to impose sets of rules, including (and perhaps especially) those rules that purport to empower, and those rules that are devised by the state and/or professional practices (also see my arguments in Smith, 2005). It is in this latter context that rights to identity-assertion and rights to need-fulfilment could be in conflict, as a person could create for themself a perspective on personal empowerment that excludes any acceptance of state support in the name of independent living. The question that now arises is what is meant by independent living, and how does this relate to principles underpinning the welfare state which have often promoted paid work as a hallmark of active citizenship and independent living?

Conditional payments and the rights to need-fulfilment of the 'active citizen'

Importantly, since the inception of the British welfare state, many rights to need-fulfilment have not been met unconditionally. Thus, while these rights are met as a matter of state obligation and duty, they also place duties on right-holders to behave in certain ways, as well as duties on the state to make available certain types of welfare provision (also see Galston, 2005: 110–26; White, 2005: 82–109, and my arguments in Smith, 1998: 121–9, 158–72). So social security benefits, guaranteeing regular cash payments from the state for unemployed people, have long been tied to behavioural conditions for those defined as 'capable of work'. Although these conditions have been increasingly applied since the 1980s by New Right and New Labour governments in their respective developments of tests to ensure that claimants are 'actively seeking work', these were conditions enshrined in Beveridge's original plan for the welfare state:

> The correlative of the state's undertaking to ensure adequate benefit for unavoidable interruptions of earnings, however long, is enforcement of the citizen's obligation to seek and accept all reasonable opportunities of work, to co-operate in measures designed to save him from habitual idleness, and to take all proper measures to be well. (Beveridge, 1942: para. 130)

So, duties are placed on the state to make provision for unemployed right-holders, but if these right-holders fail to behave in prescribed ways, they risk forfeiting their entitlement or right to social security (see also chapter 6). When it comes to disabled people, the application of this reciprocal or 'two-way' understanding of duties and rights between state and citizen has been less clear-cut. On the one hand, certain policies since the Second World War have encouraged, as much as possible, labour market participation for disabled people. On the other hand, policies reinforcing the segregation of disabled people from the wider community have also been regularly promoted, including the systematic segregation of disabled people from the labour market and social activity more generally. The implicit correlate in the latter case has been that needs should be met unconditionally and as a matter of entitlement, but through segregated institutional policies and practices.

In the aftermath of the Second World War, some government attention was focused on ensuring that disabled servicemen re-entered the workforce, assuming that disabled people (or at least disabled men) could and should make an active contribution to the economic regeneration of post-war Britain – with the principle being accepted that disabled people ought to be active contributors to their own welfare (and the economy more generally) via paid work, rather than be passive recipients of welfare provision via state services. For example, the 1944 Disabled Persons (Employment) Act positively discriminated in favour of disabled people by instituting a quota system, under which employers with over twenty employees were required to recruit at least 10 per cent of their workforce as registered disabled people (also see Smith, 1992: 2–3). However, in practice the quota system quickly ran into difficulty, as employers applied for exemptions which were very readily given by government officials, and disabled people refused to register themselves, ironically, for fear of being unfairly discriminated against by employers (also see Barnes, 1991; and my own analysis of government surveys in Smith, 1992). Consequently, when the quota system was abandoned in 1995 (being superseded by the 1995 Disability Discrimination Act, outlawing discrimination in a range of areas including employment:

Oliver and Barnes, 1998), most employers did not or could not meet the 10 per cent quota. Even those employers who did make some attempt at fulfilling it frequently employed disabled people in low-skilled menial jobs, which often non-disabled workers were unwilling to do. In short, it seems that whilst the quota system was underpinned in principle by a 'social model' attitude of inclusion and active participation for disabled people, in practice it became highly tokenistic, revealing a 'medical model' attitude to disability, dominant in the two or three decades after the Second World War. Thus, the perception is reinforced that disabled people are vulnerable and in need, and so dependent on help from others – whether this help is provided by family members, the state or a mixture of both.

The subsequent ambivalence in policy and practice raises further questions. Partly, these centre on how the social and medical models of disability are variously reflected in disability policy and as explored above. However, other questions relate to debates concerning the meaning of independent living and how so-called independence relates to paid work and competing conceptions of 'participation' and 'active citizenship'. The final section of this chapter will briefly outline some problems for the DRM and the social model arising from promoting, as an ideal, what I have called the 'myth of independent living'. It will be argued that even if financial independence is secured for disabled people through paid work (often seen as a hallmark of independent living) this so-called 'independence' is reliant, in a complex post-industrial society, on the maintenance of highly mutually supportive or interdependent relations between all individuals and groups, disabled or not.

Conclusion: the myth of independent living and the value of interdependence

The ideal of independent living for disabled people has political cachet for a society committed to the values of economic independence and self-reliance. But, as will now be argued, it represents a distortion and over-simplification of the social experiences of disabled and non-disabled people alike and of the complex moral questions arising out of these experiences – whereas understanding individual relationships and social relations as interdependent provides the basis for a more accurate account of the social and moral worlds we all occupy (also see my arguments in Smith, 2001b, 2002a, 2002b).

In general, dependency can be defined as the state in which a person or group relies upon the activities of another to meet their needs. The 'problem' of dependency, understood by policy makers in a number of different contexts, is constructed as symptomatic of both extreme and non-extreme cases. For example, as previously explored, severely disabled people are often perceived (reflecting the medical model) as being entirely dependent upon the activities of non-disabled people to meet their needs. As such, the dependency in this case is understood as essentially a medical problem, to be solved by reference to some kind of principle of justice between the 'better-off' (non-disabled) and the 'worst-off' (disabled) – establishing a right to have these medical needs met. Moreover, because of the extreme dependency, these rights are met with no conditions attached, except that the dependent person must prove their medical status as severely disabled. Once this status is proven, then no behavioural expectations, such as those found in actively seeking work tests, are attached as a condition for receiving state services and benefits.

Yet, it is arguable that, although the DRM radically challenges the myth of medically derived dependency, it still adheres to the same myth of independent living. In short, the value of independence is championed by the DRM as a fixed ideal through becoming what might be termed a 'normalised shared social goal' for all individuals, including people with impairments, understood as active citizens. Of course, the processes of 'normalisation' are conceptualised differently by the DRM as its critique refers to the social rather than medical origins of dependence. However, the medical and social models, despite these differences, define dependency as a 'social problem', whereby the ideal condition as related to independence becomes the principal aim for proponents of either model (see Smith, 2001b).

My specific claim here is that the objective of equal participation, facilitated through non-discriminatory and inclusionary policies and practices, is distinct from that of medical readjustment only in terms of the nature of its remedial solution, and not in terms of its presentation of the problem to be solved. Consequently, independent living becomes the ideal that is promoted by the DRM. Disabled people are portrayed as looking forward to, and struggling for, a future in which they can participate in the same ideal/normal independent state that non-disabled people already, supposedly, enjoy. In other words, the problem of dependency is fixed in relation to facts, whether social or medical, and it is these facts that cause the problem. Moreover, it is a problem that is 'fixable' through strategies that promote independent living, whether via social and/or medical adjustment.

At first glance, it might be thought reasonable for policy makers and practitioners to assume that securing a well-paid job offers a person financial independence, which is a route out of poverty and welfare dependence and the basis for independent living. However, this is a distorted picture of the complex and interrelated social and economic arenas that we all occupy, and as such distorts policy and practice evaluations. For example, it has been observed that since the development of public welfare provision most, if not all, people have become dependent for their prosperity upon the welfare state. Indeed, despite dominant perceptions that welfare dependants hail typically from the working (or lower) classes, various empirical studies have shown how the middle classes, in many respects, have been the principal post-war beneficiaries of increased state activity regarding welfare (for example, see Blakemore, 2003: 10–11; Le Grand and Winter, 1987). Of course, many apologists for the free-market system have argued that it is precisely this type of increasing dependence which has undermined the values of individual self-reliance across social classes. Individuals are not held to account for their actions which then encourages irresponsibility, conceived of as being an abdication of the moral responsibility that individuals (and their families) be financially independent (for example, see the respective arguments of Hayek, 2000: 90–5; Murray, 2000: 96–106; Mead, 2000: 108–18).

The contention of this chapter is that this conception of financial independence is over-narrow and over-individualistic. It has often been persuasively argued that modern capitalist economies require that welfare and economic systems are mutually supporting, in order to ensure that individuals have sufficient resources to efficiently engage in free-market activities (for example, see Gough, 2000: 234–53). For example, to obtain paid work usually (and increasingly) necessitates that the potential worker is educated and/or trained to a particular level. It has been generally recognised that the free market could not guarantee that all potential workers be educated or trained to meet the demands of employers, and more generally the demands of an increasingly competitive and technologically advanced international economy. One result of this argument is that publicly financing some kind of state-education/training system to meet these requirements is regarded as an economic necessity by most, if not all, people of whatever political persuasion – as is the priority of establishing certain forms of 'welfare rights' (also see my arguments in Smith, 2001b, 1998: 66–86).

Yet, recognising that individuals are, as a result, 'welfare dependent' because of such economic necessities seriously problematises the goal that individuals ought to be economically independent. Not only are individuals dependent on some form of state provision to secure paid employment, but modern capitalism itself is dependent upon the state financing institutions to ensure increasing efficiency and competitiveness. Therefore, the ideal of promoting financial independence as a basis for independent living should be exposed as a myth, for two reasons. First, given that the highly technical world we occupy cannot flourish without some kind of publicly funded welfare provision, it is no longer tenable to argue that individuals can, or ought to be, financially independent through paid employment. Secondly, encouraging paid work involves commitment to some kind of financial interdependence between the individual and the state for the sake of wider economic development.

More specifically, in relation to disability issues it might be argued that, if disabled people are to engage in paid work, welfare and social systems should be instituted which provide these individuals with the necessary resources for this activity to take place. Again, this position reflects well the social model of disability as it focuses on the ways in which society is organised or structured in relation to people with impairments establishing what might be broadly termed 'rights to participation'. Particular systems ensure that disabled people participate in society on the same basis as non-disabled people as a matter of entitlement, and that the state has a positive duty to subsidise this financially. Consequently, as with non-disabled people, facilitating paid work and participation entails promoting some kind of financial interdependence between the disabled individual and the state. Of course, the precise policy and practice requirements of disabled people and non-disabled people in relation to this financial interdependence will be different both within and between these groups. So, it may be that certain forms of differential treatment are justified in the name of establishing equal access to the labour market, while at other times similar treatment would be more appropriate. In either case, though, the policy objective of financial independence (linked to paid work) seems to misconstrue and distort what precisely is happening. Given the financial support needed to equip any person with the skills and knowledge necessary to engage in paid work, disabled people are not necessarily less independent than non-disabled people, only differently interdependent.

So, finally, returning to the issue of rights to need-fulfilment and rights to identity-assertion. It seems that the relationship between these rights reflects in part important ethical questions concerning how we understand 'the individual' and 'the self' in relations to 'others' and 'society'. For example, do I see my 'self' in relation to others, in reciprocal recognition, and leading a social life of common dependence, interdependence and even sacrifice? Or do I see my 'self' as an atomistic, 'independent' individual, acting independently from others and society at large? It has been argued in this chapter that, although policies and practices are often underpinned by the latter set of conceptions (derived in large part from mythologised commitments to so-called independent living), both empirical and moral realities suggest that we should seriously consider the former conception as the more compelling.

This requires that we reject, as inadequate in themselves, both rights to identity-assertion as related to independent living and also rights to need-fulfilment as a monolithic provision from the state for those who are 'vulnerable' and 'dependent'. Instead, a more reciprocal understanding of rights is recommended, assuming that all persons have something to contribute to wider society. Moreover, that we all have a right to this contribution being facilitated through various state-administered systems and services, not only underpins and promotes the value of interdependence, but also establishes a notion of universal citizenship which is active and empowering for disabled and non-disabled people alike.

9

DEVOLUTION

Devolution and the welfare state: the case of Wales

Mark Drakeford

Introduction

To provide a chapter dealing with the welfare state and devolution is, inevitably, to be drawn into the history of the Labour Party in Wales. While most of the account which follows will concentrate on developments in the post-1999 context of the National Assembly, an informed understanding of the political currents which still surround the delivery of welfare services in a devolved Wales does require some understanding of the longer-standing antecedents which surround the present day arrangement. This chapter therefore begins with a brief account of devolution issues prior to 1945. It continues with a summary of some key, formative ideas of the welfare state before going on to trace the devolution debate from Attlee to Blair. The chapter then deals, at greater length with social policy making in a devolved Wales, attempting to assess the extent to which contemporary developments draw on an earlier heritage of ideas and purposes.

Early modern devolution

It is not part of this chapter's purpose to provide a detailed or lengthy account of the political antecedents of present day devolution in Wales. That story has recently been newly illuminated in a series of papers from University of Bangor, as a result of an ESRC-funded research project into the modern history of devolution (see, for example, Tanner, 2006). Nevertheless, it is important to be aware that today's arguments and political fault-lines have their roots in far longer disputes and alignments. The tangled nature of these debates can be seen, for example, in the Gower constituency in 1886 when the Liberal David Rendall was returned to Westminster by the votes of miners and tinplate workers on a platform of 'Labour and Welsh home rule' (Griffiths, 1981: 6). Inside the Labour Party, a commitment to home rule for Wales formed part of its early programmes. Keir Hardie, in his Dowlais declaration of 14 October 1911, was forthright: 'the people of Wales fighting to repossess the land of Wales ... that is the kind of nationalism I want to see' (ibid., 1985: 12). In 1914, the Liberal MP for West Denbigh, E.T. Jones, presented a Government of Wales Bill, encompassing provision for a Welsh parliament, the sponsors including William Brace, president of the South Wales Miners' Federation.

The commitment to 'home rule all round' survived the Great War. As it came to an end, in June 1918, Arthur Henderson argued in *Welsh Outlook* that, as far as the party's plan for Welsh devolution was concerned, 'it is hardly possible to conceive an area in which a scheme of parliamentary self-government could be better established with better chances of success'. In the following month, an extraordinary congress of the South Wales Labour Federation unanimously voted in favour of a directly elected federal parliament for Wales. At the Parliamentary end, the House of Commons voted, in February 1919, to establish a Speaker's Conference to consider federal devolution to England, Scotland and Ireland – and whether this would also be 'applicable to Welsh conditions and requirements' (Griffiths, 1981: 14). When it reported in 1920, a relatively modest form of federalism was one of the options offered. In a further demonstration of the political complexity of devolution, of the four Welsh MPs who were members of the conference, only the Conservative and Unionist MP for Monmouthshire, C.L. Forestier-Walker, voted for the federal model.

The inconclusive nature of the Speaker's Conference, and the gathering storm of post-war economic and social difficulties combined to reverse the devolutionary tide which had run so strongly for more than twenty years. The notion never evaporated. Another Welsh Home Rule Bill, for example, was moved in the House of

Commons on 28 April 1922, by the Liberal MP for Wrexham but the momentum had stalled and, with it, some familiar disputes about the costs of any Welsh parliament and the relationship between different parts of Wales began to emerge more strongly. Indeed, it is not entirely encouraging that the only substantial mention of Welsh affairs in an officially sanctioned centenary history of the Labour Party (Brivati and Heffernan, 2000) is to be found in the chapter on 'Managing dissent in the party' – an indication, perhaps, not simply of Welsh Labour's chapel tradition, but of something more fissiparous in the party's make-up.

Such progress as was possible shifted from democratic to administrative devolution. An early action of the great reforming 1906 Liberal government had seen the creation, in 1907, of the Welsh Department of the Board of Education (Thomas, 1981: 2). It marked the beginning of administrative differentiation which slowly moved ahead in the interwar period. In 1938, the Welsh Parliamentary Party wrote to the prime minister, Neville Chamberlain, arguing for a secretary of state for Wales, an idea that surfaced again in 1943, in the context of post-war reconstruction, the argument being the need to protect Welsh interests in that effort (ibid.: 56). This was the state of play when Labour took office in 1945.

Key purposes of the welfare state

For the purposes of this chapter, four different core elements of the Beveridge-derived welfare state will be identified and then discussed within the devolution context. Inevitably, the account here is simplified and compressed, but has the advantage of setting in sharp relief some fundamental principles of social welfare provision and organisation.

Before embarking on that account, however, it is worth re-emphasising that, for a 1945 socialist government, social services remained an adjunct to, rather than a substitution for, economic success. Labour, famously, began not as a party of welfare, but of the trade union movement. Economic success, therefore, was to be judged from the perspective of working men and women. As Ernest Bevin put it, the 1945 Labour government was not simply about the construction of a gigantic social ambulance. At the heart of the Beveridge prescription was the responsibility, newly accepted by government, for the maintenance of full employment, backed up by decent, and rising, wages. That focus on economic prosperity is a theme to which this chapter will return in the post-devolution era.

At the heart of the Beveridge settlement[1] is a conclusion that a series of core social welfare services are better provided through the collective public effort, rather than being left to private providers in a market place or an unsustainable voluntary effort. The National Health Service remains the single most outstanding example of that proposition, while the example cited in the report was that of funeral expenses. In 1938, it had been estimated that more than 100 million funeral insurance policies were extant in Britain (Calvert, 1978: 248). These were policies held with friendly societies and commercial insurance companies. Minimal coverage was provided by them, but sufficient to avoid the ultimate shame of a 'pauper's funeral' (Fraser, 1984: 165). Such policies had sustained the industry during the lean interwar years and state 'interference' in the area had been fiercely resisted. To Beveridge, however, the argument seemed clear. The new welfare state was to provide security, and decency, 'from the cradle to the grave'. As the report put it, 'all people when they die need a funeral' (Beveridge, 1942: 151). Social insurance would provide a universal death grant, set originally at £20 but capable of being increased with 'no difficulty', Beveridge concluded, 'as the contribution required is small' (ibid.: 159). This basic argument in favour of unequivocal state provision can be seen at play in each of the services established by the 1945 Labour government. The experience of the interwar years, in health, housing and social security, as well as in the overall management of the economy, demonstrated the inadequacies and inefficiencies of un-coordinated, piecemeal provision in which the state accepted only a residual responsibility. The public interest in providing such services through collective effort, led by government, was not only social, but economic. Socially, such an approach supplied a set of new social rights of guaranteed reach and quality. Economically, it was said to secure the efficiencies to be gained through elimination of wasteful, overlapping and competing organisations while producing greater effectiveness of spending ensured that the greatest impact was felt where need was greatest. In this sense, as Tawney put it,

> the greater part of the expenditure upon the social services is not a liability, but an investment, the dividends of which are not the less substantial because they are paid, not in cash, but in strengthened individual energies and an increased capacity for cooperative effort. (Quoted in Reisman, 1997: 91)

A second linked pair of underpinning principles both of the Beveridge Report, and of the 1945 Labour government's legislative programme, were that social provision should be universal and comprehensive. Together with the insurance basis these principles would provide a contractual relationship between the citizen and the state, in which use of public services would be without stigma or dependency. Universalism guaranteed an end to humiliating means-testing, both in terms of financial inquiries and assessment of character. It was, Silburn (1994: 95) concluded, the 'one big idea in the Report which moves social policy from the margins of political concern to the centre'. It is sometimes forgotten that the policies of the 1930s, such as the hated Circular 170 of 1932, which extended the means test and aimed to cut down on free places in secondary schools, were based on widening behavioural as well as financial conditionality (Morgan, 1995: 5). The Beveridge settlement aimed for services that could be used without loss of self-respect or social esteem.

A third essential dimension of the 1945 approach was that the services to be provided would be delivered by impartial, benevolent and expert public servants, motivated by a Tawneyesque sense of public service, capable of recognising and pursuing the national interest – or, put more pejoratively, the Fabian sense that a combination of teetotalism and an excellent filing system would be sufficient to provide the expert leadership which the masses required. In the words of Beveridge's biographer, Jose Harris, the Beveridge Plan 'replaced the rule of natural law by the rule of the expert' (1977: 87).

While a certain passivity was thus built into the realisation of new citizenship rights, it is important to note that issues of representation were unlikely to loom so large in an era when mass participation in political parties and trade unions was so much more a part of the civic landscape. Membership of both the Conservative and Labour parties were at an all-time high in the post-war period (Seyd and Whiteley, 2004), while involvement with trade unions was similarly at a high water mark (Trade Union Congress, 2008). The need for the voice of users to be heard in the provision of services was not only negated by the belief, in Douglas Jay's famous phrase, that 'the gentleman in Whitehall really does know best' (1937: 317), but also by the objective fact that users were far more likely to have other means of making their views known and made effective.

Finally, the 1945 reforms were infused with an egalitarian passion in pursuit of what Ellison (2000: 422) calls 'the key objective of greater equality of outcome'. If the Labour Party has, for most of its history, had a single distinguishing characteristic it has been an enduring ambition to create greater social equality. From Tawney's famous 1931 essay 'Equality' to the more revisionist writings of Crosland in the 1950s, the belief that more equal societies bring both economic and social benefits has animated Labour's purpose (see Reisman, 1997). The experience of the 1939–45 war had emphasised the irrelevance of social distinctions in pursuit of a common cause. Famously, rationing had had the effect of improving the diet of the poorest families (Seyd and Whiteley, 2004). For the Attlee administration, therefore, equality was not some esoteric obsession with abstract ideas. It was an intensely practical matter that the government had to pursue as a common purpose.

Of course, not everything achieved by the 1945 Labour government was perfect. Universal, insurance benefits were set too low from the outset (Glennester, 1995: 41), the National Health Service contained a number of concessions to the doctors (Webster, 1998: 28) and the state-education system retained the tripartite system based on the 11-plus examination (Simon, 1991). Any social policy narrative inevitably relies on a process of selection and simplification – a point to which this chapter returns in the post-1999 context.

Devolution from Attlee to Blair

'A charge has been levelled against the 1945 Government,' wrote James Griffiths very late in his life, 'that its Welsh record was a poor one' (Griffiths, 1975: 40). In fact, in the histories of Griffiths and his great contemporary Aneurin Bevan, the essential devolution dividing line within the Welsh Labour Party was personified. For the Welsh-speaking west-walian, Jim Griffiths, architect of Labour's social insurance social security system, Wales had a natural claim to take charge of its own domestic affairs. Yet, when the case for a secretary of state for Wales was put to Attlee, as it had been put to Chamberlain in 1938, it was Bevan's opposition that was decisive. 'He was afraid', said Griffiths, 'that its effect would be to take Wales out of the mainstream of British politics and turn Welsh MPs into "local" politicians without influence on national and international affairs' (ibid.: 41).

Behind this specific decision lay a difference that continues to find an echo in today's Welsh Labour Party. Following Thomas (1981) it could be summarised as a contest between culture (Wales as a nation with its own history, language, identity) and economy (Wales as a place with particular economic characteristics: rural depopulation, industrial decline). For nearly thirty years, the compromise was to build on administrative devolution while making no concessions to political self-determination. Thus, in 1948, Labour established the advisory council for Wales and Monmouthshire in 1948 with twenty-seven members, appointed by the prime minister to represent various walks of life in Wales (Thomas, 1981: 45). In 1951, the Conservatives appointed the first minister for Welsh affairs (albeit with no specifically Welsh responsibilities), followed up by another nominated council – 'a bone without marrow – no self-respecting corgi would sniff at it' concluded Lady Megan Lloyd George, soon to be Labour MP for Carmarthen and a leading figure in the newly energised parliament for Wales campaign (Jones, 1991: 235).

A combination of devolution enthusiasts – S. O. Davies, Cledwyn Hughes – and those who feared that Wales would be disadvantaged in comparison with Scotland in any new Labour government, including James Callaghan, produced a firm commitment to a Welsh Office, headed by a secretary of state in the Cabinet. The by-now veteran James Griffiths was the charter secretary when Labour won the 1964 general election. Thereafter, for more than a decade, the office grew, gradually extending the scope of administrative devolution to the point where the case for direct, domestic political oversight of its responsibilities again became unavoidable. Yet, when a referendum came to be held in 1979, it was the force of the Labour No Assembly Campaign which swept the board. Its 'Facts to beat fantasies' document was remarkable both for its ability to tap into deep-seated fears about devolution – an assembly would produce 'conflict with the rest of Britain and disharmony within Wales' – and for the ferocity with which it attacked fellow members of the Labour Party – 'devofanatics', 'disguised nationalists', factionalist members of the 'Yesmen campaign' (Labour No Assembly Campaign Wales, 1979). Defeat by a landslide signalled, for almost every observer, the end of political devolution for Wales for a generation.

It took Mrs Thatcher to reverse that outcome and, in the 1980s and 1990s, the two dimensions of this chapter's story come together – the fate of welfare services and the political case for Wales taking responsibility, directly, for its own domestic affairs. In each general election from 1979 to 1992 Wales consistently returned a very clear majority of Members of Parliament from left-of-centre parties and throughout the period found the Welsh Office occupied by politicians from the Conservative Party. While, for a period, successive secretaries of state appeared to act in a relatively conciliatory fashion, that ended with the arrival of John Redwood, in 1990, when Wales appeared to be entered for an experiment in pushing the boundaries of neo-conservatism, rather than (somewhat passively) resisting them. The Redwood occupancy of the Welsh Office may have been brief, but it exposed sharply the fact that, whatever the rhetorical tone, Wales had been obliged to take part in every major policy initiative of the Conservative years – privatisation (where Scotland and Northern Ireland had been excluded from the sale of the water industry), poll tax, local government decline and reform, grant-maintained schools, marketisation of health services and so on.

A number of accounts now exist (Andrews, 1999; Rawlings, 2003; Tench, 2007) of both the referendum campaign itself, the founding birth pangs and subsequent development of the National Assembly for Wales. The perspective that historical distance offers is yet to be achieved, but the argument of this chapter would be relatively simple. Seventeen unbroken years of partisan Conservative rule had convinced enough Labour sceptics that an assembly would provide a bulwark against any such future experiment. The final referendum result demonstrated that, even at the Labour high water mark of 1997, Welsh voters were highly hesitant about being for the assembly. Just enough were against the idea of being governed again by the Tories to tip the balance in favour of devolution.

The assembly thus created contained sixty members, elected via a form of proportional representation in which forty constituency members, elected by the first-past-the-post, were joined by twenty others chosen from top-up lists. Because Labour dominates the constituency representation, opposition members are, overwhelmingly, drawn from the lists. Once elected, Assembly Members were, in 1999, provided with secondary legislative powers,[2] rather than the primary law-making powers available to the Scottish parliament. Nor did the assembly have an ability to raise its own revenue. Rather, it was provided, annually, with a 'block grant' from Westminster, based on what is known as the Barnett formula,[3] which the assembly is then free to allocate as it sees fit between different devolved services. These devolved matters include health, housing, education, local government, agriculture and economic development. Foreign affairs, defence, social security, taxation and macroeconomic management remain wholly un-devolved. In the case of Wales, but not Scotland, matters of crime and justice are also, for the most part (but not exclusively) reserved to Westminster. For the purposes of this chapter the important point to emphasise is that, if it were to be summarised in a phrase, the Welsh government could accurately be characterised as a social policy body. It has control of the great domestic agenda that impacts most directly on the daily lives of Welsh citizens and which, in social welfare terms, provides the assembly with four of the five giants of the Beveridge Report.

Social policy making in a devolved Wales

The second half of this chapter now turns to an examination of social policy making during what is still less than a single decade of devolved government.[4] In particular, it aims to assess the policy preferences of the first three Welsh assembly governments against the four underlying themes of the founders of the welfare state, as set out in an earlier section. In doing so, the account inevitably reflects the dominant role of the Labour Party within each of those assembly administrations. At this point it is important, too, to provide something of a health warning. If all history is biography, then what follows draws heavily on the author's own direct experience as an advisor to successive assembly cabinets throughout the period of Rhodri Morgan as first minister. It is, therefore, an explicitly insider view of policy making, and makes no claims to a more academic objectivity or even-handedness. A claim that this account would make, however, is to some avoidance of a directly party political partisanship.[5] Ever since the first stirrings towards universal suffrage during the nineteenth century Wales has, uniquely amongst the nations of the United Kingdom, demonstrated an enduring preference for left-of-centre politics. Today, the essential contest in Wales remains that between three political parties – Labour, Plaid Cymru and the Liberal Democrats – each of which would self-describe as being left of centre. Voting Conservative, as the doyen of Welsh historians, K. O. Morgan (1982: 46) puts it has always 'indelibly associated with the old social order'. While Labour has had the most practical influence over the policy developments recounted below, the claim made here would be that the ideological impulses on which they are founded would be shared across a wider range of assembly parties.

Earlier in this chapter it was suggested that, for the post-war Attlee government, achievement of full employment provided the bedrock to the rest of its social policy ambitions. While the assembly does not have responsibility for economic management, it does have substantial powers in economic development. One of the ways in which devolved government in Wales has differentiated itself from administration elsewhere has been in the continued emphasis placed on traditional regional policy economic levers. Thus, while the Department for Trade and Industry no longer exists in Whitehall – following a period in which its role and remit had gradually withered away – in Wales spending on Regional Selective Assistance for incoming firms and use of European Union funds for the development of indigenous enterprises have continued to be major drivers of the assembly government's budget. The result, according to First Minister Rhodri Morgan (2006) has been a series of 'devolution dividends'. Certainly, during the ten years of sustained economic success that followed from 1997, Wales outperformed the rest of the United Kingdom. Unemployment, having been historically higher than the UK average, moved from near the bottom of the league, to near the top. Economic inactivity rates in Wales were reduced at three times the rate in the UK as a whole. At the same time, and due in part, at least, to the enduring demand side strand in assembly government economic development policy, Wales was the only part of the UK to have seen a larger percentage increase in private sector employment than public sector jobs growth. Between the time when the assembly was established and June 2005 private sector employment in Wales rose by 10 per cent, compared to an increase of 4 per cent across the UK as a whole. When the economy hit the buffers in 2008, however, the new conditions left Wales in new, unchartered territory. The rapid devaluation of the pound, in comparison with both the euro and the dollar, in the six months after August 2008, left manufacturing industry (still a larger proportion of the Welsh economy than elsewhere in the UK) better able to compete for orders from abroad. The disproportionate impact on the automotive sector, however, also hit Wales especially hard, with its knock-on effect into supply chains and the steel industry, in particular. The distinctive impact of devolution was felt, once again, in the more interventionist policies that the assembly government pursued. Schemes to help prevent redundancies – the ProAct scheme – and to assist where jobs were lost – the ReAct scheme – were quickly established (see Welsh Assembly Government, 2009), and small-scale, but labour-intensive, public capital works brought forward from future financial years.

One positive feature of Welsh economic circumstances continued throughout the period, from good times into bad. The availability of European funding, first through the Objective One programme, and latterly through its successor programme, Convergence funding. During the seven-year Objective One period, to 2007, the level of reduction in unemployment in Objective One Wales had been four times faster than in Wales as a whole, just as household incomes rose faster in west Wales and the valleys than elsewhere in Wales. In the early part of the Convergence-funding programme, the sharp appreciation in the value of the euro has meant an unexpected bonus in the level of European funding available to Wales. In a period of economic difficulty which, in some ways, is closer to that faced by the Labour government of 1945 than at any time subsequently, the enduring importance attached to economic planning, and the role of government in helping to direct, as well as promote, economic activity means that Wales has, through devolution, readier access to a set of tools which would have been familiar sixty years ago and which, in these newly Keynesian times, are having to be rediscovered by others.

Turning now to the four key foundations of welfare state suggested earlier, there can be little doubt but that, as in the case of the economy, successive Welsh assembly governments have demonstrated an enduring preference for public services, publicly provided and delivered through cooperative, rather than competitive mechanisms. The main text here is to be found in the Welsh Assembly Government's (2004) *Making the Connections* document, which represents an explicit attempt to set out its model of public service reform. While the paper accepts that a perfectly respectable case can be made for markets as a means of allocating and delivering services, it firmly concludes that such an approach is not to be followed in Wales. In its place, the document opts for a partnership model, in which public services are to become more responsive and more efficient through greater cooperation and sharing of resources. Public service boards are the most tangible example of this mechanism, bringing together local councils, the health service, criminal justice services, the voluntary sector and others in each local authority area in order to address priority issues of common concern.

As noted earlier in this chapter it is a fool's errand to claim that each and every action of government conforms to a set of rules or principles. There are examples in Wales of services being provided by profit-making as well as third-sector organisations, especially in the field of social care. The claim made here is that, taken altogether, the record of successive assembly governments has been in the opposite direction. In Wales, education continues to be provided through recognisably comprehensive schools; hip and knee 'factories' exist for orthopaedic procedures, but these have been created within and not outside the National Health Service in Independent Sector Treatment Centres; hospital cleaning services, previously contracted out to the private sector, have been brought back within the NHS. The One Wales agreement (Welsh Assembly Government, 2007) of the then coalition administration reinforces this commitment in some important ways, notably in its intention to abolish the last vestiges of the internal market in the Welsh NHS and to end the reliance on private sector providers in acute care.

Beneath this is a recognition, which the 1945 welfare state founders would have easily recognised, that ownership matters. It has become fashionable to argue that, for users of public services, what counts is the quality of the final product, with a basic indifference to the nature of the provider. In Wales, that view is not so widely shared. The transformation of Dŵr Cymru into Glas Cymru, for example, has been widely cited as a shift in favour of a form of not-for-profit ownership which sits more easily with a Welsh view of public services (see Bennett et al., 2003 for a general review of these issues). In governmental terms, the pragmatic caution with which assembly administrations have approached the Public Finance Initiative means that the Welsh public sector is far less burdened with long-term debt repayments or with rapidly out-of-date buildings than would otherwise have been the case. Beyond pragmatism, the history of post-devolution Wales has been one in which public ownership of public assets has been the preferred model. Successive ministers, for example, have argued for local authorities to be given the ability to raise money to invest in their own housing stock, rather than having to rely on stock transfer to arrive at the same outcome. While that argument has not succeeded, the resistance of Welsh voters to transfer in Swansea and Wrexham suggests that the advantages of direct public ownerships of key assets extends beyond the political classes.

The second underpinning principle of the 1945 welfare state, suggested earlier, was that of universal and comprehensive services. Such a preference stands exactly at a major ideological fault-line in the provision of public services, between universal and means-tested (or targeted) services (see Drakeford, 2000 for an elaboration of this argument). Whereas in England, since 1979, there has been a growing preference for services provided on the basis of need (see Powell, 2008), in Wales there has been an enduring attachment to services organised on a universal basis. Thus, when charges for entry to national museums and galleries were abolished, they became free for everyone to use; when free bus passes are issued, they are free for all who qualify by age or disability; when free swimming was introduced during school holidays at local authority leisure centres, they became free for every child under sixteen; when free breakfasts were introduced in primary schools, they were free for all children; when prescription charges were abolished, they became free for every patient; when car parking charges at Welsh hospitals are abolished, parking will be free for everyone. The belief that underpins this way of providing services is the one which animated Beveridge and the 1945 Labour government – one which, in the old saying, recognises that services reserved for the poor very quickly become poor services. Universal services are not only more efficient (doing away with the elaborate administrative machinery that any form of rationing requires) but they ensure that every citizen – the articulate, as well as those who find it difficult to make their voices heard, the well-informed as much as those who struggle to navigate complex bureaucracies – has a stake in making such services as good as possible. They create, to use a phrase of Robert Owen's, a solidarity of interest which helps to bind modern, complex societies together. The centre of Welsh political gravity remains to the left of that across the United Kingdom as a whole and communitarian principles continue to have a resonance which reinforces the universal service ideal.

Over and above this approach it has been argued (see Drakeford, 2007b) that the Assembly Government has further developed the universal model through a set of measures in which the benefits of universal services are retained, but where extra resources and policy attention are paid to those whose needs are greatest. The assembly government's Health Inequalities Fund, for example, has provided well in excess of £10 million since its inception, for new and additional services in communities which need them the most. The assembly's RAISE programme has concentrated extra money in education on those schools where social and economic circumstances hold back educational attainment. Behind these decisions lies the notion of marginal utility – the judgement that, at some point in the provision of a universal service the greatest gain comes from applying new and additional resources to those in greatest need: a form of progressive universalism, in which the benefits of universalism are retained, but given a progressive twist through additional investment.

If, in these first two areas, a direct line of descent can be drawn between the animating principles of the welfare state and assembly government approaches to social welfare services, the third area identified earlier is one where greater divergence is apparent. There is a sense in which the founders of the welfare state did regard users of services as relatively passive objects of professional expertise, and there is, equally, a sense in which, in the aftermath of the war, people were grateful for whatever could be squeezed out of the highly compromised British economy. After all, Stafford Cripps, as Chancellor of the Exchequer, had made it clear that 'the result of our efforts in two worlds wars' meant that now 'our own consumption requirements have to be last in the list of priorities. First are exports . . . second is capital investment in industry; and last are the needs, comforts and amenities of the family' (quoted in Tomlinson, 1998: 63). Sixty years later neither a sense of professional omnipotence, nor of user obligation survive intact. In a Welsh context, however, the search for new ways of making services responsive to citizens has led not to marketisation, but to an emphasis on amplifying the collective voice of users, rather than finding new ways to exercise choice or exit. Beneath this preference lies a commitment to the principles of reciprocity, mutuality and trust as the enduring qualities of public service, reapplied in a twenty-first-century context. It means that co-production – the sense in which best outcomes are achieved when users and providers of services are regarded as jointly engaged in a common enterprise, each bringing something different, but of equal value to such encounters – speaks more loudly in post-devolution Wales than in the immediate post-Beveridge world. The preference for collective effort, however, would have been no surprise in an era when, as noted earlier, mass participation in collective forms of representation was stronger. School councils in every school in Wales, and retained and strengthened community health councils are just two examples of new ways in which a stronger voice for users is being developed in Welsh public services, ensuring that reform and redress are approached in ways that improve outcomes for all, rather than simply assuaging individual grievance.

Finally, to the pursuit of equality, and an enduring belief, in the Welsh context, in that simple Tawney principle of the equal worth of every human being and, as noted earlier, the practical actions which follow from a conclusion that unequal societies are wasteful economically and harmful socially. Greater equality and economic success are not enemies of one another, as so much of the neo-conservative rhetoric suggests. Rather, an equality strategy is one which harnesses the talents of all of the people in a given society, not just some. When social patterns are frozen, and intergenerational mobility is slow and difficult, then economic progress is similarly retarded. The more egalitarian a society, the more intergenerational mobility is made possible. Sweden, for example, has a far more egalitarian social structure than either the United Kingdom or the United States. It also has far higher intergenerational mobility. As Richard Wilkinson (2005: 14) has pointed out, the pursuit of equality 'is not only fairer at each point in time, but over time as well'. Inequality matters, as far as the economy is concerned, because it is as inefficient as it is unjust.

Not only do more equal societies do better economically, but they enjoy better health. There is something in the social fabric of more equal societies that, as Putnam (2000) suggests, creates a reservoir of social capital on which individuals and communities are able to draw when facing problems or in times of difficulty. Thus, more equal societies with lower economic resources have better health outcomes than less equal societies which are far better off. Health – both mental and physical well-being – is not simply a factor of how much money is spent on health services, either individually or collectively. It is closely linked to underlying senses of self-worth and social solidarity. These wider messages of being cared for, and caring for others in turn, create a social climate in which better health can be created.

The benefits which more equal outcomes produce in health are felt in other social spheres and accrue not simply to the individual, but to the collective. We live in a paradoxical era in which crime itself has fallen, but fear of crime has risen. What we also know is that more equal societies have lower levels of crime, particularly of violent crime, and that fear of crime is lower in such communities, too (Wilkinson, 2005). One of the most corrosive effects of societies that are more and more unequal is the disappearance of a shared public realm, in which we meet one another and reinforce those things which unite rather than divide us from one another. Even in societies where everyone is getting better off, those where the rate of improvement creates a widening gap between the top and the bottom reap the whirlwind in the sense of dislocation and dissatisfaction that inequality produces. Communities where fear of crime leads people to withdraw from community life, to resent strangers, to treat offers of help with suspicion and requests to contribute as an imposition, are communities where our collective freedom to act has been fundamentally reduced.

Conclusion

The creation of a National Assembly for Wales was an act of a Labour government at Westminster and, as this chapter has attempted to demonstrate, the debates that have shaped devolution in any practical sense are those which have taken place inside the Labour Party. While different strands of thought about the advisability and nature of devolution have been apparent for more than a century, the argument here has been that both Aneurin Bevan and James Griffiths, shaping forces in the creation of the welfare state, might have seen more to recognise in post-devolution social policy making in Wales than might have been apparent to them in some other parts of the United Kingdom. An enduring belief in the effectiveness of collective effort to advance the greatest good of the greatest number, in the provision of public services, publicly provided, and in the economic, social and individual benefits of greater equality provide a lasting legacy which, in very different circumstances, devolution has allowed to be applied anew in contemporary Wales.

Notes

1. The Beveridge Report itself, of course, was formally launched by Sir William himself at an event in Cardiff City Hall, where newsreel footage shows him being carried shoulder high from the civic entrance to be greeted by huge crowds outside.

2. There is no space here to trace the development of devolution since 1999. The single most important point to note is the passage of the Government of Wales Act 2006, which provided the assembly with a means of acquiring primary competence in selected areas, and which set out a means by which, following a referendum, full Scottish-style powers could be acquired. Following a referendum in 2011, the assembly has now has the power to make its own primary legislation within the devolved areas.

3. Again, the Barnett formula requires a whole paper of its own, if justice is to be done to both the complexity and importance of its subject. In 2008, the topic acquired new significance, with a commission into the workings of the formula and allied matters promised as part of the Labour/Plaid Cymru administration in Cardiff, and a convention established by the Scottish parliament (as opposed to the SNP government, with Westminster government engagement, into the same issue. Readers with a particular interest in the operation of the formula, and the funding of devolved government more generally, could consult McLean (2005) or Bell and Christie (2007)

4. It is not possible, within this chapter, to provide a detailed review of policy making in particular areas. A growing specialist literature is available to readers who wish to take a more in-depth look at, for example, health (Drakeford, 2005; Greer and Rowland, 2007), education (Egan, 2007), social work (Butler, 2007) or poverty and social exclusion (Joseph Rowntree Foundation, 2007).

5. Some aspects of the argument which follows have been rehearsed, in different contexts, in a number of other publications, including Drakeford and Chaney (2004) and Drakeford (2007).

10

THE START AND END OF LIFE

Part 1: The welfare of children since 1948

Ian Butler

In March 2008, the UK government had cause to invoke Beveridge as it set out its 'ambitions' for 'eradicating child poverty' (HM Treasury, DWP, DCSF, 2008: 3). This 'challenging ambition' would:

> require one of the most significant changes in the modern welfare state since its creation following the 1942 report by William Beveridge. The Government's approach to tackling child poverty will be consistent with Beveridge's view that nothing should be done to remove from parents the responsibility for their children, but that it is in the national interest to help parents discharge their responsibility properly. (Ibid.)

It would seem that sixty years on, at least one, and possibly two, of Beveridge's 'five giants' (want and squalor) remain to be conquered as far as children are concerned. Moreover, despite the reference to change, it seems that some of the fundamental principles of giant slaying remain unaltered, especially the ideas of 'national interest' and the tutelage of the family.

Of course, in general terms, the social conditions of children in the UK have improved beyond recognition since 1948 and have improved at a quickened pace over the last few years, partly as a result of government anti-poverty strategies. Gross measures of health, including infant mortality and rates of infectious diseases, have shown consistent positive trends for over fifty years (see Office for National Statistics, 2004) although children still face significant health challenges. In reception classes in England, almost one in four children is either overweight or obese. In year 6, this rate was nearly one in three (DoH/ DCSF, 2008: 3). The mental health and sexual health of adolescents is poor (see Office for National Statistics, 2004: chapters 12 and 6) and compared to our 'rich' neighbours, the UK ranks fifteenth amongst the twenty-five OECD countries on a range of children's health and safety indicators. It would appear that 'disease' too is an issue for children in the UK today (UNICEF, 2007).

As far as 'ignorance' is concerned, children are becoming better qualified, as higher proportions leave school with five or more GCSE grades A*–C. More children stay on at school after the age of sixteen years and more continue on to tertiary education. However, around 10,000 pupils are permanently excluded from school each year and around one in four 19-year-olds still lack NVQ2 or its academic equivalent (e.g. five or more good GCSEs) and one in twelve have no qualifications at all.[1] Perhaps, not surprisingly, in terms of educational well-being, the UK ranks twentieth out of twenty-four OECD countries (UNICEF, 2007).

As for 'idleness', that may be more a problem for their parents, but around 1.8 million children (16 per cent of all children) live in workless households, albeit down from 2.2 million a decade ago. The UK has a higher proportion of its children living in workless households than any other EU country. It is one-and-a-half times that of the EU average, one-and-a-half times that in France and Germany, and more than twice as high as that in many of the other countries.[2]

Perhaps most tellingly, on measures of subjective well-being, the UK's children and young people would appear to be the unhappiest of all of those surveyed by UNICEF. On the basis of a comparison with their OECD peers rather than the children and young people of 1940s Britain, the successes of the Beveridge welfare state are perhaps less certain than they might first appear.

In truth, young people were a relatively minor consideration for the architects of the welfare state. The state's interest in children before the war had scarcely developed beyond that of the philanthropic ambitions of the previous century. If, for the purposes of this chapter, we consider the provision of universal schooling as an economic imperative and improvements in children's health as a consequence of broader public health initiatives, then the state's interest before the 1940s was largely focused on the delinquent and the disadvantaged child.

The 1933 Children and Young Persons Act (building on the 1908 Children Act) made little distinction between the 'mad, the sad and the bad' child and although the emphasis on 'rehabilitation' in the 1933 Act was progressive, '*the concept of care [was] still nineteenth century, based on removal from the degrading environmental conditions of squalor and poverty, and [providing] a substitute family for the home which has failed*' (Heywood, 1978: 130). The 1939–45 war and the evacuation of children from the larger cities was a reminder of the continuing existence of the slum child and, from 1943, concerns had developed within government that not every child might return home. Rivalry between the Home Office and the Ministry for Health over who should be centrally responsible for children's services had precluded a speedy resolution of how such children might be managed without recourse to the Poor Law, which would have been politically distasteful, and which was, in any case, destined to be replaced by the new arrangements for health care and social security (see Parker, 1983). As is so frequently the case, it was public opinion, carefully mediated through the welfare scandal, and the purposefulness of the moral entrepreneur that prepared the ground for legislative change (see Butler and Drakeford, 2005).

Chief amongst those advocating for the reform of children's welfare services was Marjorie Allen (Lady Allen of Hurtwood). Married to Clifford Allen, a leading member of the Independent Labour Party, she had taken over the leadership of the British Nursery Association in 1942 and, inter alia, had spent the war years organising teams of craftsmen to make toys and nursery equipment out of material found on bomb sites. Through pamphlets, direct correspondence with ministers and through the press, she was determined to bring to public attention the fate of 'many thousands' of children who were being brought up in children's homes, residential schools and nurseries 'under repressive conditions that are generations out of date' and which bear the 'chilly stigma of "charity"'.[3]

In the same letter to *The Times*, quoted above, Allen argued that the current Education Bill and the White Paper on the health services had ignored 'the army of unhappy children' that the war had exposed and that a 'public inquiry, with full government support, is urgently needed to explore this largely uncivilised territory'. The government initially resisted any form of inquiry but public interest grew and the correspondence on this subject in *The Times* may have been one of the most voluminous of the whole war.

In December 1944, Herbert Morrison, the Home Secretary, announced the establishment of what came to be known as the Curtis Committee to inquire into the public care of children. Little progress followed, however, until considerable additional public interest was generated by the death, in January 1945, of 13-year-old Denis O'Neil at the hands of his foster carers in what became the first major child welfare scandal of the post-war period (see Butler and Drakeford, 2005).

The Curtis Committee set out about its task in March 1945 and produced possibly the most moving and evocative account of the lives of children 'deprived of a normal home life' that any government committee ever could. The report provides striking accounts of 'large gaunt looking buildings with dark corridors, high windows . . . traditional chocolate and buff paint . . . bare boards and draughts and a continual smell of mass cooking, soft soap and disinfectant' and of 'dirt and dreariness, drabness and over-regimentation' (Curtis Committee, 1946: paras 141 and 230).

The government formally accepted the recommendations of the Curtis Committee on 24 March 1947 and began the process of reorganising to meet the demands of the children's service that was to be given effect by the passing of the Children Act on 30 June 1948. Herbert Morrison, who had been key to the Labour Party's victory in the 1945 general election and who was now deputy prime minister and leader of the House, declared that Marjorie Allen was 'the heroine' of the new Act, although it should be noted that he might have had personal reasons for thinking so. Marjorie Allen was to decline his proposal of marriage to her and left England to work for the United Nations Emergency Fund.

At the heart of the Act was a requirement that each local authority should establish a Children's Committee and appoint a Children's Officer to oversee a Children's Department through which most of the duties that the authority had to children would be carried out. This had the effect, ultimately, of making the local state the main provider and arbiter of welfare services for children and of forming the nucleus of the discipline and practice of social work that has for sixty years taken the professional lead in this area.

The 1948 Children Act came into effect on 5 July 1948, the same day on which the other three major legislative planks of the welfare state also came into effect: the National Insurance and National Health Service Acts of 1946 and the National Assistance Act of 1948. The Children Act attracted little public attention or press comment.

This very brief sketch of the context in which the 1948 Act came into being is more than can be offered in this chapter for the intervening period to the 2004 Children Act. Public policy towards those children and young people in whom the state has a particular rather than a general interest has followed, in many ways, a similar trajectory to that of the welfare state itself; through the brief economically expansive and progressive liberalism of the 1960s and 1970s, culminating in the 1969 Children and Young People Act to the retrenching 'new politics of welfare' and the 1989 Children Act and on to the managerialist centralism of more recent times and the current legislative and policy framework.

It is important to note the almost complete bifurcation of interest in the 'bad' and the 'sad/ mad' child in the intervening period, however. Unexpectedly persistent rises in juvenile crime which followed a slight drop in the immediate post-war years were becoming a cause of concern by the time the Home Office presented its first comprehensive report on the Children's Departments in May 1953. The Home Office (and *The Times*) was still supportive of the broadly preventive approach taken towards young offenders that remained predicated on the provision or substitution of a 'happy home with its two parents living in mutual affection and confidence' but there had also 'been hints of late of a definite lacuna in the organization for dealing with a certain type of young hooligan of fourteen or fifteen, who is not eligible for Borstal, but is so brutalized that he would be a disastrous influence in an ordinary approved school'.[4]

Unfortunately, to anatomise successive UK governments' policies and programmes for young offenders is also beyond the scope of this chapter. The reference is made here to illustrate a further enduring characteristic of children's position in relation to the institutions, political environment and economics of the welfare state. As well as being considered perpetually as an 'investment' in the future of the nation and an object of the state's 'disciplinary' functions (in a Foucauldian sense), children are a politically normative category. Whilst the new sociologists of childhood recognise childhood as neither a fixed nor certain set of experiences or structures but rather a socially produced and reproduced set of social relations, it is much more straightforward for most politicians. Childhood is certainly not what it was nor what it ought to be.

Supported by a more or less scientific psychological 'developmentalism', children and young people have been offered little standing, means or opportunity to engage in the making or shaping of the welfare state either by those who design or operate it. And it is this that differentiates children and young people most clearly from most others for whom the welfare state might be claimed to operate. Almost the entire political economy of the welfare state, both in respect of its 'universal' offerings as well as those targeted at more troubled and troublesome groups, has, until very recently, embedded and reinforced a politically neutered construction of childhood. In this it has operated in tandem with the generational interests of the time, no doubt, and it is this democratic deficit, the gap that still exists for children and young people between 'marginality and citizenship' (Wintersberger, 1996) that may account for how singularly unhappy the current generation of young people would appear to be. The welfare state in which they live has done little to ensure that it is meeting their welfare needs as children and young people experience and understand them.

To be disenfranchised is one thing but to be systematically represented as dangerous, difficult, unbiddable or worse is another. I have written elsewhere of how there has been a comfortable alignment between the technocratic practices of social workers, teachers and other children's professionals and the social authoritarianism and low trust of the 2007–2010 Blair/Brown government and its vision for the welfare state (see Butler and Drakeford, 2001, 2005; Butler and Pugh, 2004). The popular representation of a feral, generation of ASBOs NEETs, constantly under CCTV surveillance or subject to data exchange on a scale that would have alarmed Arthur Eric Blair (George Orwell) as much as that other Mr Blair have all been given substance by the Acts and actions of the post-1997 government of New Labour (see Butler and Drakeford, 2001; Garrett, 1999, for example).

The anxieties of the libertarian left over the 'policy child' of the current regime have their echo in the conservative right who seem alarmed (as always) over the erosion of parental authority and the strain that is being put on intergenerational relations by the child protection industry's mania with vetting, which:

- fuels suspicions among adults about each other;
- transmits negative signals about adults to children;
- undermines the ability of adults to take responsibility for children;
- diminishes adult authority and damages community relations.

(Furedi and Bristow, 2008)

The precise nature of the 'policy child' is more clearly debatable than this chapter is able to articulate, but I would argue that a compelling case can be made for a dominant political vision of childhood that is far more anxious, uncertain, pessimistic and lacking in imagination than that which ran through the corridors of the Home Office and the columns of *The Times* in the early 1940s.

However, that may be changing, at least in some parts of the UK. The contrast in the rhetoric of child poverty in Wales and England could not be greater (see Butler, 2007; Crowley, 2007). In Wales, the challenge of child poverty for the government is not its threat to the future or the social order but,

> Our duty as a Government is to use our powers to their maxi-
> mum potential and effect on behalf of those children who face

poverty in their daily lives in Wales. It is a matter of both entitlement and social justice. Freedom from poverty is a basic human right. (National Assembly for Wales, 2005: 34)

This argument captures a conception of the citizenship of children and young people that remains unfamiliar to many in Westminster and Whitehall; on 14 January 2004, the National Assembly had unanimously adopted the United Nations Convention on the Rights of the Child as the formal basis of policy making for children.

Reflecting a communitarian political tradition that was much more Welsh Labour than New Labour, the assembly government has given real substance to that commitment ever since. It was Wales that saw the appointment of the first Children's Commissioner; in Wales, the single children and young people's plans that local authorities have to compile are structured to meet the rights and entitlements of children and young people; the assembly and the assembly government have taken a principled stand in opposition to the corporal punishment of children; Wales has had an influential children's 'parliament' (Funky Dragon) since 2000; it is a statutory requirement in Wales for every school to have a school council; Wales is seeking powers to give children independent rights of audience to key tribunals; in Wales, the emphasis is on 'teach not test' and so there are no league tables or SATs (and broadly equivalent educational achievement); early years education is being reformed along Nordic lines in a way that places play at the centre of learning; Wales remains one of the few European countries to have a play policy, and so on.

The institutions of government in Wales are in the early stages of their development and many of its policies remain to be judged by their outcomes, although the latter is true of many current initiatives by the UK government. The point is that the Assembly Government has adopted a participatory, emancipatory, progressive and confident view of the capacity of the local and national state and of the creativity, competence and commitment of its young people. Marjorie Allen might have approved of that.

Part 2: The welfare of older people since 1948

Liz Lloyd

What needs are particular to later life and who should take responsibility for meeting these? These apparently straightforward questions provoke debate not only about the role and function of the welfare state in its capacity to ward off the 'five giants' but also about the social and cultural values that underpin welfare provision and the social status of older people. In 2010, one of the last policies of the outgoing Labour government was to reform social care for older people, with the aim of altering the relationship between the individual and the state in favour of greater individual responsibility and promoting increased individual choice and control over services. Recent pension reforms have also emphasised individual over state responsibility for ensuring an adequate income in old age. This is therefore an opportune moment to reflect on changes in older people's circumstances as well as on continuities and changes in welfare state provision since the post-war years.

The first most striking contrast between 1948 and now is the difference in life expectancy. One's chances of growing to old age are far greater now than they were in 1948, when average life expectancy at birth for men was sixty-six years and for women seventy years. In 2008, the equivalent figures are 78.3 and 82.1 respectively. Coupled with this, over the past twenty-five years there has been a dramatic increase in life expectancy among the oldest age groups. Life expectancy at age sixty-five is now at its highest level ever for both men and women. If current trends continue men aged sixty-five could expect to live for another 16.9 years on average, and women a further 19.7 years. In 2007, there were 11,000 centenarians and it is estimated that by 2036 the number will rise to 61,000, making them the fastest growing age group in the population (Self, 2008).

Increased life expectancy has profound implications for individual experiences of ageing. However, when changes in patterns of mortality and a reduced birth rate are also taken into account we see a picture of an ageing population, which has profound implications also for welfare policies. The changed age structure of the UK population means that in 2008 for the first time in history the proportion of the population aged below sixteen is lower than that over pensionable age. This change is a crucially important issue for a welfare state funded from taxation. In 1942, when the Beveridge report was written, 20.6 per cent of the population of Great Britain was aged below fifteen, 67.5 per cent were of working age and 12.0 per cent over state pension age. This gave an old age support ratio of 5.6 per cent. By 2004, with the ageing of the 'baby-boom generation' the equivalent support ratio had fallen to 3.3 per cent (Hills, 2006). This reduction in the support ratio has generated concerns – sometimes expressed in somewhat cataclysmic terms – about the affordability of welfare for older people. It is a great irony that the significant progress that has been made towards the goal of eliminating premature death has become recast as the 'problem' of an ageing society. Arguably, the picture is more complex, requiring a wider range of factors to be taken into account.

First, it is important to remember that the baby-boom generation is exactly that – a generation. Overall, birth rates have fallen as longevity has increased and the likelihood is that the proportions of older to working-age people within the population will eventually change again. Projections about the future age structure of the population are very uncertain, as we have no way of foretelling what future birth rates or death rates will be. In addition, it is necessary to consider that the concept of the 'working age' is a political and social artefact, which has proved to be very elastic over time. For example, since the welfare state was founded, the age at which young people leave full-time education has risen several times and recently the age at which women qualify for a state pension has also risen.

It is also important to consider that the concept of support (or dependency) ratios is based on the assumption that retired people are always beneficiaries of and not contributors to the welfare system. However, this is clearly open to challenge in a number of ways. Older people pay taxes on their income and they also make a considerable contribution to the economy, for example in the unpaid care of grandchildren, which enables sons and daughters to take up paid employment, as well as in unpaid work for charitable organisations and community groups. Older people also make up a sizeable proportion of those who provide unpaid care for adult relatives. Buckner and Yeandle (2005) point out that 1.5 million of the 6 million carers identified in the 2001 census are aged over sixty.

Nevertheless, concerns about the increasing numbers of older people and the reduction in support ratios have a profound effect on policy making. We might question why it is that the perception that older people are a burden is so deeply entrenched, whether in the relatively affluent contemporary context or in the impoverished post-war years.

The issue of financial security in old age has remained an issue throughout the past sixty years. Policy debates have consistently focused on the question of entitlements to cash benefits and the relative merits of universal pensions and means-tested benefits as a means of preventing poverty. Financial security has also been at the heart of campaigns by older people's groups and remains so today. Contemporary debates on pension reforms reflect those that took place in the 1940s when retirement pensions were introduced through the National Insurance Act (Hills, 2006).

The spirit of universalism evident in the 1940s was reflected in the flat rate retirement pension, based on individual National Insurance contributions. Indeed, in order to make these contributions affordable for the lowest paid workers, the level of contributory benefits was deliberately set low. In the view of the then minister of National Insurance: 'The speed of the convoy is that of the slowest ship' (Fraser, 1984: 229). The Labour government of the day introduced the retirement pension at the full rate, rather than phase it in over twenty years, as envisaged by Beveridge. This decision generated concerns over whether retirement pensions were affordable, particularly given the insecure state of the post-war economy, and meant that the level of the state retirement pension had to be kept low.

Throughout its history, therefore, the state pension has had to be supplemented with means-tested benefits in order for retired people to avoid living in poverty. Supplementary income arrangements have varied over the years; currently anyone who relies on state benefits in old age is entitled to claim pensioner credits. However, a serious concern about pensioner credits is that an estimated one-third of those entitled to claim it do not, meaning that around 1 million older people are living below the official poverty line (Department for Work and Pensions, 2007b). Campaigns continue to call for action to ensure that people obtain the benefits to which they are entitled (Age Concern and Help the Aged, 2009).

From the outset, gender inequalities have persisted in the provision of pensions and cash benefits. When the welfare state was established it was taken for granted that women's financial security would be ensured through that of their husbands or fathers. Over the years, campaigns for gender equality in pension provision have produced reforms, although women's disadvantaged position within the labour market still generates income inequalities in retirement. The 2007 Pensions Act makes provision for some (mostly women) who give up paid employment to care for children or for sick and disabled relatives through individual savings accounts and carer credits. Carers' organisations have long pointed out that the increased individualisation of pension arrangements and dependence on a combination of earnings-related contributions and savings left most carers facing a bleak future in terms of their own financial security.

Universalism was famously challenged in the 1980s when the Thatcher government decided to de-index pensions from earnings, to cut by half the State Earning-Related Pension Scheme that had been introduced in the 1970s and to encourage private pensions in place of state-supported pensions. It was expected then that the state pension would 'wither on the vine'. This view was maintained for some time after the election of the Labour government in 1997. However, failure to regulate the private market led to mis-selling of private pensions resulting in a loss of income for an estimated 3 million people (Walker and Foster, 2006). Compensation for those who were mis-sold pensions has not made up for the amount of pension lost to individuals, nor does it cover everyone who was affected. The 2007 Pensions Act restored the link between pensions and earnings and confirmed the continuing place of the state pension as a central plank in financial security in retirement. However, it parts company with the Beveridge approach in the idea of the flat-rate contribution, which, it was argued, simply meant that there were never enough resources to push people over the poverty line.

However, the pressure for reform of the pensions system was much wider than concerns about the poorly regulated pensions market. Demographic trends, changed expectations about living standards in retirement, the cost of state provision and the need to encourage personal savings all generated pressure for a different approach and a sense of urgency, as reflected in this statement by Peter Hain (2008), the then secretary of state for work and pensions:

> People are living longer, are more active and expect to be able to enjoy the type of lifestyle in retirement they had while working. Around three quarters of people say they will need more than the State Pension to live on. But actions do not match words – only around four in 10 working age people are saving into a private pension. With increasing longevity, if we don't tackle the challenge of under-saving, by around 2050 we face the nightmare of a pensions crisis with people of working age struggling to pay for an ageing population. The state, individuals and employers all share in the responsibility to avert such a crisis – so we must act decisively now to renew the social contract between us.

Today's pension system still reflects the pattern set out in the Beveridge Report. Retired people still receive a flat-rate pension, based on National Insurance contributions, which is supplemented by an occupational or private pension or savings or means-tested cash benefits from the state. However, the 2007 reforms also produced a new form of contractual arrangement between the individual and the state in the National Pensions Saving Scheme. The reformed pension system can be seen as a response to more flexible or insecure employment patterns, since the scheme is 'portable' and not dependent on long-term employment with a single employer, as well as having the capacity to compensate those who give up paid employment in order to provide care.

What improvements have been made to older people's health? Improved standards of living have, without doubt, been the major influence on health and longevity. However, the introduction of the NHS with health care free at the point of delivery has played a highly significant part in treating the diseases that would have caused premature death and those associated with old age, which previously would have caused suffering. The three major causes of death in Britain in 1948 were heart disease, stroke and infectious diseases. Since then, mortality from all three of these has fallen, cancer now being the biggest single cause of death. However, the added years of life are not necessarily spent in good health (Evandrou, 2005; Evandrou and Falkingham, 2000). The diseases now most commonly associated with old age are heart disease, circulatory and musculo-skeletal diseases and cancer. In addition, rates of cognitive impairment (Alzheimer's disease and other forms of dementia) are greatest in the oldest age groups and there are relatively high levels of depression that only in recent years are being recognised.

As Victor (2005) points out, the majority of older people live relatively independent lives and do not require health care to do so. It is therefore important to guard against making assumptions about illness in old age. However, the numbers of older people requiring health care is an important policy issue. One notable change in the NHS is that specialist geriatric services have been significantly reduced. Whether or not there is a need for such specialist services is a contentious point. There is a strong argument that older people's health care should not be differentiated from that of other age groups but there is a counter argument in favour of retaining specialists who are able to understand the complexities and interrelatedness of age-related health problems.

The improvements in overall life expectancy in Britain throughout the twentieth century have been reflected in improvements in levels of inequality in health between social classes (Marmot et al., 2010; Wilkinson and Pickett, 2009). These remain quite striking, particularly among men. In east Glasgow, for example, average life expectancy at birth for men is 68.1 years, ten years below the national average and for women it is 76.0 years, six years below the national average. Such persistent inequalities raise questions about the role and capacity of welfare services to achieve their aim of combating inequalities.

A further point to consider is older people's usage of services. Evidence of age-related inequalities in health service provision raise questions about older people's disadvantaged position in society and demonstrate that not only do welfare services fail to combat inequalities, they in fact play a role in reinforcing these. Health problems, such as depression, frequently remain undiagnosed or regarded simplistically as an inevitable by-product of ageing. Older people are routinely not offered the same range of treatment options and at the end of life they are under-represented in palliative care and hospice services (Grande et al., 2006). Such age-related inequalities go to the very heart of welfare state values and focus attention on older people's citizenship status and entitlements.

The provision of shelter for people who are vulnerable by reason of age was a core aim of the founders of the welfare state but the history of the workhouse could not be fully eradicated. In the post-war years residential care homes were intended to provide shelter more akin to that of a hotel than a workhouse. However, Townsend's seminal work 'The last refuge' (published in 1962) concluded that residents in care homes were often there not for reasons of frailty but because they were poor. They were often isolated from friends and family, they lacked meaningful occupation, suffered loss of privacy and identity and the capacity for self-determination. Continuing evidence of the abuse of older people in care homes reinforced the drive, which remains today, to enable them to remain in their own homes. Recognition of the effects of institutionalisation can be seen in the numerous policies over the past sixty years, including the 1990 NHS and Community Care Act. The provision of sheltered housing, domiciliary care services, housing adaptations, day care and a range of other services and technical innovations that assist older people in their mobility and their security are all intended to enable them to remain in their own homes (Means and Smith, 1998).

However, institutionalisation, which is generally associated with large-scale institutions, is also evident when services are provided at home. Thus, older people are dependent on the schedules and procedures of care providers rather than being able to determine for themselves how their everyday lives should be conducted, what time they should eat or when they should be helped to go to bed. In addition, it is also the case that the abuse of older people by care staff and by family members continues within their own homes (Eastman and Harris, 2004).

The 1946 National Health Service Act and the 1948 National Assistance Act distinguished between older people who were sick and in need of medical attention and those who were in need of care and attention (Means and Smith, 1998). This distinction is another example of a continuing theme in welfare services for older people, whose entitlement to health services free at the point of delivery depends on the definition given to their need. Today, the labelling of some needs as 'social care' is highly contentious, since it means that older people are obliged to pay for services. Debates surrounding support for older people in need of long-term care encapsulates many of the wider debates about welfare state values, with consideration being given to who should provide care, how eligibility for services should be assessed, how care should be organised and in what location and, perhaps most contentiously, who should pay for it.

Looking back over sixty years, it is striking how the roots of many of the issues currently being debated can be traced to the post-war years. It is also striking how services reflect and sometimes reinforce the socially disadvantaged position of older people. Means and Smith argued that ageism has been embedded in the history of welfare services for elderly people, so that they 'have been a low priority for resources, the services offered have often been of a low standard, they have been patronised by policy-makers and sometimes abused by practitioners' (1998: 331). In 1948, it was hoped that the National Assistance Act would spell an end to the stigma associated with the old system of poor relief but the low take-up of benefits and entitlements suggests that stigma associated with asking for state help persists to the present day.

Today there is increased recognition of older people's rights and individuality and new perspectives on age discrimination. A recent policy debate has focused on the right of older patients to return home on discharge from hospital against medical advice. The right to take such risks is an important aspect of independence and autonomy. However, in the absence of adequate support at home it is likely to be very difficult for many older people to exercise such a choice. Older people's current campaigns reflect the continuing need for equality of opportunity and an end to the patronisation of older people within welfare but also for better quality services, an end to poor standards of care in hospitals and at home, and better advice so that older people are aware of their entitlements to cash benefits.

Without doubt, the welfare state has brought benefits to older people, with better health care, better standards of housing and greater financial security. Now, as when Beveridge published his report in 1942, the vast majority of older people live independently in their own homes and, except for drawing their state pensions, are relatively independent of the welfare state. However, when older people's lives are understood in the contemporary social context it is evident that the welfare state has not brought with it the desired change in their social status and the changed age structure of the population has exacerbated long-standing anxieties about the affordability of welfare. In the post-war years the aim was to provide for those in need of care and attention. Today, such needs remain and the circle still to be squared is how to provide services in ways that promote older people's health, well-being, security and dignity.

Notes

1. *www.poverty.org.uk.*
2. *www.poverty.org.uk.*
3. Letter to *The Times*, 15 July 1944.
4. *The Times*, 23 May 1953.

CONCLUSIONS

Taking Stock

Victoria Winckler

This collection of essays is a timely review of the achievements, and shortcomings, of the British welfare state. So ubiquitous have the various services provided by the welfare state become that their provision is in many ways taken for granted, although there is vigorous debate about the detailed provision of those services. As a measure of the extent to which the welfare state has become ingrained, it is virtually impossible to find among political agendas any credible proposals to dismantle it, either in whole or in part. Even in one of the most contested areas, welfare benefits – where arguments rage about the level of benefit and the conditions attached to its receipt – there are few serious suggestions that welfare support for people who are unemployed should end altogether. Similarly, whilst there is much argument about the role and merits of different types of school (faith, foundation, academy and so on, as highlighted in chapter 3), there are no public proposals that challenge the principle of an 'entitlement' to education.

Indeed, the persistence of the welfare state – despite having undergone not inconsiderable tinkering – is surely an achievement in itself. Chapter after chapter, throughout this book, track that tinkering through successive reforms and initiatives – some of the most radical attempts to restructure the welfare state being during the Thatcher and Major years. Most chapters note that the subsequent Labour government of 1997–2010 continued to reform the welfare state in a similar vein, with increasing marketisation of the NHS for example, constraints on benefits and pensions, and an emphasis on individual choice and responsibility. Nevertheless, I would argue, the welfare state is substantially intact. So is this cause for celebration? It would seem not. There is a striking ambivalence about the achievements of the welfare state found in all the contributions to this book.

On the one hand, there is recognition of the undoubted improvements in people's quality of life brought by the welfare state since 1948. In terms of education, for example, Rees argues that the welfare state has provided the context for an enormous expansion in educational opportunities, and notes that the state has become the provider of those opportunities in ways that would be 'unrecognisable' to those who lived earlier in the twentieth century. Looking at one of the challenges to the welfare state, that of the welfare of children, Butler notes that 'the social conditions of children in the UK have improved beyond recognition since 1948'. Other chapters make similar points.

However, the claims made about the achievements of the welfare state are qualified: various authors rightly point out that the welfare state's achievements are tempered by its shortcomings. Crucially, the welfare state has not succeeded in eradicating Beveridge's 'five giants'. As successive chapters point out, want, squalor, disease, ignorance and idleness all persist today – albeit in some instances in new forms compared with pre-welfare state days. Kenway (chapter 1) is very clear that, from a modern perspective, the welfare state 'most certainly did not' eradicate poverty and cites the proportion of children and pensioners who continue to live in households whose income is below the relative poverty threshold. In discussing health (chapter 2), Sullivan points out that, although life expectancy has increased, the gap between the life expectancy of different social groups has not only persisted but has widened over the last sixty years. Similarly, Rees concludes that notwithstanding its massive achievements 'the education system has fallen short of the ambitions that have been espoused for it' (p. 81). Puzey (chapter 4) and Byrne (chapter 5) also highlight ways in which the welfare state has failed to eradicate, respectively, 'squalor' and 'idleness'. Byrne charts the changes in worklessness over the decades, during which Beveridge's model of the 'idle' as the almost exclusively male, adult constituency of the unemployed has morphed into a more diverse, if still 'idle', group of unemployed, incapacitated, non-working lone parents and NEETS (young people who are not in education, employment or training). Puzey argues that although the nature of the housing crisis has changed since the immediate post-war period, the problems persist not just as street homelessness but as other forms of housing stress and shortage.

That the welfare state has apparently fallen so significantly short is surely a cause for deep concern. How can it be that, after sixty years, some people are still without an adequate home, young people still leave school unable to read and write, and ethnic minority groups do not get the health care to which they are entitled? These are not just rhetorical questions, but are issues that concern ordinary people who, at a most basic level, see the taxes that they pay failing to deliver the services that they expect. The welfare state's failures pose real challenges to its own future.

However, whether the welfare state's failures outweigh its successes is a moot point. Taking a long view, the welfare state has brought unarguable improvements to people's lives. Most of the criticisms of the welfare state in these contributions look through a contemporary lens, in that they use modern standards to appraise the welfare state's achievements. But as Kenway points out, using Beveridge's own standards rather than current ones suggests a rather better performance, at least in terms of eradicating 'want'. Similarly, life expectancy has increased by more than twelve years during this time, homelessness is a fraction of its post-war levels, and so on. If there is any doubt about the changes brought by the welfare state, a reading of accounts of pre-war life, whether fictional or factual, such as the reports of local medical officers, should eliminate it.

The shortcomings are not so much failings of the welfare state per se, but a sign of its limited capacity to eradicate class differences. For example, Rees says, 'Access to educational opportunities remains stubbornly divided according to people's social backgrounds' (p. 81), whilst in terms of health, Sullivan likewise points to the deterioration in the relative position of adults in manual social classes compared with the rest of the population (p. 58). In other words, the tide of well-being may have risen, but the relative position of the socio-economic boats that float upon it has not changed.

This brings us to the second key theme in the book, namely that of inequality. It is clear from the five chapters on challenges that the welfare state has failed to address many inequalities in society. Shaw,

Williams, Smith, Butler and Lloyd all make powerful arguments that the welfare state has not served particular groups – respectively women, ethnic minorities, disabled people, children and older people – well. Indeed, in what is probably the most critical chapter, Williams goes so far as to assert that the principles underpinning the welfare state have 'failed to serve the needs of ethnic minority groups' (p. 142).

It is of course important to remember that the welfare state was a product of the post-war era. It understandably predicated its provision on the socio-economic circumstances of the time. So, for example, the specific needs of ethnic minority groups did not feature in the post-war welfare state because, in 1948, the population was overwhelmingly (and unquestioningly) British. The provision for pensions, unemployment benefits and social care assumed a family unit of working male and non-working female, because that was the dominant household form. The state pension assumed a life expectancy beyond retirement of just a few years, because that was the norm.

What the welfare state did not do, however, was respond and adapt to subsequent and quite dramatic changes in social structure. Shaw charts the increase in the number of lone parents, for example, while Williams highlights the impact of immigration to the UK of various ethnic minority groups. Lloyd does likewise with the increase in the proportion of older people. Thinking and attitudes have also changed during the welfare state's sixty years. Smith points out how conceptions of disability have shifted from the 'medical model' to the 'social model', whilst Butler points out the way in which young people, as present in 1948 as today, were a 'relatively minor consideration' for the architects of the welfare state (p. 196). These critiques are powerful and bring into some question whether the welfare state has been an unequivocally 'good thing' for all groups of people, as might be widely assumed.

There are parallels between the conclusions of chapters in part 2 – on race, gender, disability and age – and part 1's discussions of the 'five giants'. Both sets of contributions conclude that the welfare state has fallen short of expectations, in that whilst there has been a general improvement in socio-economic conditions, the welfare state has not improved the lot of all people equally. Whether the divisions are class, or gender, race, age and disability, not only have some people systematically benefited less from the welfare state than others but in some instances inequalities have widened and become more deeply entrenched.

Rees concludes that it is unrealistic to expect that education can, alone, achieve the kinds of social change that is espoused for it. The point is summed up concisely in a phrase Rees quotes from Bernstein: that 'education cannot compensate for society' (Bernstein, 1970: 344). This conclusion applies just as well to other elements of the welfare state and to inequality by gender, race, age and disability as well as class. Devised and delivered in a post-war society that was riven by class differences, was racist and ageist, was highly patriarchal and viewed disabled people as incapacitated, it is hardly surprising that the welfare state has reflected rather than addressed these issues. What is more surprising is that the changes necessary to ensure that the welfare state does eradicate inequality do not seem to have been clearly articulated, nor has the way in which the welfare state should be part of a wider programme to eliminate inequality.

Perhaps inevitably, the various chapters have relatively little to say about the future directions for the welfare state. Surveys of public opinion suggest that some aspects of the welfare state, notably the NHS, are high in the public's affections whilst other elements, particularly benefits, are much less well regarded. The recent survey and debate on modern social evils undertaken by the Joseph Rowntree Foundation (2009) suggest, however, that the concerns of the public today are less about the 'five giants' and more about behaviour and values – drugs and alcohol, crime and violence, family breakdown, loss of shared values, inequality and lack of community were key themes that emerged. None of these are overtly addressed by the welfare state.

If and how the welfare state will develop in the future is far from clear. The emphasis – at least in recent government policy emanating from Westminster, both under New Labour and since May 2010, the Conservative/Liberal Democrat coalition – on personal responsibility, choice and marketised provision seems unlikely to be reversed in the short to medium term, whichever government is in power, and may well increase. Whether it increases to such an extent that the welfare state is no longer defined by universal and collective provision, (mostly) free at the point of delivery, remains to be seen. Interestingly, recent work on the relative reduction in the value of welfare benefits for the unemployed (Kenway, 2009) argues that the fundamental case for raising the level of job-seeker's allowance (JSA) is a moral and political one, as the evidence on the impact of the value of the benefit on labour market behaviour is inconclusive. Kenway suggests that the failure to up-rate unemployment benefits reduces their role as a 'safety net' for all people, which in turn reduces the public's support for them. The implication of this argument is that the welfare state depends on the universalism and quality of its services to maintain its legitimacy. Targeting of services – to the extent that substantial proportions of the population are excluded from them, and cutting them back, either in monetary value or quality – risks undermining support for those services in the long term. As the financial constraints following the current recession take hold, there is a powerful agenda in favour of cuts and targeting. Elements of the UK welfare state that have been unchallenged for decades, such as child benefit, are being questioned. It remains to be seen what the impact of any cuts will be on support for the welfare state.

In Wales, the direction of travel has been somewhat different. Drakeford (chapter 9) argues very clearly that both Beveridge and Bevan would recognise in Wales today the principles that underpinned the welfare state sixty years ago. Similarly Butler and Lloyd (chapter 10) argue that, in terms of education and young people, Wales has a more 'democratic' and collectivist approach, and has also made concerted attempts to take account of and respond to the needs of children, ethnic minority groups and others. Drakeford implies that popular support for publicly provided services, as well as politics within Wales, is likely to see a broad continuation of the approach taken to date. However, the recession is prompting renewed and vigorous debate about public service reform – for which read reform of the welfare state. Whilst the focus is mainly on delivery (for example, mergers of public bodies, collaboration between providers and greater efficiency), there will undoubtedly be cuts too, in the second decade of the twenty-first century. Free public transport for over sixties and free NHS prescriptions have already been identified as possible casualties of public spending cuts.

Whichever approach is taken wherever in the UK, it is vital that the failings of the welfare state are addressed. The persistence of poverty and injustice within welfare state provision as well as outside is a serious challenge to the public and political support on which the welfare state's future depends. Rees concludes that in Wales, as elsewhere, the welfare state needs to be embedded within a wider programme of restructuring of economic and social opportunities if it is to achieve social justice objectives. Williams (chapter 7) proposes 'welfare frameworks' that are based on local self-determination and empowerment, coupled with much better understanding of multicultural needs and practices. To this can be added the needs of different genders, ages and abilities.

Interesting approaches to the welfare state are emerging from policy and practice on regeneration and community development. Instead of being the deliverer of services to an essentially passive population, the welfare state is also recognised as an employer of large numbers of people and as a tool for improving quality of life. Underlying these new approaches is the idea that recipients of services are not consumers or clients (or even, as the marketisers would have it, customers) but 'co-producers' of the service. 'Co-production' in its formal sense has to date mostly involved people outside paid work and has typically used 'time banking' as the means of recognising service users' contribution. This has tended to limit the wider application and mainstreaming of the co-production approach.

However, a similar principle underlies other developments in the welfare state, particularly in Wales and most notably in housing. Much of Wales's council housing stock is being transferred to mutually owned and controlled housing associations. The large-scale house renovation programmes that then follow the stock transfer are being used to create employment and training for local residents, whilst the purchase of building materials is helping to support local businesses. It is, however, ironic that the transfer of housing out of ambit of the welfare state has been a prerequisite for the home improvements. On a smaller scale there have been similar moves to help socially excluded people to take up employment in the very community programmes that are designed to help them, for example as youth workers. Although there have been calls for public sector employers to build routes into employment for socially excluded groups on a larger scale, these have mostly been unheeded.

The overwhelming conclusion of these chapters seems to be that the British welfare state since its inception has brought unprecedented improvements in socio-economic conditions to the great majority of the population. However, unless the additional, specific steps are taken to ensure that the 'five giants' are eradicated, and that deep-seated inequalities are not perpetuated, then the welfare state will not have succeeded. The recent recession and banking crisis, together with the ensuing impact on the UK's finances, will make this task all the more difficult.

REFERENCES

Abbot, E. and K. Bompas (1943). *The Woman Citizen and Social Security: A Criticism of the Proposals Made in the Beveridge Report as they Affect Married Women*, private publication.

Abel-Smith, B. (1964). *The Hospitals 1800–1948*, London, Heinemann.

Abel-Smith, B. and P. Townsend (1965). *The Poor and the Poorest: A New Analysis of the Ministry of Labour's Family Expenditure Surveys of 1953–4 and 1960*, London, Bell.

Acheson, D. (1998). *Independent Inquiry into Inequalities in Health*, London, The Stationery Office.

Addison, P. (1982). *The Road to 1945*, London, Quartet.

Age Concern and Help the Aged (2009). *More Money in Your Pocket*, London, Age Concern and Help the Aged, *www.ageconcern.org.uk* (accessed 27 March 2009).

Ahmad, W. (ed.) (1993). *'Race' and Health in Contemporary Britain*, Buckingham, Open University Press.

Ainley, P. and B. Bailey (1997). *The Business of Learning: Staff and Student Experiences of Further Education in the 1990s*, London, Cassell.

Aldrich, R. (ed.) (2002). *A Century of Education*, London, Routledge.

Alibhai-Brown, Y. (2000). *After Multiculturalism*, London, Foreign Policy Centre.

Andrews, L. (1999). *Wales Says Yes*, Bridgend, Seren Books.

Atkinson, J. (2005). 'Reaching beyond the New Deal', *Employment Studies*, 2, Institute of Employment Studies, University of Sussex.

Bacon, J. (2002). 'Moving between sickness and unemployment', *Labour Market Trends*, April 2002, 195–205.

Bailey, B. (2002). 'Further education', in R. Aldrich (ed.), *A Century of Education*, London, Routledge Falmer.

Ball, S. J. (1981). *Beachside Comprehensive*, Cambridge, Cambridge University Press.

Ball, S. J. (2008). *The Education Debate*, Bristol, Policy Press.

Banks, O. (1955). *Parity and Prestige in English Secondary Education: A Study in Educational Sociology*, London, Routledge and Kegan Paul.

Barker, K. (2004). *The Barker Review of Housing Supply*, London, HMSO.

Barnes, C. (1991). *Disabled People in Britain and Discrimination*, London, Hurst and Calgary.

Barnett, C. (1996). *The Audit of War: The Illusion and Reality of Britain as a Great Nation*, London, Pan.

Barton, D. (1963). *A Hope for Housing?*, London, Mayflower.

Bates, I. and G. Riseborough (eds) (1993). *Youth and Inequality*, Buckingham, Open University Press.

Beecham, J. (2006). *Beyond Boundaries: Citizen-centred Local Services for Wales*, Cardiff, Welsh Assembly Government.

Bell, D. and A. Christie (2007). 'Funding devolution: the power of money', in A. Tench (ed.), *Devolution and Power in the United Kingdom*, Manchester, Manchester University Press.

Benn, C. and C. Chitty (1996). *Thirty Years On: Is Comprehensive Education Alive and Well or Struggling to Survive?*, London, David Fulton.

Bennett, J., E. Iossa and G. Legrenzi (2003). 'The role of commercial non-profit organisations in the provision of public services', *Oxford Review of Economic Policy*, 19, 335–47.

Bernstein, B. (1970). 'Education cannot compensate for society', *New Society*, 377, 344–7.

Bevan, A. (1952). *In Place of Fear*, New York, Simon & Schuster.

Beveridge, W. (1942). *Social Insurance and Allied Services Report*, Cmd 6404, London, HMSO.

Beveridge, W. (1944). *Full Employment in a Free Society*, London, Allen and Unwin.

Bhavnani, K. and R. Bhavnani (1985). 'Racism and resistance in Britain', in D. Coates, G. Johnson and R. Bush (eds), *A Socialist Anatomy of Britain*, Cambridge, Polity Press.

Blair, T. (1998). *The Third Way: New Politics for a New Century*, London, Fabian Society.

Blakemore, K. (2003). *Social Policy: An Introduction*, 2nd edn, Milton Keynes, Open University Press.

Blunkett, D. (2005). 'A new England: an English identity in Britain', speech to the Institute of Public Policy Research, March 2005, *www.ippr.org.uk* (accessed 10 September 2008).

Bochel, H., C. Bochel, R. Page and R. Sykes (2005). *Social Policy: Issues and Developments*, Harlow, Pearson Education.

Bradshaw, J. and J. Millar (1990). *Lone-parent Families in the UK; Final Report to DSS, Volume 1*, London, HMSO.

Bradshaw, J., S. Middleton, A. Davis, N. Oldfield, N. Smith, L. Cusworth and J. Williams (2008). *A Minimum Income Standard for Britain: What People Think*, York: Joseph Rowntree Foundation, *http://www.jrf.org.uk/bookshop/eBooks/2226-income-poverty-standards. pdf* (accessed 1 January 2009).

Breen, R. (ed.) (2004). *Social Mobility in Europe*, Oxford, Oxford University Press.

Briggs, A. (1961). 'The welfare state in historical perspective', *European Journal of Sociology*, 2, 221–58.

Brivati, B. and R. Heffernan (eds) (2000). *The Labour Party: A Centenary History*, Basingstoke, Macmillan.

Brown, P. and A. Hesketh (2004). *The Mismanagement of Talent: Employability and Jobs in the Knowledge Economy*, Oxford, Oxford University Press.

Bryan, B., S. Dadzie and S. Scafe (1985; 1992). *The Heart of the Race*, London, Virago Press.

Buckner, L. and S. Yeandle (2005). *Older Carers in the UK*, London, Carers UK.

Butler, I. (2007). 'Children's policy in Wales', in C. Williams (ed.), *Social Policy for Social Welfare Practice in a Devolved Wales*, Birmingham, BASW/Venture Press.

Butler, I. and M. Drakeford (2001). 'Which Blair project: communitarianism, social authoritarianism and social work', *Journal of Social Work*, 1, 7–20.

Butler, I. and M. Drakeford (2005). *Scandal, Social Policy and Social Welfare*, 2nd edn, Bristol, Policy Press.

Butler, I and R. Pugh (2004). 'The politics of social work research', in R. Lovelock, K. Lyons and J. Powell (eds), *Reflecting on Social Work: Discipline and Profession*, Aldershot, Ashgate.

Butler, J. (1992). *Patients, Policies and Politics*, London, Open University Press.

Calvert, H. (1978). *Social Security Law*, London, Sweet and Maxwell.

Carpenter, M. (1980). 'Left orthodoxy and the politics of health', *Capital and Class*, 11, 73–98.

Castles, F. G., S. Leibfried, J. Lewis and H. Obinger (eds) (2010). *The Oxford Handbook of the Welfare State*, Oxford, Oxford University Press.

Child Poverty Action Group (2004). *Poverty: The Facts*, *http://www.cpag.org.uk* (accessed 1 December 2008).

Child Poverty Action Group (2008). *Poverty: The Stats*, *http://www.cpag.org.uk/info/briefingspoverty/* (accessed 1 December 2008).

Clarke, K. (2007). 'New Labour: family policy and gender', in C. Annesley, F. Gains and K. Rummery (eds), *Women and New Labour Engendering Politics and Policy?*, Bristol, Policy Press.

Coburn, D. (2000). 'Income inequality, social cohesion and the health status of populations: the role of neo-liberalism', *Social Science and Medicine*, 51, 135–46.

Coburn, D. (2004). 'Beyond the income inequality hypothesis: class, neo-liberalism, and health inequalities', *Social Science and Medicine*, 58, 41–56.

Commission for Racial Equality (2006). *At the Turning of the Tide*, London, Commission for Racial Equality.

Commission for Racial Equality (2007). *A Lot Done, A Lot to Do*, London, Commission for Racial Equality.

Commission for Rural Communities (2007). *A8 Migrant Worker in Rural Areas*, Briefing Paper, *http://www.ruralcommunities.gov.uk* (accessed 21 March 2009).

Commission of the European Communities (2008). *Implementation of the Barcelona Objectives Concerning Childcare Facilities for Pre-school-age Children*, COM 638 final, *http://register.consilium.europa.eu/pdf/en/08* (accessed 10 April 2010).

Conservative Research Department (1951). *All the Answers to 100 Vital Questions*, London, Conservative Research Department.

Cook, R. (1988). *Life Begins at 40: In Defence of the NHS*, London, Fabian Society.

Cooper, A. (2008). 'Welfare: dead, dying or just transubstantiated?', *Soundings*, 38, 29–41.

Coote, A. (2009). 'Green well fair', *Bevan Foundation Review*, 12, 6–7.

Coote, A. and J. Franklin (2009). *Green Well Fair: Three Economies for Social Justice*, London: New Economics Foundation.

Cox, A. and M. Mead (eds) (1975). *A Sociology of Medical Practice*, London, Collier-Macmillan.

Craig, G. (2007). '"Cunning, unprincipled, loathsome": the racist tail wags the welfare dog', *Journal of Social Policy*, 36, 605–23.

Crowley, A. (2007). 'Child poverty in Wales', in C. Williams (ed.), *Social Policy for Social Welfare Practice in a Devolved Wales*, Birmingham, Venture Press.

Curtis Committee (1946). *Report of the Care of Children Committee*, presented by the Secretary of State for the Home Department by the Minister for Health and the Minister for Education by the command of His Majesty, London, HMSO.

Dale, J. and P. Foster (1986). *Feminists and State Welfare*, London, Routledge and Kegan Paul.

Davey-Smith, G., D. Dorling, R. Mitchell and M. Shaw (2002). 'Health inequalities in Britain: continuing increases up to the end of the 20th century', *Journal of Epidemiology and Community Health*, 56, 434–5.

Deacon, B. (1983). *Socialism and Social Policy*, London, Pluto Press.

Deaton, A. (2001). 'Relative deprivation, inequality, and mortality', unpublished paper, Centre for Health and Well-being, Princeton University.

Department for Education and Skills (1998). *National Childcare Strategy*, *http://www.poverty/org.uk/policies/childcare* (accessed 12 April 2004).

Department for Education and Skills (2003). *Every Child Matters*, London, The Stationery Office.

Department for Education and Skills (2005). *Extended Schools: Access to Services and Opportuntiies for All*, *http://www.teacher.net.gov.uk/* (accessed 14 December 2008).

Department for Education and Skills (2007). *Every Parent Matters*, London, The Stationery Office.

Department for Work and Pensions (2006a). *Helping Lone Parents*, London, Department of Work and Pensions, *http://www.dwp.gov. uk/welfarereform/c3.asp* (accessed 3 December 2008).

Department for Work and Pensions (2006b). *Security in Retirement: Towards a New Pension System*, Cm 6841, London, Department of Work and Pensions.

Department for Work and Pensions (2007a). *Opportunity for All: Indicators Update 2007*, London, Department for Work and Pensions.

Department for Work and Pensions (2007b). *Ready for Work: Full Employment in Our Generation*, Cm 7290, *http://www.dwp.gov.uk/welfarereform/readyforwork/07chapter2.htm* (accessed 3 December 2008).

Department for Work and Pensions (2008a). *No One Written Off: Reforming Welfare to Reward Responsibility*, Cm 7363, *www.dwp.gov.uk/docs/noonewrittenoff-summary.pdf* (accessed 27 March 2009).

Department for Work and Pensions (2008b). *Raising Expectations and Increasing Support: Reforming Welfare for the Future*, Cm 7506, *http://www.dwp.gov.uk/welfarereform/raisingexpectations/* (accessed 27 March 2009).

Department of Health (1962). *A Hospital Plan for England and Wales*, Cmnd. 1604, London, HMSO.

Department of Health (2008). *Tackling Health Inequalities: 2005–07 Policy and Data Update for the 2010 National Target*, London, Department of Health.

Devine, P., A. Pearmain and D. Purdy (eds) (2009). *Feelbad Britain: How to Make it Better*, London, Lawrence and Wishart.

DHSS (1980). *Inequalities in Health: Report of a Research Working Group* (The 'Black Report'), *http://www.sochealth.co.uk/Black/black.htm* (accessed 7 May 2012).

Dilnot, A.W., J. A. Kay and C. N. Morris (1984). *The Reform of Social Security*, Oxford, Oxford University Press.

Disabled People's International (1993). 'Constitution', *http://v1.dpi.org/lang-en/index?page=4* (accessed 4 January 2008).

DoH/DCSF (2008). *National Child Measurement Programme: 2006/07 School Year, Headline Results*, The Information Centre, *http://www.ic.nhs.uk/* (accessed 1 December 2008).

Doherty, J., D. Manley, E. Graham, R. Hiscock and P. Boyle (2005). *Mixing Housing Tenures: Is it Good for Social Well-being?*, St Andrews,

Centre for Housing Research, *urbanrim.org.uk/cache/Mixing%20 Tenure%20(draft).pdf* (accessed 30 April 2012).

Donkin, A., P. Goldblatt and K. Lynch (2002). *Inequalities in Life Expectancy by Social Class 1972–1999*, London, Office for National Statistics.

Dorling, D. (2010). *Injustice: Why Social Inequality Persists*, Bristol, Policy Press.

Drakeford, M. (2000). *Privatisation and Social Welfare*, London, Longman.

Drakeford, M. (2005). 'Health policy in Wales: making a difference in conditions of difficulty', *Critical Social Policy*, 26, 543–61.

Drakeford, M. (2007a). 'Governance and social policy', in C. Williams (ed.), *Social Policy for Social Welfare Practice in a Devolved Wales*, Birmingham, Venture Press.

Drakeford, M. (2007b). 'Social justice in a devolved Wales', *Benefits*, 15, 171–8.

Drakeford, M. and P. Chaney (2004). 'Making social policy in Wales', in C. Bochel, N. Ellison and M. Powell (eds), *Social Policy Review*, Bristol, Policy Press.

DSS (1998). *A New Contract for Welfare*, London, The Stationery Office.

Dwelly, T. (2006). 'Social housing isn't working', in T. Dwelly and J. Cowans (eds), *Rethinking Social Housing*, London, Smith Institute.

Dwyer, P. (2004). *Understanding Social Citizenship: Themes and Perspectives for Policy and Practice*, Bristol, Policy Press.

Eastman, M. and J. Harris (2004). *Placing Elder Abuse within the Context of Citizenship: A Policy Discussion Paper*, London, Action on Elder Abuse.

Egan, D. (2007). *Combating Child Poverty in Wales: Are Effective Education Strategies in Place?*, York, Joseph Rowntree Foundation.

Elliott, L. and D. Atkinson (2007). *Fantasy Island*, London, Constable.

Ellison, N. (2000). 'Labour and welfare politics', in B. Brivati and R. Heffernan (eds), *The Labour Party: A Centenary History*, Basingstoke, Macmillan.

English, J. (1992). 'Building for the masses', in C. Grant (ed.), *Built to Last? Reflections on British Housing Policy*, London, ROOF Magazine.

Equalities Review (2007). *Fairness and Freedom*, London, The Stationery Office.

Essex, S., B. Smith and P. Williams (2008). *Affordable Housing in Wales: A Report to the Deputy Minister for Housing*, Cardiff, Welsh Assembly Government.

Evandrou, M. (2005). 'Health and wellbeing', in *Focus on Older People*, London, Office for National Statistics.

Evandrou, M. and J. Falkingham (2000). *Looking Back to Look Forward: Lessons from Four Birth Cohorts for Ageing in the 21st Century*, London, Office for National Statistics.

Felstead, A., D. Gallie, F. Green and Y. Zhou (2007). *Skills at Work 1986–2006*, Oxford, SKOPE.

Ferguson, R. (2004). 'Discourses of exclusion: reconceptualising participation among young people', *Journal of Social Policy*, 33, 289–320.

Finch, J. and D. Groves (1983). *A Labour of Love, Woman, Work and Caring*, London, Routledge and Kegan Paul.

Fisk, M. (2000). 'Historical perspectives on housing development', in R. Smith, T. Stirling and P. Williams (eds), *Housing in Wales: The Policy Agenda in an Era of Devolution*, Coventry, Chartered Institute of Housing.

Fitz, J., B. Davies and J. Evans (2006). *Education Policy and Social Reproduction: Class Inscription and Symbolic Control*, London, Routledge.

Fleurbaey, M. and E. Schokkaert (2009). 'Unfair inequalities in health and healthcare', *Journal of Health Economics*, 28, 73–90.

Floud, J., A. H. Halsey and F. M. Martin (1956). *Social Class and Educational Opportunity*, London, Heinemann.

Foot, M. (1973). *Aneurin Bevan: 1945–1960*, London, Paladin.

Forbes, I. (ed.) (2001). *Health Inequalities: Poverty and Policy*, London, ALSISS.

Fothergill, S. and I. Wilson (2007). 'A million off incapacity benefit: how achievable is Labour's target?', *Cambridge Journal of Economics*, 31, 1007–23.

Fraser, D. (1984). *The Evolution of the British Welfare State*, 2nd edn, Basingstoke, Macmillan.

Fraser, D. (2009). *The Evolution of the British Welfare State*, 4th edn, Basingstoke, Macmillan.

Freud, D. (2007). *Reducing Dependency, Increasing Opportunity: Options for the Future of Welfare to Work*, London, Department of Work and Pensions.

Furedi, F. and J. Bristow (2008). *Licensed to Hug: How Child Protection Policies are Poisoning the Relationship between the Generations and Damaging*, London, Civitas.

Galston, W. A. (2005). 'Conditional citizenship', in L. M. Mead and C. Beem (eds), *Welfare Reform and Political Theory*, New York, Russell Sage Foundation.

Garrett, P. M. (1999). 'Mapping child-care social work in the final years of the twentieth century: a critical response to the "looking after children" system', *British Journal of Social Work*, 29, 27–47.

Garrett, P. M. (2007). '"Making anti-social behaviour": a fragment on the evolution of ASBO politics', *British Journal of Social Work*, 37, 839–56.

Giddens, A. (1998). *The Third Way: The Renewal of Social Democracy*, Cambridge, Polity Press.

Giddens, A. (2000). *The Third Way and its Critics*, Cambridge, Polity Press.

Gilroy, B. (1976). *Black Teacher*, London, Cassell.

Gilroy, P. (1998). *There Ain't No Black in the Union Jack*, London, Routledge.

Glendinning, C. and J. Millar (1987). *Women and Poverty in Britain*, Brighton, Wheatsheaf.

Glennerster, H. (1995). *British Social Policy since 1945*, Oxford, Blackwell.

Glennerster, H. (2004). 'Poverty policy from 1900 to the 1970s', in H. Glennerster, J. Hills, D. Piachaud and J. Webb (eds), *One Hundred Years of Poverty and Policy*, York, Joseph Rowntree Foundation.

Goodhart, D. (2006a). *Progressive Nationalism: Citizenship and the Left*, London, Demos.

Goodhart, D. (2006b). 'National anxieties', *Prospect Magazine*, 123, June.

Goodin, R. E. (1985). *Protecting the Vulnerable: A Re-analysis of Our Social Responsibilities*, Chicago, University of Chicago Press.

Goodin, R. E. (1988). *Reasons for Welfare: The Political Theory of the Welfare State*, Princeton, Princeton University Press.

Gorard, S. and G. Rees (2002). *Creating a Learning Society? Learning Careers and Policies for Lifelong Learning*, Bristol, Policy Press.

Gordon, D. et al. (2000). *Social Exclusion in Britain*, York, Joseph Rowntree Trust.

Gordon, D., S. Middleton and J. R. Bradshaw (2002). *Millennium Survey of Poverty and Social Exclusion, 1999* [computer file], 2nd edn, Colchester, Essex: UK Data Archive [distributor].

Gough, I. (2000). 'Social welfare and competitiveness', in C. Pierson and F. G. Castles (eds), *The Welfare State Reader*, 2nd edn, Cambridge, Polity Press.

Government Equalities Office (2008a). *Women's Representation in the UK FactSheet, http://www.equalities.gov.uk/research_facts_and_figures/ factsheets.aspx* (accessed 26 March 2009).

Government Equalities Office (2008b). *What Has the Government Achieved for Women?*, factsheet, *http://www.equalities.gov.uk/research_ facts_and_figures/factsheets.aspx* (accessed 26 March 2009).

Graham, H. (2007). 'Women's poverty and caring', in C. Glendinning and J. Millar (eds), *Women and Poverty in Britain*, Brighton, Wheatsheaf.

Grande, G. E., M. C. Farquhar, S. I. G. Barclay and C. J. Todd (2006). 'The influence of patient and carer age in access to palliative care services', *Age and Ageing*, 35, 3, 267–73.

Greer, S. L. (2004). *Territorial Politics and Health Policy: UK Health Policy in Comparative Perspective*, Manchester, Manchester University Press.

Greer, S. L. (2008). 'Devolution and divergence in UK health policies', *British Medical Journal*, 337, 78–80.

Greer, S. L. and D. Rowland (2007). *Devolving Policy, Diverging Values?*, London, Nuffield Trust.

Gregg, P. (2008). *Realising Potential: A Vision for Personalised Conditionality and Support*, London, Department of Work and Pensions.

Griffith, B., S. Iliffe and G. Rayner (1987). *Banking on Sickness: Commercial Medicine in Britain and the USA*, London, Lawrence and Wishart.

Griffiths, J. (1975). 'Welsh politics in my lifetime', in E. Jones (ed.), *James Griffiths and his Times*, Cardiff, Labour Party Wales.

Griffiths, R. (1981). *Turning to London: Labour's Attitude to Wales 1898–1956*, Abertridwr, Welsh Republican Socialist Movement.

Griffiths, R. (1985). 'The left and the national question in Wales', unpublished MA thesis, Cardiff University.

Griggs, J. with R. Walker (2008). *The Costs of Child Poverty for Individuals and Society: A Literature Review*, York, Joseph Rowntree Foundation.

Hain, P. (2008). Press statement prior to the second reading of the Pensions Bill in the House of Commons, 7 January. London, Department of Work and Pensions.

Hantrais, L. (2007). *Social Policy in the European Union*, 3rd edn, Basingstoke, Palgrave Macmillan.

Harrington , B., K. Smith, D. Hunter, L. Marks, T. Blackman, L. McKee, A. Greene, E. Elliott and G. Williams (2009). 'Health inequalities in England, Scotland and Wales: stakeholders' accounts and policy compared', *Public Health*, 123, 24–8.

Harris, J. (1977). *William Beveridge*, Oxford, Clarendon Press.

Harris, J. (1981). 'Social policy making in Britain during the Second World War', in W. Mommsen (ed.), *The Emergence of the Welfare State in Britain and Germany*, London: Croom Helm.

Hart, J. T. (1975). 'The inverse care law', in S. Cox and M. Mead (eds), *A Sociology of Medical Practice*, London, Collier-Macmillan.

Hart, J. T. (1988). *A New Kind of Doctor*, London, Merlin Press.

Hayek, F. A. (2000). 'The meaning of the welfare state', in C. Pierson and F. G. Castles (eds), *The Welfare State Reader*, 2nd edn, Cambridge, Polity Press.

Helm, T. (2011). 'Shirley Williams plunges NHS reforms into fresh turmoil', *Guardian*, 3 September, *http://www.guardian.co.uk/politics/2011/sep/03/shirley-williams-nhs-reforms-turmoil* (accessed 5 September 2011).

Henderson, P. and R. Kaur (1999). *Rural Racism*, London, CDF/SIA.

Her Majesty's Stationery Office (1998). *Meeting the Childcare Challenge: A Childcare Strategy for Scotland, http://www.archive.official-documents.co.uk/document/cm39/3958/3958.htm* (accessed 22 April 2009).

Heywood, A. (2004). *Political Theory: An Introduction*, 3rd edn, Basingstoke, Palgrave.

Heywood, J. S. (1978). *Children in Care: The Development of the Service for the Deprived Child*, London, Routledge and Kegan Paul.

Higgins, J. (1988). *The Business of Medicine*, London, Macmillan.

Hills, J. (2006). *From Beveridge to Turner: Demography, Distribution and the Future of Pensions in the UK*, CASE/110, London, Centre for Analysis of Social Exclusion, London School of Economics and Political Science.

Hills, J. (2007). *Ends and Means: Where Next for Social Housing?*, London, Centre For Analysis of Social Exclusion, London School of Economics and Political Science.

Hills, J., J. Ditch and H. Glennerster, H. (1994). *Beveridge and Social Security: An International Retrospective*, Oxford, Clarendon Press.

Hills, J. et al. (2010). *An Anatomy of Economic Inequality in the UK: Report of the National Equality Panel*, London: Government Equalities Office.

Hirsch, D. (2006). *What Will it Take to End Child Poverty? Firing on All Cylinders*, York, Joseph Rowntree Foundation.

HM Revenue and Customs (2007). *Child and Working Tax Credit Statistics, http://www.hmrc.gov.uk/stats/personal-tax-credits/cwtc-dec07. pdf* (accessed 23 July 2008).

HM Treasury (2006). *Public Expenditure: Statistical Analyses, http://www. hm-treasury.gov.uk/media/C/E/cm6811_comp.pdf* (accessed 23 July 2008).

HM Treasury, DfES, DWP and DTI (2004). *Choice for Parents, the Best Start for Children: A Ten Year Strategy for Childcare, http://www. everychildmatters.gov.uk/files* (accessed 22 April 2009).

HM Treasury/ DWP/ DCSF (2008). *Ending Child Poverty: Everybody's Business*, London, HM Treasury.

HMSO (1956). *Report of the Committee of Enquiry into the Cost of the National Health Service* (chairman: C. W. Guillebaud), London, HMSO.

Hoggart, L. and S. Vergeris (2008). 'Lone parents and the challenge to make work pay', in J. Strelitz and R. Lister (eds), *Why Money Matters: Family Income, Poverty and Children's Lives*, London, Save the Children.

Holmans, A. (2003). *Who's Counting? Demand for Housing in Wales 1998–2016*, London, Council of Mortgage Lenders.

Hosain, M. and E. Breen (2007). *New Deal Plus for Lone Parents Qualitative Evaluation*, Leeds, Department of Work and Pensions research report 426, London, Department for Work and Pensions.

House of Commons Health Committee (2009). *Third Report: Health Inequalities, http://www.publications.parliament.uk/pa/cm200809/cmselect/cmhealth/286/28602.htm* (accessed 7 May 2012).

Hunter, C. and J. Nixon (2001). 'Taking the blame and losing the home: women and anti-social behaviour', *Journal of Social Welfare and Family Law*, 23, 4, 395–410.

Hunter, D. (2009). 'The case against choice and competition', *Health Economics, Policy and Law*, 4, 489–501.

Iliffe, S. (1988). *Strong Medicine: Health Politics for the Twenty-first Century*, London, Lawrence and Wishart.

Institute for Fiscal Studies (2007). *Fiscal Facts, http://www.ifs.org.uk/ff/indexben.php* (accessed 21 January 2009).

Istance, D. and G. Rees (1994). 'Education and training in Wales: problems and paradoxes revisited', *Contemporary Wales*, 7, 7–27.

Jacobs, S. (1985). 'Race, empire and the welfare state: council housing and racism', *Critical Social Policy*, 13, 6–28.

Jay, D. (1937). *The Socialist Case*, London, Faber and Faber.

Jones, G. E. (1982). *Controls and Conflicts in Welsh Secondary Education 1889–1944*, Cardiff, University of Wales Press.

Jones, G. E. (1990). *Which Nation's Schools? Direction and Devolution in Welsh Education in the Twentieth Century*, Cardiff, University of Wales Press.

Jones, G. E. (1997). *The Education of a Nation*, Cardiff, University of Wales Press.

Jones, G. E. and G. W. Roderick (2003). *A History of Education in Wales*, Cardiff, University of Wales Press.

Jones, M. (1991). *A Radical Life: The Biography of Megan Lloyd George*, London, Hutchinson.

Joseph Rowntree Foundation (2007). *Monitoring Poverty and Social Exclusion in Wales 2007*, York, Joseph Rowntree Foundation.

Joseph Rowntree Foundation (2009). *Contemporary Social Evils*, Bristol, Policy Press.

Kenway, P. (2008). *Addressing In-work Poverty*, York, Joseph Rowntree Foundation.

Kenway, P. (2009). *Should Adult Benefit for Unemployment Now Be Raised?*, York, Joseph Rowntree Foundation.

Kerchoff, A., K. Fogelman, D. Crook and D. Reeder (1996). *Going Comprehensive in England and Wales: A Study of Uneven Change*, London, Woburn Press.

Kilkey, M. (2006). 'New Labour and reconciling work and family life: making it a father's business?', *Social Policy and Society*, 5, 167–85.

Klein, R. (1989). *The Politics of the NHS*, London, Longman.

Kynaston, D. (2007). *Austerity Britain: 1945–51*, London: Bloomsbury.

Labour No Assembly Campaign Wales (1979). 'Facts to beat fantasies', Blackwood, Labour No Assembly Campaign Wales.

Lammi-Taskula, J. (2006). 'Nordic men on parental leave: can the welfare state change gender relations?', in A. Ellingsaeter and A. Leira (eds), *Politicising Parenthood in Scandinavia: Gender Relations in Welfare States*, Bristol, Policy Press.

Le Grand, J. (2007). 'The giants of excess: challenges to a nation's health', *Journal of the Royal Statistical Society*, 171, 843–56.

Le Grand, J. (2009). 'Choice and competition in publicly funded health care', *Health Economics, Policy and Law*, 4, 479–88.

Le Grand, J. and D. Winter (1987). 'The middle classes and the welfare state under Conservative and Labour governments', *Journal of Public Policy*, 6, 399–430.

Levitas, R. (1996). 'The concept of social exclusion and the new Durkheimian hegemony', *Critical Social Policy*, 16, 5–20.

Levitas, R. (2005). *The Inclusive Society? Social Exclusion and New Labour*, Basingstoke, Palgrave Macmillan.

Levy, A. (2004). *Small Island*, London, Headline Book Publishing.

Lewis, G., S. Gerwitz and J. Clark (2000). *Multiculturalism and Social Policy in 'Rethinking Social Policy'*, London, Sage.

Liachowitz, C. H. (1988). *The Social Construction of Disability*, Philadelphia, University of Pennsylvania Press.

Lister, R. (2006). 'Children (but not women) first: New Labour, child welfare and gender', *Critical Social Policy*, 26, 315–35.

Lister, R., F. Williams, A. Anttonen, J. Bussemaker, U. Gerhard, J. Heinen, S. Johansson, A. Leira, B. Siim and C. Tobio with A. Gavanas (2007). *Gendering Citizenship in Western Europe*, Bristol, Policy Press.

Little, K. (1947). *Negroes in Britain*, London, Routledge Kegan Paul.

Lloyd, T. (2007). 'Housing', in J. Cruddas et al., *Closer to Equality? Assessing New Labour's Record on Equality after 10 Years in Government*, London, Compass.

Local Government Data Unit (2008). *Welsh Housing Statistics 2007*, *http://www.dataunitwales.gov.uk/Documents/Publications/lgd02010_Welsh_Housing_Statistics_2007_eng.pdf* (accessed 29 October 2009).

McCleod, M., D. Owen and C. Kahamis (2001). *Black and Minority Ethnic Voluntary and Community Organisations: Their Role and Future Development in England and Wales*, London, Policy Studies Institute.

McCrone, D. (2006). 'Who do we think we are?', in Commission for Racial Equality, *At the Turning of the Tide*, London, Commission for Racial Equality.

McCulloch, G. (1991). *Philosophers and Kings: Education for Leadership in Modern Britain*, Cambridge, Cambridge University Press.

McCulloch, G. (1998). *Failing the Ordinary Child? The Theory and Practice of Working-class Secondary Education*, Buckingham, Open University Press.

MacDonald, R. (ed.) (1997). *Youth, the Underclass and Social Exclusion*, London, Routledge.

McIntosh, M. (2006). 'Feminism and social policy', in C. Pierson and F. G. Castles (eds), *The Welfare State Reader*, 2nd edn, Cambridge, Polity Press.

MacKay, R. R. (1998). 'Unemployment as exclusion: unemployment as choice', in P. Lawless, R. Martin and S. Hardy (eds), *Unemployment and Social Exclusion*, London, Jessica Kingsley.

McLaughlin, E. and G. Boucher (2007). 'Rising or falling to the challenges of diversity in Europe? Social justice and differentiated citizenship', *Social Policy Review*, 19, 221–40.

McLean, I. (2005). *The Fiscal Crisis of the United Kingdom*, Basingstoke, Palgrave.

McPherson, W. (1998). *Inquiry into the Death of Stephen Lawrence*, London, HMSO.

Malpass, P. (2004). '50 years of British housing policy: leaving or leading the welfare state?', *European Journal of Housing Policy*, 4, 209–27.

Marmot, M. et al. (2010). *Fair Society, Healthy Lives* ('The Marmot review: executive summary'), *www.ucl.ac.uk/marmotreview* (accessed 24 March 2010).

Marshall, T. H. (1963). 'Citizenship and social class', in T. H. Marshall *Sociology at the Crossroads and Other Essays*, London: Heinemann.

Marshall, T. H. (1972). 'Value problems of welfare capitalism', *Journal of Social Policy*, 1, 15–32.

Mead, L. (2000). 'The new politics of the new poverty', in C. Pierson and F. G. Castles (eds), *The Welfare State Reader*, 2nd edn, Cambridge, Polity Press.

Mead, L. M. (1997). *From Welfare to Work*, London, IEA.

Means, R. and R. Smith (1998). *From Poor Law to Community Care: The Development of Welfare Services for Elderly People 1939–1971*, 2nd edn, Bristol, Policy Press.

Melzer, D., B. McWilliams, C. Brayne, T. Johnson and J. Bond (1999). 'Profile of disability in elderly people: estimates from a longitudinal study', *British Medical Journal*, 318, 1108–111.

Millar, J. (1987). 'Lone mothers', in C. Glendinning and J. Millar (eds), *Women and Poverty in Britain*, Brighton, Wheatsheaf.

Millar, J. (2003). 'Employment policies for lone parents', in J. Millar and M. Evans, *Lone Parents and Employment: International Comparisons of What Works*, London, Department for Work and Pensions.

Mirza, H. S. (1997). *Black British Feminism*, London, Routledge.

Mirza, H. S. and D. Reay (2000). 'Spaces and places of black educational desire: rethinking black supplementary schools as a new social movement', *Sociology*, 345, 521–44.

Mitchell, R., M. Shaw and D. Dorling (2000). *Inequalities in Life and Death: What If Britain Were More Equal?*, Bristol, Policy Press.

Mooney, G. and C. Williams (2007). 'Forging new "ways of life": social policy and nation building in devolved Scotland and Wales', *Critical Social Policy*, 26, 587–607.

Morgan, K. O. (1982). *Rebirth of a Nation, Wales: 1880–1980*, Oxford, Oxford University Press.

Morgan, K. O. (1995). *Democracy in Wales from Dawn to Deficit*, Cardiff, British Broadcasting Corporation.

Morgan, R. (2006). *Wales Can Do It*, Cardiff, Welsh Assembly Government.

Morris, J. (1991). *Pride against Prejudice*, London, Women's Press.

Murray, C. (1990). *The Emerging British Underclass*, London, Institute of Economic Affairs.

Murray, C. (2000). 'The two wars against poverty', in C. Pierson and F. G. Castles (eds), *The Welfare State Reader*, 2nd edn, Cambridge, Polity Press.

National Assembly for Wales (2001). *Better Homes for People in Wales*, Cardiff, National Assembly for Wales.

National Assembly for Wales (2005). *The Official Record of the National Assembly for Wales, 9/02/05*, Cardiff, National Assembly for Wales.

Navarro, V. and L. Shi (2001). 'The political context of social inequalities and health', *Social Science and Medicine*, 52, 481–91.

No Turning Back Group (1988). *The NHS: A Suitable Case for Treatment*, London, Conservative Political Centre.

Northern Childcare Partnership (2009). DHSS, Training and Employment Agency and Department of Education Northern Ireland (1999). *Children First: The Northern Ireland Childcare Strategy, http://northernchildcare.compublications.htm* (accessed 22 April 2009).

OECD (2008). *Family Database, http://www.oecd.org/els/social/family/database* (accessed 30 October 2008).

Office for National Statistics (2004). *The Health of Children and Young People*, London, Office for National Statistics.

Office for National Statistics (2008a). *Social Trends*, 38, *http://www.statistics.gov.uk/socialtrends38* (accessed 2 December 2008).

Office for National Statistics (2008b). *Gender Work and Family, http://www.statistics.gov.uk/* (accessed 26 March 2009).

Oliver, M. (1996). *Understanding Disability: From Theory to Practice*, London, MacMillan.

Oliver, M. and C. Barnes (1998). *Disabled People and Social Exclusion: From Exclusion to Inclusion*, London, Longman.

Osborne, S. (2007). 'Work-focused interviews: recent rules and research', *Welfare Rights Bulletin*, 198, London, Child Poverty Action Group.

Owen, D. (1948). *Guide to the National Insurance Act 1946*, London: New Chronicle.

Palmer, G., T. MacInnes and P. Kenway (2008). *Monitoring Poverty and Social Exclusion 2008*, York: Joseph Rowntree Foundation, *http://www.npi.org.uk/reports/mpse%2008.pdf* (accessed 1 December 2008).

Parekh, B. (2000). *The Future of Multi-ethnic Britain*, London, Runnymede Trust.

Parker, R. A. (1983). 'The gestation of reform: the Children Act 1948', in P. Bean and S. MacPherson (eds), *Approaches to Welfare*, London, Routledge and Kegan Paul.

Parmar, P. (1982). 'Gender, race and class: Asian women and resistance', in Centre for Contemporary Cultural Studies, *The Empire Strikes Back: Race and Racism in 70s Britain*, London, Routledge.

Pascal, G. (1986). *Social Policy: A Feminist Analysis*, Basingstoke, Tavistock.

Pateman, C. (2006). 'The patriarchal welfare state', in C. Pierson and F. G. Castles (eds), *The Welfare State Reader*, 2nd edn, Cambridge, Polity Press.

Paterson, L. and C. Iannelli (2007a). 'Patterns of absolute and relative social mobility: a comparative study of England, Wales and Scotland', *Sociological Research Online*, 12, *http://www.socresonline.org. uk/12/6/15.html* (accessed 12 May 2012).

Paterson, L. and C. Iannelli (2007b). 'Social class and educational attainment: a comparative study of England, Wales and Scotland', *Sociology of Education*, 80, 330–58.

Paul, K. (1997). *Whitewashing Britain: Race and Citizenship in the Post-war Era*, Ithaca and London, Cornell University Press.

Phillips, M. (1987), 'Faith in NHS endures', *Guardian*, 23 October 2010, cited in M. Sullivan (1996), *The Development of the British Welfare State*, New York, Prentice Hall.

Phillips, M. and T. Phillips (1998). *Windrush: The Irresistible Rise of Multicultural Britain*, London, Harper Collins.

Phillips, R. (2003). 'Education policy, comprehensive schooling and devolution in the disunited kingdom: an historical "home international" analysis', *Journal of Education Policy*, 18, 1–17.

Pierson, C. and F. G. Castles (eds) (2006), *The Welfare State Reader*, 2nd edn, Cambridge, Polity Press.

Pilkington, A. (2003). *Racial Disadvantage and Ethnic Diversity in Britain*, Basingstoke, Palgrave Macmillan.

Pimlott, B. (1992). 'Giants of poverty yet to be slain', *The Independent*, 1 December, *http://www.independent.co.uk/opinion/giants-of-poverty-yet-to-be-slain-fifty-years-after-beveridge-want-disease-squalor-ignorance-and-idleness-persist-ben-pimlott-calls-for-a-new-visionary-to-fashion-a-social-policy-for-our-age-1560853.html* (accessed 17 July 2009).

Player, D. and D. Barbour-Might (1988). *Health for All: The Practical Socialism of the NHS*, London, Tribune.

Powell, M. (1997a). 'Socialism and the British National Health Service', *Healthcare Analysis*, 5, 3, 187–94.

Powell, M. (1997b). *Evaluating the NHS*, Buckingham, Open University Press.

Powell, M. (ed.) (2008). *Modernising the Welfare State*, Bristol, Policy Press.

Putnam, R. D. (2000). *Bowling Alone: The Collapse and Revival of American Community*, New York, Simon & Schuster.

Ratcliffe, P. (2004). *'Race', Ethnicity and Difference: Imagining the Inclusive Society*, Milton Keynes, Open University Press.

Rawles, S. (2008). 'Portraits of respect', *Guardian*, 26 March, *http://www.guardian.co.uk/society/2008/mar/26/longtermcare.socialcare* (accessed 27 March 2008).

Rawlings, R. (2003). *Delineating Wales: Constitutional, Legal and Administrative Aspects of National Devolution*, Cardiff, University of Wales Press.

Rawls, J. (2001). *Justice as Fairness: A Re-statement*, Cambridge, Mass., Harvard University Press.

Rees, G. (2004). 'Democratic devolution and education policy in Wales: the emergence of a national system?', *Contemporary Wales*, 17, 28–43.

Rees, G. and D. Stroud (2001). 'Creating a mass system of higher education: participation, the economy and citizenship', in R. Phillips and J. Furlong (eds), *Education, Reform and the State: Twenty-five Years of Politics, Policy and Practice*, London, Routledge-Falmer.

Rees, G. and C. Taylor (2006). 'Devolution and the restructuring of participation in higher education in Wales', *Higher Education Quarterly*, 60, 370–91.

Reisman, D. (1997). *Crosland's Future: Opportunity and Outcome*, London, Macmillan.

Rex, J. and S. Tomlinson (1979). *Colonial Immigrants in a British City: A Class Analysis*, London, Routledge and Kegan Paul.

Rowlingson, K. and S. McKay (2002). *Lone Parent Families Gender, Class and State*, Harlow, Pearson Education Limited.

Rowntree, S. and G. R. Lavers (1951). *Poverty and the Welfare State*, London, Longman Green.

Rummery, K. (2007). 'Caring, citizenship and New Labour: dilemmas and contradictions for disabled and older women', in C. Annesley, F. Gains and K. Rummery (eds), *Women and New Labour: Engendering Politics and Policy?*, Bristol, Policy Press.

Rustin, M. (2008). 'Contradictions in the welfare state', *Soundings*, 38, 42–55.

Ryan, R. and A. Sparrow (2008). 'No. 10 plays down Flint's social housing plan', *Guardian*, 5 February.

Segal, R. and D. Marsland (1989). *Cradle to Grave: Comparative Perspectives on the State of Welfare*, London, Macmillan.

Self, A. (ed.) (2008). *Social Trends 38*, *www.statistics.gov.uk/socialtrends38* (accessed 1 December 2008).

Selvon, S. (1979). *The Lonely Londoners*, London, Longman: Caribbean Writers.

Seyd, P. and P. Whiteley (2004). 'British party members: an overview', *Party Politics*, 10, 4, 355–66.

Shakespeare, T. (2006). *Disability Rights and Wrongs*, London, Routledge.

Shaw, M., G. Davey-Smith and D. Dorling (2005). 'Health inequalities and New Labour: how the promises compare with real progress', *British Medical Journal*, 330, 1016–21.

Shaw, S. M. I. (1992). 'Conflicting experiences of lone parenthood', in M. Hardey and G. Crow (eds), *Lone Parenthood*, Hemel Hempstead, Harvester Wheatsheaf.

Shelter Cymru (2007). *An Unnatural Disaster: Report of the Commission of Inquiry into Homelessness and Poor Housing Conditions in Wales*, Swansea, Shelter Cymru.

Silburn, R. (1994). 'Beveridge and the war-time consensus', *Journal of Social Policy and Administration*, 25, 80–6.

Simon, B. (1991). *Education and the Social Order 1940–1990*, London, Lawrence and Wishart.

Sivanandan, A. (1990). *Communities of Resistance*, London, Verso.

Smith, D. (2005). *On the Margins of Inclusion*, Bristol, Policy Press.

Smith, S. R. (1992). 'Disabled in the labour market', *Economic Report*, 7, 1 July/August, Employment Policy Institute, London.

Smith, S. R. (1998). *The Centre-left and New Right Divide? Political Philosophy and Social Policy in the Era of the Welfare State*, Aldershot, Ashgate.

Smith, S. R. (2001a). 'The social construction of talent: a defence of justice as reciprocity', *The Journal of Political Philosophy*, 9, 19–37.

Smith, S. R. (2001b). 'Distorted ideals: the "problem of dependency" and the mythology of independent living', *Social Theory and Practice*, 27, 579–98.

Smith, S. R. (2002a). 'Fraternal learning and interdependency: celebrating differences within reciprocal commitments', *Policy and Politics*, 30, 47–59.

Smith, S. R. (2002b). *Defending Justice as Reciprocity: An Essay on Social Policy and Political Philosophy*, Lampeter, Edwin Mellen.

Smith, S. R. (2005). 'Equality, identity and the disability rights movement: from policy to practice and from Kant to Nietzsche in more than one uneasy move', *Critical Social Policy*, 25, 554–76.

Standing, K. (1999). 'Lone mothers and "parental" involvement: a contradiction in policy?', *Journal of Social Policy*, 28, 479–95.

Sullivan, M. (2000). 'Labour, citizenship and social policy: a retreat from social democracy?', inaugural lecture, Swansea University, Swansea.

Sunley, P., R. Martin and C. Nativel (2001). 'Mapping the New Deal: local disparities in the performance of welfare-to-work', *Transactions of the Institute of British Geographers*, 26, 484–512.

Swain, J., S. French and C. Cameron (2003). *Controversial Issues in a Disabling Society*, Buckingham, Open University Press.

Tanner, D. (ed.) (2006). *Debating Nationhood and Governance in Britain 1995–1945: Perspectives from the 'Four Nations'*, Manchester, Manchester University Press.

Tawney, R. H. (1931). *Equality*, London, Unwin Books.

Taylor-Gooby, P. (2001). 'Preface', in Peter Taylor-Gooby (ed.), *Welfare States under Pressure*, London: Sage.

Tench, A. (ed.) (2007). *Devolution and Power in the United Kingdom*, Manchester, Manchester University Press.

Thatcher, M. (1977). 'Speech to Zurich Economic Society', 14 March, *http://www.margaretthatcher.org/document/103336* (accessed 29 April 2012).

Thatcher, M. (1993). *The Downing Street Years*, London, HarperCollins.

Thomas, A. (2007). *Lone Parent Work Focused Interviews: Synthesis of Findings*, Leeds, Department for Work and Pensions research report 443, London, Department for Work and Pensions.

Thomas, B. and D. Dorling (2004). 'Know your place: housing wealth and inequality in Great Britain 1980–2003 and beyond', in D. Dorling, J. Ford, A. Holmans, B. Thomas and S. Wilcox (eds), *The Great Divide: An Analysis of Housing Inequality*, London, Shelter.

Thomas, I. C. (1981). *The Creation of the Welsh Office: Conflicting Purposes in Institutional Change*, Centre for the Study of Public Policy, University of Strathclyde.

Timmins, N. (2001). *The Five Giants: A Biography of the Welfare State*, rev. edn, London: HarperCollins.

Tisdall, E. (2006). 'Antisocial behaviour legislation meets children's services: challenging perspectives on children, parents and the state', *Critical Social Policy*, 26, 101–20.

Tomlinson, J. (1998). 'Why so austere? The British welfare state of the 1940s', *Journal of Social Policy*, 27, 63–77.

Torgersen, U. (1987). 'Housing: the wobbly pillar under the welfare state', in B. Turner, J. Kemeny and L. Lundqvist (eds), *Between State and Market: Housing in the Post-industrial Era*, Goteborg, Almqvist & Wiksell.

Townsend, P. (1962). *The Last Refuge*, London, Routledge and Kegan Paul.

Townsend, P., N. Whitehead and M. Whitehead (1988). *Inequalities in Health*, Harmondsworth, Penguin.

Trade Union Congress (2008). *How has Trade Union Membership Changed in Recent Years?*, *http://www.bized.co.uk/compfact/tuc/tuc15. htm* (accessed 19 March 2008).

Underdown, A. (2007). *Young Children's Health and Well-being*, Maidenhead, Open University Press.

UNICEF (2007). *Child Poverty in Perspective: An Overview of Child Well-being in Rich Countries*. (Innocenti Report Card 7), Florence, UNICEF Innocenti Research Centre.

UPIAS (1976). *Fundamental Principles of Disability*, London, Union of the Physically Impaired Against Segregation.

Victor, C. (2005). 'The epidemiology of ageing', in M. L. Johnson (ed.), *The Cambridge Handbook of Age and Ageing*, Cambridge, Cambridge University Press, pp. 95–105.

Walby, S., J. Armstrong and L. Humphreys (2008). *Research Report 1: Review of Equality Statistics*, London: Equality and Human Rights Commission, *http://www.equalityhumanrights.com/uploaded_files/research/ 1_review_of_equality_statistics_241008.pdf* (accessed 5 February 2010).

Walker, A. and L. Foster (2006). 'Caught between virtue and ideological necessity: a century of pensions policy in the UK', *Review of Political Economy*, 18, 3, 427–48.

Webster, C. (ed.) (1991). *Aneurin Bevan on the National Health Service*, Oxford, Wellcome Unit for the History of Medicine.

Webster, C. (1998). *The National Health Service: A Political History*, Oxford, Oxford University Press.

Webster, W. (1998). *Imagining Home: Gender, 'Race' and National Identity 1945–64*, London, University College London Press.

Welsh Assembly Government (2004). *Making the Connections*, Cardiff, Welsh Assembly Government.

Welsh Assembly Government (2005). *Childcare is for Children*, Cardiff, Welsh Assembly Government, *http://wales.gov.uk/topics/ educationandskills/publications/guidance/Thechildcarestrategyforwales? lang=en&ts=1* (accessed 22 April 2009).

Welsh Assembly Government (2007). *One Wales: A Progressive Agenda for the Government of Wales*, an agreement between the Labour and Plaid Cymru groups in the National Assembly, Cardiff, Welsh Assembly Government.

Welsh Assembly Government (2009). '£68 million boost to skills economy', press release, 28 January, Cardiff, Welsh Assembly Government.

White, S. (2005). 'Is conditionality illiberal?', in L. M. Mead and C. Beem (eds), *Welfare Reform and Political Theory*, New York, Russell Sage Foundation.

Whitehead, M. and D. Drever (1997). *Health Inequalities: Decennial Supplement*, London, The Stationery Office.

Wilcox, S. (2006). *Young, Working and Still Homeless: Housing Market Affordability in Wales in 2005*, Cardiff, Chartered Institute of Housing Cymru.

Wilcox, S. (ed.) (2008). *UK Housing Review 2008/09 Edition*, Chartered Institute of Housing, York.

Wilkinson, R. (2005). *The Impact of Inequality: How to Make Sick Societies Healthier*, London, Routledge.

Wilkinson, R. and K. Pickett (2009). *The Spirit Level: Why Equality is Better for Everyone*, Harmondsworth, Penguin.

Williams, C. (1995). 'Race and racism: some reflections on the Welsh context', *Contemporary Wales*, 8, 113–31.

Williams, C. (2006). 'The dilemmas of civil society: black and ethnic minority associations in Wales', in G. Day, D. Dunkerley and A. Thompson , *Civil Society in Wales*, Cardiff, University of Wales Press.

Williams, C. (ed.) (2007). *Social Policy for Social Welfare Practice in a Devolved Wales*, Birmingham, Venture Press.

Williams, C. and P. De Lima (2007). 'Devolution, multicultural citizenship and race equality: from laissez faire to nationally responsible policies', *Critical Social Policy*, 26, 498–522.

Williams, C. and M. R. D. Johnson (2010). *Race and Ethnicity in a Welfare Society*, Buckingham, Open University Press.

Williams, F. (1989). *Social Policy: A Critical Introduction*, Cambridge, Polity Press.

Winckler, V. (ed.) (2009). *Equality Issues in Wales: A Research Review: Equality and Human Rights Commission, Research Report 11*, London, Equality and Human Rights Commission.

Wintersberger, H. (1996). 'Children on the way from marginality to citizenship', in H. Wintersberger (ed.), *Childhood Policies: Conceptual and Practical Issues*, Vienna, European Centre for Social Welfare Policy and Research.

Wintour, P. (2008). 'Labour: if you want a council house, find a job: housing minister Flint's plan to make tenants actively seek work', *Guardian*, 5 February.

Wolf, A. (2002). *Does Education Matter? Myths about Education and Economic Growth*, London, Penguin.

World Health Organisation (1995). *The World Health Report 1995 – Bridging the Gaps, http://www.who.int/whr/1995/en/index.html* (accessed 7 May 2012).

Worley, C. (2005). '"It's not about race. It's about the community"': New Labour and "community cohesion"', *Critical Social Policy*, 25, 483–96.

INDEX

Acheson, Donald 59, 60
age 6, 12–13, 217, 219, 195–211
    passim
agriculture 69, 77, 185
alcohol 61, 217
Allen, Clifford 197
Allen, Marjorie 197, 198, 202
'anti-social behaviour' 128, 201
assimilation 11, 143, 147, 156
asylum 152
Attlee, Clement v, 12, 45, 182, 183
autonomy 161, 166, 167, 168, 211

Barker, Kate 94
Barnett Formula 185, 194
Bentham, Jeremy 118
Bernstein, Basil 217
Bevan, Aneurin v, 2, 3, 5, 14, 44,
    46, 47, 49, 86, 91, 92, 97,
    183, 193
Beveridge, William v, 3, 5, 6, 8, 9,
    10, 12, 14, 19, 20, 23, 24, 25,
    26, 27, 28, 33, 35, 36, 37, 38,
    39, 40, 43, 46, 63, 65, 71, 83,
    99, 105, 107, 110, 116, 118,
    121, 180, 190, 195, 196, 205,
    207, 211
'Beveridge consensus' 20, 30–2
Beveridge Report 1, 2, 20, 23, 24,
    25, 45, 65, 83, 105, 109, 126,
    181, 185, 194, 204, 207
Bevin, Ernest 179
Black Report 59
Blaenau Gwent 10, 74
Blair, Tony 12, 59, 62, 183, 201
Brace, William 178
Breadline Britain Survey 59
British Medical Association 4, 60

British Nursery Association 197
Britishness 147, 157
Brown, Gordon 115, 201
Bryan, Beverley 144
Butetown 152
Butler, Ian xiii, 12–13, **195–202**,
    214, 216
Byrne, David xiii, 9–10, **98–121**,
    214

Calder, Gideon xiii, **1–14**
Callaghan, James 53, 183
capitalism 44, 99, 119
Cardiff 150, 151, 152, 194
caring, role of 10 125, 126, 127,
    130, 205, 206
Carmarthen 183
Castle, Barbara 52
Chamberlain, Neville 179, 183
charity 162
child benefit 26, 32, 39, 42, 218
child poverty 19, 37, 39, 40, 60,
    102, 133, 201
Child Support Act 1991 132
Child Support Agency 107
Child Tax Credit 109
childcare 138
children v, 5, 12, 19, 22, 23, 26, 27,
    32, 34, 36, 37, 40, 127, 128,
    136, 140, 195–202 *passim*
Children Act 2004 199
Children and Young People Act
    1969 199
Children and Young Persons Act
    1933 197
Children's Act 1948 198, 199
Children's Commissioner for Wales
    13, 202

'choice' 85, 161, 167, 168, 203, 211
Churchill, Winston v
citizenship 10, 11, 13, 62, 66, 67, 125, 129, 135, 145, 155, 160, 161, 162, 163, 168, 169, 171, 175, 202
Civil Partnership Act 2004 131
civil partnerships 131
civil society 155
Clarke, Kenneth 56
class 6, 57, 58, 69, 72, 75, 79, 86, 173
coal 69, 77
cohabitation (of couples) 131, 132
Commission for Racial Equality 156
commodification 83, 138
Commonwealth 11, 141, 143, 144, 148
communism 46
Community University of the Valleys 13
competitive tendering 52, 55
comprehensive schools 72, 73
conditional access to welfare 134
Conservative Party 1, 3, 8, 9, 44, 48, 50, 53, 54, 55, 59, 62, 64, 73, 86, 87, 88, 89, 102, 108, 118, 120, 132, 142, 178, 182, 184, 185, 217
contributions 23, 24, 29
Cook, Robin 51
council housing 9, 86, 87–8, 89, 90, 117, 145, 219
Craig, Gary 152
crime 4
Cripps, Stafford 191
Crosland, Anthony 182
Curtis Committee 198

Dadzie, Stella 144
Davies, S. O. 183

democracy 66, 80
democratic participation 66
dependency 11, 85, 91, 102, 125, 126, 160, 172
devolution v, 11, 69, 118, 125, 130, 154, 177–194 *passim*
diet 62
disability v, 6, 11, 29, 115, 126, 140, 160–76 *passim*, 217
Disability Discrimination Act 1995 170
Disability Rights Movement 160, 162–9, 171, 172, 173
Disabled Persons (Employment) Act 1944 170
discrimination 147–8, 152–3, 159, 164, 170
'disease' (as one of 'Five Evils'/ 'Five Giants') v, 6, 7, 44–64 *passim*, 214
divorce 131
Dorling, Daniel 4
Drakeford, Mark xiii, 12, **177–94**, 218

education v, 6, 8, 65–83 *passim*, 92, 128, 130, 148, 149, 185, 194, 213
Education Act 1944 71, 75, 81
Edwards, Huw v
elementary education 71
elitism 4
Ellison, Nick 182
'employability' 114
Employment Support Allowance 117
empowerment 11, 159, 166, 168
England 61, 63, 64, 69, 71, 72, 76, 81, 90, 93, 102, 119, 178, 201
equality 11, 74, 80, 151, 154, 182, 192
Equality Act 2006 156

Essex Review 95
ethnic minorities 142, 143, 148, 216
eugenicism 151
European Parliament 130
European Union 126, 135–8, 187

Fabian Society 92
fairness 68
families 10, 22, 35, 103, 107,
    125–40 *passim*, 146, 196, 217
family allowances 29–30, 32, 42,
    121
Family Income Supplement 108
feminism 126
'Five Evils' v, 5, 63, 195, 203, 214,
    217, 220
'Five Giants', *see* 'Five Evils'
Flint, Caroline 117, 119
Foot, Michael 46, 85
Forestier-Walker, C. L. 178
Foucault, Michel 200
free school milk 26
Freud, David 111, 116, 119
further education 76, 78

Garw 87
Gass, Jeremy xiv, **1–14**
gender v, 4, 6, 10, 79, 105, 107–8,
    125–40 *passim*, 206, 217, 219
Germany 105
Gilroy, Beryl 144
Glasgow 208
globalization 2, 5, 154
Glyncorrwg 87
Goodhart, David 142
Government of Wales Act 2006
    194
Gower 178
Gregg, Paul 100–1
Griffiths, James 183, 184, 193
Guillebaud Committee 49
Guyana 144

Hain, Peter 207
'handicap' 163
Hardie, Keir 178
Harris, Jose 181
Hart, Julian Tudor 47
health v, 1, 4, 6, 7, 13, 44–64 *passim*,
    128, 130, 133, 148, 162, 184,
    185, 188, 192, 196, 209
Health and Social Care Act 2012
    16
Health and Social Care Bill 2011 1
Health Services Act 1980 52
Heath, Edward 88
higher education 68, 75, 79, 80
Hills, John 92
Hills Report 4, 92
House of Commons 129
House of Lords 1
housing v, 9, 84–97 *passim*, 128,
    148, 162, 185, 194, 209,
    214
housing associations 90, 219
Hughes, Cledwyn 183
Hunter, David 63, 64
Huxley, Elspeth 145

Iceland 104
identity 6, 148, 153, 161, 166, 168,
    175
ideology 11, 12, 88–91, 150, 151
'idleness' (as one of 'Five Evils'/
    'Five Giants') v, 6, 45,
    98–121 *passim*, 196, 214
'ignorance' (as one of 'Five Evils'/
    'Five Giants') v, 6, 8, 45,
    65–83 *passim*, 196, 214
immigration 2, 5, 11, 142, 143,
    151, 152
impairment 12, 163, 164
Incapacity Benefit 111, 116, 117
income transfers 19
Independent Labour Party 197

independent living 11–12, 13, 160,
        161, 169, 171
inequality 4, 5, 8, 11, 45, 47, 50, 56,
        60, 61, 62, 64, 67, 80, 81, 90,
        141, 148, 206, 215, 217
infant mortality 58
Inter-Departmental Committee on
        Social Insurance and Allied
        Services 20
inter-generational disadvantage
        128, 192
internal markets 54, 55
Ireland 178
Italy 106

Jamaica, immigrants from 143
Jay, Douglas 182
Job-Seeker's Allowance 10, 103,
        104, 111, 116, 117, 118, 218
Johnson, Linton Kwesi 146
Jones, E. T. 178
Joseph Rowntree Foundation 10,
        41, 217

Kenway, Peter xiv, 7, **19–43**, 214,
        215
Keynes, John Maynard 28, 85, 96
Keynesianism 85, 96, 188
Klein, Rudolf 48

labour market 66, 75, 81, 98, 99,
        108, 116, 126, 140, 170, 218
Labour Party (*see also* New Labour)
        v, 2, 7, 8, 9, 12, 19, 44, 46,
        48, 55, 63, 64, 72, 86, 98,
        102, 116, 117, 142, 156, 178,
        179, 182, 185, 186, 193, 198,
        202, 203, 205, 213
Large Scale Voluntary Transfers 90
Lawrence, Stephen 156
Laws, David 120
Le Grand, Julian 63, 64

legal aid 1
Levitas, Ruth 112
Levy, Andrea 145
Lewis, Gail 150
Liachowitz, Claire 163
Liberal Democrats 1, 3, 8, 48, 62,
        120, 217
liberalism 68, 152, 199
life expectancy 57, 58, 203
literacy 4
Little, Ken 150
Lloyd, Liz xiv, 12–13, 43, **203–211**,
        216
Lloyd George, Megan 183
London 107
lone parents 10, 107, 115, 128,
        131–4, 140
long-term sickness 111
'Lord Kitchener', *see* Roberts,
        Aldwyn

Major, John 106, 213
Malpass, Peter 87, 88, 89
managerialism 154, 199
market, role of 9, 85, 89
marketization of welfare provision,
        51, 184, 191, 213, 217, 219
Marmot, Michael 4, 60
Marmot Report 4, 60, 61, 200
marriage 23, 24, 125, 126, 131–2
Marshall, T. H. 129
Mead, Lawrence 114
means-testing 7, 24, 34, 38, 41, 42,
        120
'medical model' of disability 12,
        160, 163, 164, 172
meritocracy 68, 78
Merrill-Glover, Kirsten xiv, **1–14**
Merthyr Tydfil 74
metal manufacture 69, 77
miners 69, 178
'modernization' 3

Monmouthshire 183
Morgan, Kenneth O. 186
Morgan, Rhodri 186, 187
Morrison, Herbert 198
multiculturalism 142, 146, 147, 150, 155
musicians 115
Muslims 110, 157

National Assembly for Wales 8, 61, 69, 70, 73, 82, 177, 193, 201
National Assistance 33
National Assistance Act 1948 199, 210
National Health Service 1, 2, 3, 11, 44–64 *passim*, 141, 148, 155, 180, 182, 208, 213, 217, 219
National Health Service Act 1946 199, 210
National Insurance 23, 30, 31, 42, 207
National Insurance Act 1946 15, 28, 30, 199
nationalization 85
needs 11–12, 142, 162, 167, 175, 190
NEETS 104, 112, 201, 214
neo-liberalism 143, 146
New Deal 100, 113–20
New Labour 8, 9, 11, 37, 63, 64, 73, 103, 108, 112, 113, 118, 128, 129, 133, 139, 140, 142, 154, 155, 156, 169
New Poor Law 1834 108
New Right 3, 128, 169
NGOs 147
NHS and Community Care Act 1990 126, 209
No Turning Back Group 55
nonconformism, religious 68
Northern Ireland 106, 118, 119, 143, 150
nurseries 70

Offe, Claus 3
Office for National Statistics 42, 57
Ogmore 87
older people 203–11 *passim*
Oliver, Mike 166, 167
O'Neil, Denis 198
Orwell, George 200
Owen, Robert 190

Parekh Report 151
parental leave 137
Paul, Kathleen 144, 150
pensioners 35, 37, 38
pensions 13, 23, 37, 38, 138, 205
Pensions Act 2007 206
Phillips, Melanie 58
Pickett, Kate 4, 208
Pimlott, Ben 45
Plaid Cymru 186
poll tax 184
poverty 7, 9, 19, 35, 37, 38, 39, 40, 56, 60, 64, 92, 102, 133–4, 140, 149, 194, 201
Poverty and Social Exclusion Survey of Britain 60
Powell, Enoch 146
power 2, 14
Powys 74
prejudice 4
private health insurance 53–4
privatization 184
Public Finance Initiative 189
Purnell, James 102, 119
Putnam, Robert 192
Puzey, John xiv, 9, **84–97**, 214

race 11, 110, 141–159 *passim*, 217
racism 142, 144, 147, 148, 217
Rathbone, Eleanor 29, 30
reciprocity 12, 142, 170, 175
Redwood, John 184

Rees, Gareth xv, 8–9, **65–83**, 215, 216, 219
Rendall, David 178
responsibilities 155, 203, 217
retirement 23, 25
'Right to Buy' (council housing) 84, 89, 193
rights 12, 62, 66, 129, 130, 155, 160, 161–2, 168
Roberts, Aldwyn ('Lord Kitchener') 143, 146
Rowntree, Seebohm 34, 35

Scafe, Suzanne 144
school meals 26
Scotland 61, 63, 64, 81, 118, 143, 150, 158, 178, 185
Scottish National Party 194
Scottish Parliament 130, 151
secondary education 68, 71, 72, 73, 75, 81
Selvon, Sam 145
sexual division of labour 125–40 *passim*
Shaw, Sandra xv, 10–11, **125–40**, 215
Silburn, Richard 181
Sinfield, Adrian 101
Smith, David 107
Smith, Steven R. xvi, 11–12, **160–76**, 215
smoking 61, 62
social capital 155
social cohesion 154
social democracy 62–4, 99
social exclusion 4, 12, 71, 80, 112, 159, 194
social inclusion 66, 154, 158, 163, 171, 172
Social Insurance 20, 21, 24, 27, 28, 39, 43
social mobility 67, 78–81, 82, 91

'social model' of disability 12, 160, 163, 164, 171, 172, 174
social justice 8
Social Security v, 7, 21, 23
social services v, 148, 162
socialism 46
solidarity 142, 153, 190, 192
South Wales Miners' Federation 178
Spain 106
'squalor' (as one of 'Five Evils'/ 'Five Giants') v, 6, 45, 84–97 *passim*, 214
SS Empire Windrush 143, 146, 147
Sullivan, Michael xvi, 7–8, **44–64**, 216
Swansea 189
Sweden 192

Tawney, R. H. 181, 192
Taylor-Gooby, Peter 5
technology 5, 66
terrorism 152
Thatcher, Margaret 51, 84, 102, 106, 146, 154, 184, 206, 213
third sector 11, 147, 156–7, 158, 188
Thomas, Ian C. 183
Timmins, Nicholas 5
Titmuss, Richard 89
Townsend, Peter 61, 209
transport 69, 77, 219
tuition fees (university) 79

unemployment 5, 23, 27, 29, 39, 41, 42, 75, 98–121 *passim*, 188, 214
United Nations Convention on the Rights of the Child 202
United States of America 101, 192
universalism (of provision) 7, 11, 39, 42, 116, 138, 141, 146, 147, 158, 190, 196, 200, 205, 217

vocational education 67, 68, 76
voluntary sector, *see* third sector
vulnerability 160

Wales 2, 5, 7, 8, 12, 57, 63, 65–83
    passim, 87, 90, 93, 97, 118,
    119, 143, 150, 158, 177–94
    passim, 201, 218, 219
'want' (as one of 'Five Evils'/ 'Five
    Giants') v, 6, 7, 19–43 *passim*,
    214, 215
Webster, Wendy 144
Welfare Reform Act 2012, 16
Welfare Reform Bill 2011, 1
Welsh (Assembly) Government 12,
    61, 70, 73, 95, 97, 130, 190
Welsh Home Rule Bill 1922 178–9
West Indies, immigrants from 143
Whiteside, Noel 88

Wilkinson, Richard 4, 192, 208
Williams, Charlotte xvi, 11,
    141–59, 216, 219
Williams, Fiona 144, 150, 151
Williams, Shirley 1
Wilson, Harold 52
Winckler, Victoria xvi, 13,
    213–220
Working Families Tax Credit 109,
    138
World War I 2, 121, 178
World War II 34–5, 45, 63, 85, 96,
    164, 170, 171
Wrexham 189

Young, Michael 67–8
young people 13, 110, 112–13
youth justice system 128
youth work 220